The Aeolic Style in Architecture

THE AEOLIC STYLE IN ARCHITECTURE

A Survey of Its Development in Palestine, the Halikarnassos Peninsula, and Greece, 1000-500 *B.C.*

by Philip P. Betancourt

PRINCETON UNIVERSITY PRESS

Library of Congress Cataloging in Publication Data

Betancourt, Philip P.   1936–
    Aeolic style in architecture.

    Bibliography: p.
    Includes index.
    1. Architecture, Aeolic—Palestine.
2. Architecture—Palestine.   3. Palestine—
Antiquities.   4. Architecture, Aeolic—Muğla,
Turkey (Province)   5. Architecture—Muğla,
Turkey (Province)   6. Muğla, Turkey
(Province)—Antiquities.   7. Architecture,
Aeolic—Greece.   8. Architecture—Greece.
9. Greece—Antiquities.
I. Title.
NA245.P34B47   722   76-45890
ISBN 0-691-03922-4

For Mary

Contents

Introduction   3

Abbreviations   7

List of plates   10

List of text figures   12

List of maps   13

PART I

   I The Bronze Age Background   17

PART II

   II Palestine   27

      Hazor   27

      Megiddo   29

      Samaria   34

      Shechem   35

      Unknown Site, Said to be
        "in Transjordan"   36

      Jerusalem   37

      Ramat Raḥel   40

      Medeibîyeh   43

      Historical Development   44

III The Halikarnassos Peninsula   50

      Alâzeytin   51

      Historical Development   55

IV Aeolis, Northern Ionia, and
   the North Aegean   58

      Old Smyrna   58

      Neandria   63

      Larisa on the Hermos   73

      Klopedi   82

      Mytilene   87

      Eressos   88

      Thasos   88

      Delos   91

      Paros   92

Contents

Historical Development   93

V Attica   99

Historical Development   108

PART III

VI A Summary of the Stylistic Development in the Eastern Mediterranean   115

VII The Relation between the Aeolic and Ionic Orders   122

Catalogue   134

Appendix A. Sites Yielding Aeolic Balusters and Illustrations of Balustrades with Volute Capitals   142

Appendix B. Athenian Vases Illustrating Aeolic Columns   145

Appendix C. Vases from the Northeast Aegean with Illustrations of Aeolic Columns   152

Glossary   154

Selected Bibliography   157

Index   163

The Aeolic Style in Architecture

Introduction

Although it has been nearly a century since the first Aeolic capital to be unearthed in modern times was presented to the academic world, no general study of the Aeolic style has ever been undertaken. Yet many of the buildings whose capitals had vertically rising volutes were outstanding architectural monuments, and they must have exerted considerable influence on the development of Archaic architecture. The style appeared in many cities, and it is important both for its own sake and for its possible relation to the development of the Ionic order of Classical Greece. The present study makes no pretense at being the full treatment the style deserves; while much new evidence has appeared in recent years, the information is still insufficient for a complete analysis. The basis here is the three regions in the eastern Mediterranean where the evidence is most complete. An attempt is made to learn something of the internal development within these specific localities and of the relationships between local styles. The chief difference between this and previous analyses (like those of Ciasca and Wesenberg) is its more comprehensive nature and the fact that it treats the Aeolic elements within their architectural settings rather than piecemeal, as isolated details of decoration.

Only two regions—Palestine and Greece—have yielded substantial numbers of stone buildings with Aeolic columns or pillars. On the whole, there is a great difference between the styles in the two regions, and their relationship appears (to the present writer) to have been indirect rather than direct. A consideration of that relationship demands the inclusion of a discussion of the two Aeolic buildings from the Halikarnassos peninsula, as does also the fact that these structures used pillars and pilasters in the Palestinian structural way even though the artistic style of the supports is in appearance more Greek than Near Eastern. Unfortunately, the evidence from other areas is virtually all from secondary sources (carved facades for tombs or stelai, paintings, reliefs, etc.). Since one of the principal aims of the present work has been to examine the role of the Aeolic capitals within their architectural contexts, regions where such architectural contexts do not exist and where the evidence is from secondary sources have been considered in the text where they shed light on the main subject of discussion rather than in separate chapters of their own. In any case, two of those regions—Etruria and Cyprus—have already been published very fully in recent years, and the reader is referred to the

3

writings of Ciasca and Masson for a more comprehensive treatment of their styles.

First, a word about nomenclature is necessary. Exactly what to call the capitals with vertically rising volutes has posed a problem, and a cross section of the literature shows considerable confusion. The examples from Aeolis itself, which capped free-standing columns, have been called "Proto-Ionic" (W. B. Dinsmoor), "Aeolic" (K. Schefold; D. S. Robertson; E. Akurgal), "Éolo-ionic" (R. Vallois), and both "Aeolisch-Ionisch" and "Ionisch-äolisch" (J. Durm). Their counterparts from Palestine, Cyprus, Halikarnassos, and elsewhere, which were used with pilasters, have been called "Proto-Aeolian" (Y. Yadin *et al.*, in *Hazor*), "Proto-Aeolic" (J. Boardman; W. F. Albright), "Proto-Ionic" (H. G. May; D. Ussishkin), "Aeolic" (W. Radt), and simply "volute capitals" (A. Ciasca; B. Wesenberg). To further complicate matters, the term "Aeolic" has also been applied to certain capitals decorated with palm leaves (W. B. Dinsmoor). The palm capitals are distinct from the others, and the idea of calling them "Aeolic" has had few adherents, but there is no clear way to divide the remaining examples into two well-defined groups. The best suggestion, ably stated by John Boardman (*Antiquaries Journal* 39 [1959] p. 215), attempted a division on geographic, structural, and decorative lines by placing all engaged pilaster capitals with volutes springing from a central triangle in one group (*i.e.* the capitals from Palestine and Cyprus) and all capitals for true columns without the central triangle in another group (*i.e.* the examples from Aeolis). Discoveries made since Boardman's suggestion, however, have obscured these lines. We now have Palestinian capitals from Hazor without central triangles, theories which place free-standing Aeolic columns in the tradition of the *bit hilani* of North Syria and Palestine, and sixth-century B.C. engaged pilaster capitals (used exactly like the early Palestinian ones) from the Halikarnassos peninsula. It has recently been suggested that some of the Palestinian capitals were true architectural supports, not simply decorative doorjambs or engaged pilasters. And finally, there is the problem of the "true" capital from Shechem and of certain clay models from Palestine and Cyprus that show engaged half-columns without the basal triangle but which may reflect engaged half-columns with the triangle. Perhaps the time has come to clarify and simplify. It is here suggested that the term "Aeolic style" be used for all architectural supports with vertically rising volutes, just as the words "Doric" and "Ionic" are used for general stylistic divisions. The name "Aeolic" goes back to the nineteenth century, and it has been gaining in popularity for some time because it implies no theory about the lines of stylistic development (as do words with the prefix "proto"). It need not imply that the capital originated in Aeolis any more than the name Ionic requires that that capital be of Ionian origin. Here the term "Aeolic" is used in this generic sense for both columns and pilasters. With the exception of the final Archaic stage in the north Aegean, the phrase "Aeolic style" is preferred to "Aeolic order" to avoid any suggestion that the Aeolic system is to be taken as parallel to the Doric or Ionic orders. Capitals with vertically rising volutes but with additional elements that place the members in a separate tradition (like those of the Egyptian Late Bronze Age) are called simply volute capitals or Aeolic-related capitals, and (following Ciasca and Wesenberg) the Near Eastern capitals are usually called "volute capitals" also.

The Aeolic style had a great flowering in the Greek region of Aeolis, but the fashion also extended as far west as Spain and as far east as the limits of Alexander's empire. Chronologically, its beginnings go back to the Bronze Age, while a few late variations were still being constructed in the time of the Roman empire. The choice of areas discussed in this study does not imply any *a priori* assumptions about the relative importance of the regions where the style was in vogue. On the contrary, many areas not discussed here—in both Italy and the Near East

—seem to have had developments of profound importance for the history of architecture in general. The choice of regions discussed is based solely on the fact that sufficient evidence exists for tentative judgments to be made about the architectural development.

Since our aim is to present the evidence for the development of Aeolic architecture in a concise and readable survey, and not to persuade the reader to subscribe to a particular set of theories, we have tried to present alternate solutions as honestly and completely as possible. A conclusion has been drawn if the evidence seems to warrant it, but it has seemed better in some cases simply to state both sides of the argument and to offer no solution at this time. It is to be hoped that future investigations will be able to clarify some of these questions.

For the purpose of this study, capitals and fragments of capitals have been examined from the following sites: Medinet Habu; Megiddo (no. 3); Neandria; Larisa on the Hermos (nos. 20–21); Klopedi; Mytilene; Paros (no. 32); Athens (nos. 34–36 and 38); and Sykaminon. Much additional material, including the Assyrian reliefs in the British Museum and in the Oriental Institute in Chicago, was also inspected at first hand, and the building sites at Klopedi, Larisa, and Neandria were also observed (in the summer of 1971).

This work could not have been completed without the assistance and suggestions of so many individuals and organizations that it is impossible to name them all. Those who kindly lent permission to reproduce photographs and other visual material are named in the appropriate captions. Portions of the travel and research in connection with the work were supported by a grant-in-aid for research from Temple University, in Philadelphia. Special thanks are also due all those who helped make it possible to study the material at first hand at the building sites and in museums in Greece, Turkey, Great Britain, and the United States. For the Greek material, the writer's appreciation is extended especially to J. R. McCredie and E. Vanderpool

of the American School of Classical Studies at Athens, to the Department of Antiquities and Restoration of Greece, and to G. Dontas, Director of the Akropolis Museum, who made it possible to include much material that would otherwise not have been available. The writer is also very grateful to T. Leslie Shear, Jr., Director of the Agora Excavations, for permission to include the unpublished Aeolic fragment from the Agora (no. A 4273). Information and assistance in connection with the Athenian vases was kindly offered by Dietrich von Bothmer, Curator of the Department of Greek and Roman Art at the Metropolitan Museum in New York, and by Michael Eisman of the Department of History at Temple University. For the material from Turkey, I would like to thank N. Dolunay, Director of the Archaeological Museums, Istanbul. Special appreciation is extended to Wolfgang Radt, who made available photographs and information from his researches at Alâzeytin. For the information about Gordion, and for many helpful comments, the study is indebted to the late Rodney S. Young, formerly Curator of the Mediterranean Section of the University Museum of the University of Pennsylvania. Several helpful suggestions concerning the Palestinian capitals were made by Yigal Shiloh, of the Institute of Archaeology, the Hebrew University, Jerusalem, and assistance with the Palestinian evidence was extended by Mrs. Inna Pommerantz of the Department of Antiquities and Museums in Israel. The Palestinian section was read by James B. Pritchard, Associate Director of the University Museum of the University of Pennsylvania, for whose help I am extremely grateful. For assistance with the bibliographical references in Hebrew, thanks are extended to my colleague Abraham Davidson, of Temple University. Helpful suggestions on the Bronze Age aspects of the volute motif were offered by Machteld Mellink, Professor of Classical and Near Eastern Archaeology at Bryn Mawr College. For permission to include the fragment of a volute capital recently discovered near Cádiz, I would like to thank Concepción Blanco, of the

Museo Provincial, Cádiz. The text was read by Homer A. Thompson, of the Institute for Advanced Study in Princeton, whose advice was especially welcome, and by Brunilde Sismondo Ridgway, of Bryn Mawr College, who also made many valuable suggestions. And finally, a word of thanks must be extended to the many friends and colleagues who offered encouragement, bibliographical leads, and advice on many individual points.

Abbreviations

The citations of ancient texts employ the abbreviations listed in *The Oxford Classical Dictionary*, N. G. L. Hammond and H. H. Scullard (eds.), Oxford, 1970.

Other bibliographical abbreviations include:

AA
Archäologischer Anzeiger

AAA
Ἀρχαιολογικὰ Ἀνάλεκτα ἐξ Ἀθηνῶν (*Athens Annals of Archaeology*)

AASOR
Annual of the American Schools of Oriental Research

ABV
J. D. Beazley, *Attic Black-figure Vase-painters* (Oxford, 1956)

Äolische Kapitell
K. Schefold, "Das äolische Kapitell," *JOAI* 31 (1939) 42–52.

AJA
American Journal of Archaeology

Akropolis
B. Graef, and E. Langlotz, *Die antiken Vasen von der Akropolis zu Athen*, unter mitwirkung von P. Hartwig, P. Wolter, und R. Zahn (Berlin, 1925)

AntJ
Antiquaries Journal

ArchEph
Ἀρχαιολογικὴ Ἐφημερίς

Architecture of Ancient Greece
W. B. Dinsmoor, *The Architecture of Ancient Greece* (London, New York, Toronto, and Sidney, 1950)

ARV²
J. D. Beazley, *Attic Red-figure Vase-painters* (Oxford, 1963)

ASAA
Annuario della Scuola Archeologica di Atene e delle Missioni Italiane in Oriente

AthMitt
Mitteilungen des deutschen archäologischen Instituts, Athenische Abteilung

BA
Biblical Archaeologist

BASOR
Bulletin of the American Schools of Oriental Research

7

BCH
Bulletin de correspondance hellénique

BIA
Bulletin of the Institute of Archaeology, University of London

BSA
British School of Archaeology at Athens, Annual

Capitello Eolico
A. Ciasca, *Il Capitello detto Eolico in Etruria* (Florence, 1962)

Catalogue
G. Mendel, *Catalogue des sculptures grecques, romaines, et byzantines* (Constantinople, 1912) vol. II

CP
Classical Philology

CQ
Classical Quarterly

Deltion
Ἀρχαιολογικὸν δελτίον

Figuralkapitelle
E. von Mercklin, *Antike Figuralkapitelle* (Berlin, 1962)

Greek and Roman Architecture
D. S. Robertson, *A Handbook of Greek and Roman Architecture* (Cambridge, 1943)

Greek Architecture
A. W. Lawrence, *Greek Architecture* (Baltimore, 1962)

Hazor
Y. Yadin *et al., The James A. de Rothschild Expedition at Hazor* (Jerusalem, 1958–1961)

Histoire de l'art
G. Perrot and C. Chipiez, *Histoire de l'art dans l'antiquité* (Paris, 1882–1914)

IEJ
Israel Exploration Journal

IstMitt
Mitteilungen des deutschen archäologischen Instituts, Abteilung Istanbul

JdI
Jahrbuch des deutschen archäologischen Instituts

JHS
Journal of Hellenic Studies

JOAI
Jahreshefte des österreichischen archäologischen Instituts

Kapitelle und Basen
B. Wesenberg, *Kapitelle und Basen. Beobachtungen zur Entstehung der griechischen Säulenformen* (Düsseldorf, 1971)

Kunst Anatoliens
E. Akurgal, *Die Kunst Anatoliens von Homer bis Alexander* (Berlin, 1961)

Larisa I
J. Boehlau and K. Schefold, *Larisa am Hermos* I: *Die Bauten* (Berlin, 1940)

Larisa II
L. Kjellberg, *Larisa am Hermos* II: *Die architektonischen Terrakotten* (Stockholm, 1940)

Larisa III
J. Boehlau and K. Schefold, *Larisa am Hermos* III: *Die Kleinfunde* (Berlin, 1942)

MdI
Mitteilungen des deutschen archäologischen Instituts

Megiddo I
R. S. Lamon and G. M. Shipton, *Megiddo* I (Chicago, 1939)

Megiddo II
G. Loud, *Megiddo* II (Chicago, 1948)

MRMC
H. G. May, *Material Remains of the Megiddo Cult* (Chicago, 1935)

Neandria
R. Koldewey, *Neandia* (51. Programm zum Winckelmannsfeste der archäologischen Gesellschaft zu Berlin, 1891)

Nimrud Ivories
R. D. Barnett, *A Catalogue of the Nimrud Ivories with other examples of ancient Near Eastern ivories in the British Museum* (London, 1957)

Paralipomena
J. D. Beazley, *Paralipomena: Additions to Attic Black-figure Vase-painters and to Attic Red-figure Vase-painters* (Oxford, 1971)

PEQ
Palestine Exploration Quarterly

Praktika
Πρακτικὰ τῆς ἐν ᾿Αθήναις ᾿Αρχαιολογικῆς ᾿Εταιρείας

Problème des ordres
R. Martin, "Problème des origines des ordres à volutes," *Etudes d'archéologie classique* 1 (1955–1956) 117–131

PW
A. Pauly, G. Wissowa *et al., Paulys Realencyclopädie d. classischen Altertumswissenschaft* (1893–)

QDAP
The Quarterly of the Department of Antiquities in Palestine

Ramath Raḥel 1954
Y. Aharoni, "Excavations of Ramath Raḥel, 1954," *IEJ* 6 (1956) 137ff.

Ramat Raḥel 1959–60
Y. Aharoni *et al., Excavations at Ramat Raḥel Seasons 1959 and 1960* (Rome, 1962)

Ramat Raḥel 1961–62
Y. Aharoni *et al., Excavations at Ramat Raḥel Seasons 1961 and 1962* (Rome, 1964)

Samaria-Sebaste 1
J. W. Crowfoot, K. M. Kenyon, and E. L. Sukenik, *Samaria-Sebaste* 1: *The Buildings* (London, 1942)

Technik und Form
A. Raubitschek, "Zur Technik und Form der altattischen Statuenbasen," *Bulletin de l'institut archéologique bulgare (Bulgarska akademiia na naukite). Sofia, Arkheologicheski institut, Izvestiia*, 2nd Series, 12 (1938) 132ff.

List of Plates

1. Cast bronze stand from Egypt
2. Foundation tablet from Sippar
3. Medinet Habu, relief depicting a cluster-column with a composite capital
4. Hazor, capital from a pillar
5. Hazor, bifacial capital from a pillar
6. Hazor, reconstruction of pillars with volute capitals
7. Aerial view of Area B at Hazor
8. Megiddo, capitals M 5339 and M 5340
9. Megiddo, capital from a pillar
10. Megiddo, capital from a pillar
11. Megiddo, reconstruction of Building 338
12. Megiddo, suggested use of volute capitals in Building 338
13. Megiddo, pottery shrine with engaged volutes at the corners, above sphinxes
14. Megiddo, fragment of a miniature capital
15. Samaria, capital for a pillar
16. Detail of the facade of glazed bricks from Babylon, showing a two-tiered volute capital from one of the decorative columns
17. Shechem, fragment of a capital
18. Pottery shrine said to be from Transjordan, with the entrance flanked by columns with volute capitals
19. Megiddo, ivory plaque with incised decoration
20. Golgoi, Cyprus, stele with paired volutes, heraldic sphinxes, and floral elaboration
21. Jerusalem, capital from a pillar
22. Ramat Raḥel, capital from a pilaster
23. Ivory plaque from the Nabu temple, Khorsabad
24. Tell Tainat, relief illustrating a volute column, part of the throne for a large seated statue
25. Medeibîyeh, capital from the east gate of the citadel
26. Series of limestone balusters from the principal building of the citadel at Ramat Raḥel
27. Broken frieze from Ramat Raḥel depicting columns or balusters with capitals with vertical volutes
28. Fragment of a stele found near Cádiz, Spain, showing an Aeolic pilaster capital with the volutes rising from a triangle
29. Alâzeytin, capital from a pilaster, from Building 30
30. Alâzeytin, capital from a pilaster, from Building 30
31. Alâzeytin, back of the capital with the heart-shaped figure between the whorls, from Building 30
32. Alâzeytin, capital from Building 31
33. Alâzeytin, capital from Building 31
34. Alâzeytin, back of capital from Building 31
35. Alâzeytin, fragment of capital from Building 31

36. Old Smyrna, leaf drum from the Archaic temple
37. Thasos, leaf drum from a capital
38. Phokaia, column drum and capital or leaf drum from an Archaic building
39. Larisa, building model with the upper part of a column
40. Larisa, building model with the upper part of a column
41. Neandria, capital from the Archaic temple, with three superimposed elements
42. Larisa, capital with vertical volutes incorrectly restored above a leaf drum from another column
43. Samos, bronze plaque illustrating a design like that of the Aeolic capital, with paired volutes rising from a leaf drum
44. Larisa, reconstruction of the large stone capital as the crowning member of an isolated column
45. Reconstruction of the Old Palace, showing the front facade, Larisa
46. Larisa, Aeolic capital with small holes for metal sheathing, assigned to the Old Palace
47. Larisa, fragment of the left volute of an Aeolic capital, assigned to the Old Palace
48. Larisa, fragment of a small Aeolic capital, probably from a votive column
49. Klopedi, Aeolic capital from the temple
50. Mytilene, capital with double margins and eyes bored completely through the stone
51. Eressos, Aeolic capital
52. Athens, fragment of an Aeolic capital found in a well in the Agora
53. Athens, capital for a votive column, found on the Akropolis

54. Athens, capital for a votive column, found on the Akropolis
55. Athens, capital for a votive column, found on the Akropolis
56. Athens, capital from a small building or shrine, found on the Akropolis
57. Athens, capital from a small building or shrine, found on the Akropolis
58. Athens, capital from a small building or shrine, found on the Akropolis
59. Athens, nineteenth-century drawing of a painted Aeolic capital found on the Akropolis
60. Athens, cavetto capital with double-volute design, from a gravestone
61. Athens, sphinx on lyre capital, from a gravestone
62. Athens, plaster cast of sphinx on lyre capital with color restored
63. Black-figured plaque no. 2547, from Athens
64. Black-figured plaque no. 2549, from Athens
65. Tamassos, Cyprus, carved tomb, showing volute capitals crowning pilasters
66. Calyx krater illustrating the slaying of the Minotaur by Theseus
67. Attica, capital found built into a church at Sykaminon, near Oropos
68. Skyphos showing an Aeolic column
69. Fragments of plaster from the Persian period at Gordion, illustrating an Aeolic column
70. Tell Tainat, column base in the portico of the *bît hilani*
71. Detail of a skyphos illustrating the ransom of Hektor

List of Text Figures

1. Painted column from the tomb of Nefer-Secheru at Zâwijet el-Mêtin, Egypt
2. Composite floral capital from the tomb of Sennedjem at Thebes
3. Column with composite floral capital from a relief in an eighteenth-dynasty tomb at Thebes
4. Map of Palestine
5. Building 1723 and its courtyard at Megiddo
6. Restoration of Building 1723 following the researches of D. Ussishkin
7. Plan of the *bît hilani* at Tell Tainat
8. Fragment of a miniature stone capital from Megiddo
9. Capital from a grave stele, from Golgoi, Cyprus
10. Plan of the citadel at Ramat Raḥel
11. Assyrian relief from the palace of Sennacherib at Nineveh (ancient Kuyunjik)
12. Plan of the fortifications around the site at Medeibîyeh
13. Capital from a grave stele, from Trapeza, Cyprus
14. Map of Egypt and the eastern Mediterranean
15. Building 30 at Alâzeytin (upper building)
16. Pilaster capital with palmette, from Building 30 at Alâzeytin
17. Pilaster capital with heart-shaped form between the volutes, from Building 30 at Alâzeytin
18. Cross section of Building 31 at Alâzeytin
19. a., Ground plan of the upper level of Building 31 at Alâzeytin
    b., Two fragmentary pilaster capitals from Building 31
20. Capital from Old Smyrna
21. Assyrian relief from the palace of Assurbanipal at Nineveh
22. Map of Aeolis and northern Ionia
23. Leaf drum from an unknown context, found at Aigai
24. State plan of the temple at Neandria
25. Volute elements from the temple at Neandria
26. Smaller volute element from the temple at Neandria
27. The smaller leaf drums from the temple at Neandria
28. The larger leaf drums from Neandria
29. Three-tiered reconstruction of the capitals from Neandria
30. The temple at Neandria restored as a simple cella with a central "spine" of columns
31. The temple at Neandria restored as a peripteral building
32. Restoration of the elements from Neandria with a single leaf drum below the volutes
33. Plan of the major buildings on the akropolis of Larisa on the Hermos
34. The large Aeolic capital from Larisa

35. Plan of the Old Palace at Larisa
36. Palace P at Pasargadae
37. Plan of the early temple at Larisa
38. Plan showing the Archaic temples at Larisa
39. Plan of the smaller temple at Klopedi
40. Plan of the larger temple at Klopedi
41. Capital, column base, and one of the drums from the Aeolic temple at Klopedi
42. Elevation of the temple at Klopedi
43. The Aeolic capital from Eressos
44. Map of Greece, the Aegean, and coastal Anatolia
45. Aeolic votive capital from Delos
46. Aeolic column used as a base for statuary, from Paros
47. Fragment of an Aeolic capital found in a well in the Agora, Athens
48. Capital from a column to support statuary, from the Athenian Akropolis
49. Aeolic capital from the Athenian Akropolis
50. Reconstruction of a sphinx and its Ionic capital from Cyrene

51. Restoration of the capital from the Naxian column at Delphi
52. Capital from a sphinx column on a pelike by the Syleus painter
53. Persian composite capital from Susa
54. Column base from the temple of Hera at Samos
55. Column base from the temple of Artemis at Ephesos
56. Reconstructed columns from the temple of Artemis at Ephesos
57. Column from the temple of Apollo at Naukratis
58. Necking from the upper part of the shaft of one of the columns of the temple of Apollo at Naukratis
59. Column base from the Aeolic temple at Klopedi
60. Rectangular block used as a capital in wooden architecture

List of Maps

Fig. 4. Palestine, p. 28
Fig. 14. Egypt and the eastern Mediterranean, p. 52

Fig. 22. Aeolis and northern Ionia, p. 62
Fig. 44. Greece, the Aegean, and coastal Anatolia, p. 90

PART I

Chapter I

THE BRONZE AGE BACKGROUND

Double-spiral designs were already established as a decorative motif for jewelry and ceramics by the Early Bronze Age. Their use continues throughout history, but the pattern is such a simple one that independent invention in a number of different areas is much more likely than a theory of unilateral transmission. By the late second millennium B.C. the design had been joined to the current styles of floral decoration where it appeared as the curvature of flower petals, palm fronds, and tendrils. Since we are concerned here only with the application of the motif to the structural parts of architecture, the decorative and symbolic uses which are related in form but not in architectural function are not a proper part of this study.[1] They are considered only incidentally when they shed light on the main subject of research.

That the roots of the architectural tradition reach earlier than the Iron Age is very apparent.

Many similar patterns existed in the Late Bronze Age, leaving little doubt that at least the outward form of the double-volute designs was already widely disseminated in the second millennium B.C.; the transition to stone architecture must have occurred at about the end of the Late Bronze Age. Since these Bronze Age designs (as later representations in the minor arts) used all possible combinations of vertical and horizontal volutes both singly and in series, the establishment of a unified theory to explain the style's beginnings is a complex matter.

Research into the origins of the Aeolic column has concentrated on comparisons with this earlier body of art. One of the many theories resulting from such comparisons suggests a development from Bronze Age palm designs like the "sacred tree."[2] According to this proposal, the Aeolic capital would have had its origins in the art of Assyria and Mesopotamia and would have spread from there to North Syria, Pales-

---

[1] For an extensive listing of decorative and symbolic uses, see that compiled by H. Danthine, *Le Palmier-Dattier et les arbres sacrés* (Paris, 1937).

[2] For a good presentation of this theory, see R. M. Engberg, "Tree Designs on Pottery, with Suggestions Concerning the Origin of Proto-Ionic Capitals," in *MRMC*, 35ff. The theory has been preferred by most of the scholars who have studied

the Palestinian series. See A. Ciasca, "I capitelli a volute in Palestina," *Rivista degli studi orientali* 36 (1961) 189–197; D. Auscher, "Le Problème des chapiteaux dits 'Proto-Ioniques,'" in "Les Relations entre la Grèce et la Palestine avant la conquête d'Alexandre," *Vetus Testamentum* 17 (1967) 27–30.

tine, and elsewhere. In a second theory the tradition is traced to Egypt where it is seen as an outgrowth of Egyptian lotus and lily capitals.[3] A third theory suggests a Hittite origin, transmitted to North Syria by Neo-Hittite population elements at the end of the Bronze Age.[4] A fourth would like to see a nascence in the art of the Mycenaeans and Minoans.[5]

The theory that traces the columns to early palm designs must rely almost entirely on comparisons from nonarchitectural contexts. It uses a large corpus of bilaterally symmetrical plant motifs, mostly based on the "sacred tree,"[6] which can be enumerated from a wide area extending all the way from beyond the Tigris and Euphrates valleys to the Mediterranean coast and from there to Anatolia, the Aegean, and Egypt. Occurring in a variety of media from carved reliefs and murals to pottery, from seals and metalwork to ivories,[7] the designs are often clearly columnar.

In their ancestry, these Asian representations often reflect the date palm. In fact, an unbroken sequence from very naturalistic trees to highly abstract columnlike patterns can be easily put together,[8] since naturalistic examples persisted alongside their more abstract counterparts until Classical times. It is the more abstract motifs, of course, which seem most related to Aeolic architecture. Many details on these "sacred trees" have close counterparts from the later architectural usage. A cast bronze stand from Egypt, now in the Field Museum of Natural History in Chicago (pl. 1), can serve to illustrate both the wide dissemination of the motif and the possible analogies with later designs. The piece,[9] found with a matching bronze jar, is decorated with openwork and includes an elegant plant form flanked by goats. It has been dated to the second half of the Eighteenth dynasty,[10] since in Egypt this type of "sacred tree" is usually associated with the period after Amenhotep II. In this example the trunk is constricted to form a small column from which spring two well-formed volutes. Their whorls have a single turn, exactly as in the earliest capitals from the Palestinian Iron Age (pls. 8 and 14). The fruit of the palm (or perhaps it is the female inflorescence), which hangs below the volutes and stretches to the ground, may be the stylistic ancestor of the small petals below the volutes on many later capitals. At the top are additional fronds, in matched pairs. They form a major part of the elaboration on this work, although some Bronze Age examples are more reserved in this area. Similar designs appear in later times as well

[3] L. Borchardt, *Die aegyptische Pflanzensäule* (Berlin, 1897) 18ff. For the lotus, see W. H. Goodyear, *The Grammar of the Lotus* (London, 1891) 71ff. and *passim*. The most closely comparable designs are those in the decorative arts, not those of the architectural tradition. For examples of the latter, see G. Foucart, *Histoire de l'ordre lotiforme* (Paris, 1897); G. Jéquier, *Manuel d'archéologie égyptienne. Les Elements de l'architecture* (Paris, 1924) 167ff. The possible Egyptian antecedents are fairly well known. They were discussed in some detail by O. Puchstein, *Die ionische Säule als klassisches Bauglied orientalischer Herkunft* (Leipzig, 1907) *passim*, and later writers have followed Puchstein's lead.

[4] Martin, *Problème des ordres*, 129.

[5] See D. Fimmen, *Die kretisch-mykenische Kultur* (Leipzig and Berlin, 1921) 202; A. Persson, *New Tombs at Dendra near Midea* (Lund, 1942) 129–132.

[6] The term should not imply that all such representations always had a religious significance. As H. Frankfort has noted, "A tree or plant occurs as the centre of an antithetical group from the earliest times. . . . Whether or not it possessed a symbolic significance in addition to its decorative value is . . . irrelevant" (*Cylinder Seals* [London, 1939] 204–205).

[7] See above, note 1.

[8] *MRMC*, 40 n. 30.

[9] Dia. 0.095 m.; ht. 0.072 m. Published by G. Steindorff, "Ein bronzener Gefässuntersatz," *Zeitschrift für ägyptische Sprache und Altertumskunde* 73 (1937) 122, pl. 12. Steindorff saw the floral motif as Egyptian, not Asian.

[10] W. S. Smith, *The Art and Architecture of Ancient Egypt* (Harmondsworth, Baltimore, and Mitcham, 1958) 137.

(pls. 18–20) where they have sometimes been regarded as the predecessors of the central palmettes on Archaic Greek capitals.

Many of the features on the bronze stand appear regularly in the Late Bronze Age, and by the Iron Age the motif was being applied to architecture. The earliest Aeolic-related palm column from a good architectural context seems to be the foundation tablet from Sippar in the British Museum (pl. 2). Illustrating King Nabu-apal-iddin before the god Shamash, the tablet dates from the ninth century B.C.[11] On the plaque the god's canopy is supported by a wooden post with paired volutes on both capital and base, and the origin of the column is confirmed by the treatment of its shaft in imitation of a palm's trunk. We do not know when the first such palm column was employed, but the highly stylized example on the tablet from Sippar suggests the end of a long development.

The custom of carved wooden supports can be traced much farther back in Egypt where canopies of this type appear by the second half of the eighteenth dynasty.[12] Their symbolism, however, reflects the lotus and the lily instead of the palm (figs. 1–3), and one can assume that the Egyptian movement began as a native tradition. The carved and perhaps stuccoed columns, known from painted representations in a number of Theban tombs, usually include several superimposed elements, with flowerlike forms occurring regularly. They are the earliest known architectural columns with Aeolic-like designs. Their volutes sometimes rise from triangles like those of the later Palestinian or Cypriote series,[13] and small forms are occasionally suspended below the volutes in the same position as the later

petals (fig. 2). Occasional pistils or stamens could be regarded as the progenitors of the palmette.

Yet there is little evidence that the transition from symbolic floral motif to stone architectural support occurred in Egypt itself. Certain architectural slabs with Aeolic-like decorations from the fortified temple complex of Ramses III at Medinet Habu (pl. 3)[14] illustrate the final stage of the Bronze Age development in Egypt, and their form stops well short of the volute style of the Iron Age.

Ramses III built a vast complex at Medinet Habu, planned as both a temple and a fortified citadel. The slabs[15] were found at the western gateway of the precinct's main defense wall where they had apparently been set into the walls of one of the side chambers of the fortified gate. Cuttings at their tops once accommodated a wooden lintel, and fragments of flat limestone blocks found with them imply a stone-lined niche with the reliefs at the sides.

The designs on the two limestone blocks are identical. Three elements form the capitals, which rise from shafts carved to simulate bundles of reeds. Lotus blossoms are just above the shafts, open papyrus clusters rise above them, and lilies form the crowning elements. Bright colors, chiefly blue, red, green, yellow, and black, were used to complete the scheme.

Architecturally, the slabs from Medinet Habu are far removed from the later development of the Aeolic style. While they seem to have supported a wooden lintel, their engaged columns are little more than high reliefs. It is the blocks themselves and not their surface decorations which act as structural supports. The architec-

[11] For a brief discussion, see A. Parrot, *Nineveh and Babylon* (London, 1961) 168–169, figs. 213 and 215.

[12] The bibliography of this motif was collected by J. Capart, *L'Art égyptien* (Paris, 1922) 35–36, pl. 152. For the dating, see F. Thureau-Dangin *et al., Arslan-Tash* (Paris, 1931) 99.

[13] An alternative theory, that the triangle owes its origin to religious symbolism, must also be considered. For bibliography and discussion of this view,

see P. Cintas, "The 'Sign of Tanit,'" *Archaeologia Viva* 1 (1968) 4ff.

[14] U. Hölscher, *The Excavation of Medinet Habu* (Chicago, 1934–1954) IV, 1–11, pls. 1–4, 6–11, 41. A good recent summary is A. Badawy, *A History of Egyptian Architecture* III (Berkeley and Los Angeles, 1968) 462ff.

[15] Cairo Mus., no. 59891; Chicago, Oriental Institute, no. 14089.

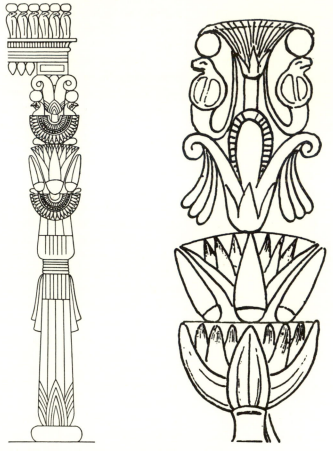

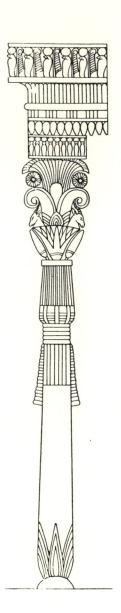

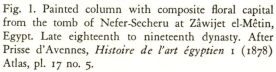

Fig. 1. Painted column with composite floral capital from the tomb of Nefer-Secheru at Zâwijet el-Mêtin, Egypt. Late eighteenth to nineteenth dynasty. After Prisse d'Avennes, *Histoire de l'art égyptien* 1 (1878) Atlas, pl. 17 no. 5.

Fig. 2. Composite floral capital from the tomb of Sennedjem at Thebes. Twentieth dynasty. After L. Borchardt, *Die aegyptische Pflanzensäule* (1897) fig. 34.

Fig. 3. Column with composite floral capital from a relief in an eighteenth-dynasty tomb at Thebes. After Prisse d'Avennes, *Histoire de l'art égyptien* 1 (1878) Atlas, pl. 17 no. 4.

tural function is purely secondary, and the main purpose of the design is the abstract symbolism of its floral embellishment.

Artistically, however, the lily elements have several details that recall later Near Eastern volute capitals. Small objects hang at the sides in the same position as the fruit on the date palm, just like the small petals on Palestinian, Cypriote, and Phoenician capitals. The sepals enclosing the lily's petals are triangular, and one could have been expanded to form the triangle at the base of many capitals from the same later series (pls. 8–10, 15–16, 20–22, 24–25, and 28). The shape between the petals, while clearly not a palmette, is strongly reminiscent of the ovals in this position on certain seventh-century B.C. baluster capitals from Ramat Raḥel (pl. 26), and an even closer correspondence exists with the Iron Age capitals from Hazor (pls. 4–6).

In other words, both Egyptian and Asian designs can be compared favorably with later volute designs. A simple morphological comparison cannot solve the question of the volute capital's antecedents, because by the Late Bronze Age both Egyptian flower motifs and Asian tree motifs used details like those of the later capitals.

It would seem that in the eighteenth and nineteenth dynasties, during what has been termed the "International Style,"[16] floral motifs were widely disseminated throughout the Near East. Forms which survived into later times as the Aeolic style appeared in many parts of the eastern Mediterranean during this era, and they must have influenced one another extensively. It was this that led to the use of double-volute patterns in Mycenaean and Minoan contexts, as well as in the Hittite designs of the Anatolian Bronze Age. Palms, lilies, and other floral patterns were used side by side, in many different contexts. Their details seem mutually interrelated. Since these details bear a striking resemblance to aspects of the architectural fashion, one must suppose the volute capital had its nascence in this "International Style." A single origin, if

it ever existed, can no longer be ascertained. Both lilies and palms probably affected the style's early course, so that a unilateral development from either is probably too simple a theory to explain the situation adequately. The designs were evidently applied to wooden posts from a very early date.

While the locality where the transition to monumental stone architecture first occurred is not known with certainty, several pieces of evidence point toward the Syro-Palestinian coast. As will be seen in the following chapters, this region is the only common denominator linking several areas with vigorous architectural traditions in the immediately succeeding periods. An alternate theory, which would substitute an origin in Mesopotamia or Assyria, does not take the Egyptian comparisons into consideration.[17] While these eastern areas undoubtedly played an early role in the style, a few features (like the application to architectural supports) clearly appear first in the Nile Valley, and an Egyptian flavor seems likely in many of the floral embellishments.

The Syro-Palestinian coast was a crossroad for artistic influences, where both Egyptian and Asiatic fashions were brought together again and again. The resulting styles placed great emphasis on exotic floral motifs with abstract symbolic meaning, and the floral capital with its underlying connotations of the "sacred tree" fits well into this pattern. A Syro-Palestinian origin corresponds very well with what we know of the style in general, and the earliest Iron Age capitals that have survived (from Megiddo, pl. 8) are also from this area. Since the blocks from Megiddo are extremely conservative, suggesting a recent and cautious application to stonework, a remote source is not justified. It is much more likely that the inspiration was from close at hand.

An additional piece of evidence would strongly reinforce this theory, provided the dating suggested by its original discoverer is accepted.

[16] W. S. Smith, *Interconnections in the Ancient Near East* (New Haven and London, 1965) chap. II and *passim*.

[17] Auscher (supra n. 2); F. Krischen, *Weltwunder der Baukunst in Babylonien und Jonien* (Tübingen, 1956).

The excavation of the Canaanite temple at Shechem by Ernst Sellin in the 1920s yielded a stone fragment that seems to be part of a capital with vertical volutes (pl. 17).[18] If it dates from the Late Bronze Age, it is the earliest extant fragment of a stone volute capital.

Shechem had an important sacred precinct with a monumental temple as early as the Middle Bronze Age. Sellin assigned the fragment to this building, but the piece was not found *in situ*, and a Middle Bronze Age dating is surely too early. More recent excavations have helped clarify the picture of Bronze Age Shechem,[19] and its situation is now more fully understood. Since a Late Bronze Age temple has now been recognized, it is much more likely that the block should be dated no earlier than this later period. The sacred precinct at Shechem was completely destroyed at the end of the Bronze Age. Only granaries were erected in this area in the Iron Age, suggesting that a later dating, while possible, would mean that the block had been moved from some more distant area of the city.

Very little is known of the Late Bronze Age phase of the temple at Shechem. In the Middle Bronze Age the structure had been a massive rectangle with several interior supports. A similar temple type is found at Megiddo, but it is otherwise rather rare in Bronze Age Palestine. The building was burned at the end of the Middle Bronze Age, and the site was not occupied for about a century. When the temple was rebuilt (about the second half of the fifteenth century B.C.), it was given a slightly different orientation. Repairs and renovations in the thirteenth century B.C. resulted in a new altar, a new floor, and undoubtedly other changes as well, but so little remains of the Late Bronze Age building that no adequate reconstruction

of either of the late phases can be attempted. Analogies from other Canaanite sites suggest a broad-roomed structure with an entrance in one of the long sides and a base for the cult statue against the other long wall.[20] The placement of the capital, if indeed it belongs to one of these temple phases, is not known.

The style of the fragment is somewhat different from that of the Iron Age volute capitals from this area (see below, chap. 11). Since the block is so fragmentary, its full design cannot be restored with certainty, but it clearly had neither the marginal borders that delineate details on later examples nor the central triangle that usually occurs on Palestinian Iron Age capitals. A comparison may be made with the capitals from Hazor (pls. 4–5), which have no triangles, because the markings on the capital from Shechem correspond rather closely with the lower portions of the examples from the more northern context, but the collation is not exact. The capital from Shechem was certainly higher, and its volutes must have been more vertical. In spite of these differences, however, the Iron Age dating is probably to be preferred. While a final answer must await further excavation, the analogy of the capitals from Hazor suggests a date of about the ninth century B.C. as the best working hypothesis.[21]

The creation of a style in stone must not imply that the tradition of the volute capital was then fully formed. The custom must have existed in a climate that included many related artistic modes in wood and even in the minor arts. These would have constantly modified the style, imbuing it with new ideas that led to fresh artistic variations. Much of this aspect of the tradition is irretrievably lost. Of one thing, however, we may be sure. The many Bronze Age

[18] E. Sellin, "Die Ausgrabung von Sichem," *Zeitschrift des Deutschen Palästina-Vereins* 49 (1926) 310, pl. 39B. The block was published only in preliminary reports. Sellin's final manuscript was destroyed in the bombing of Berlin in 1943.

[19] R. J. Bull, "A Re-examination of the Shechem Temple," *BA* 23 (1960) 110ff.; G. E. Wright, *She-*

chem: The Biography of a Biblical City (New York, 1964) with additional bibliography.

[20] Wright (supra n. 19) 97.

[21] An eighth-century B.C. date was proposed by G. Welter, "Stand der Ausgrabungen in Sichem," *AA* (1932) col. 313.

designs show the style had already formed by the end of the Late Bronze Age. The Iron Age simply expanded an existing tradition, with perhaps a metamorphosis from wood into stone.

The volute column seems to have begun as floral and palm symbolism applied to wooden supports. Eighteenth dynasty Egypt provides the earliest extant examples of Aeolic-like designs in architecture, but the Egyptian colonnettes are composite floral patterns with only a general resemblance to the columns and pilasters of the Iron Age. The maturation of the motif and its application to stone architecture must have occurred in the years that marked the transition between the Bronze and Iron Ages. A wedding of abstract religious symbolism with practical architectural function seems to have been a part of the style at its inception, and this symbolism may have persisted during much of its subsequent history.[22]

[22] See especially W. Andrae, *Die ionische Säule, Bauform oder Symbol?* (Berlin, 1933); for the same author's more recent views, see "Die griechischen Säulenordnungen," in *Kleinasien und Byzanz* (Berlin, 1950) 1–9.

PART II

Chapter II

PALESTINE

Stone capitals with vertically rising volutes first appear in Palestinian architecture in the tenth or ninth century B.C.,[1] during or immediately after the Israelite monarchy of David and Solomon. They have been recovered from a number of different sites, and although few can be assigned with certainty to their original architectural contexts, several tentative theories about their use have been proposed. The capitals almost always occur in the largest and most splendid architectural complexes, where they were used with especially fine buildings.

There is some local variation in the design of individual capitals, but in the group as a whole there are many common stylistic points, and it should probably be regarded as constituting a single artistic tradition. In general, the designs of the capitals are more simple and functional than their Bronze Age antecedents, and the exotic floral elaboration of their predecessors is largely eliminated. The blocks were usually employed with pilasters rather than columns, and their clear structural function probably helped determine their decorative style.

In the following subsections, the Palestinian sites are arranged geographically because of the uncertain chronology of many individual capitals.

HAZOR

The ancient city of Hazor[2] was situated in the Huleh plain, north of the Sea of Galilee (fig. 4). Its commanding position overlooking the north-south trade arteries made it a natural strong point, one of the more important cities in ancient Palestine, and its settlement began at a very early period. The site figured prominently in Middle and Late Bronze Age history; in the Iron Age it came under the control of the Israelites, and its dominant position continued.

The earlier city was completely destroyed in the thirteenth century B.C., presumably by the Israelites, and there was only sparse occupation at the site until it was rebuilt during the tenth century B.C. (Stratum X). With a casemate wall pierced by a magnificent gateway like those of contemporary Gezer and Megiddo, the city now boasted a royal quarter set off from the remainder of the town. The casemate wall was still used in Stratum IX, probably to be assigned to the next century, but in the succeeding period (Stra-

---

[1] For a possible earlier example see the discussion of the fragment from Shechem in chapter I.

[2] Y. Yadin *et al., Hazor* I–IV.

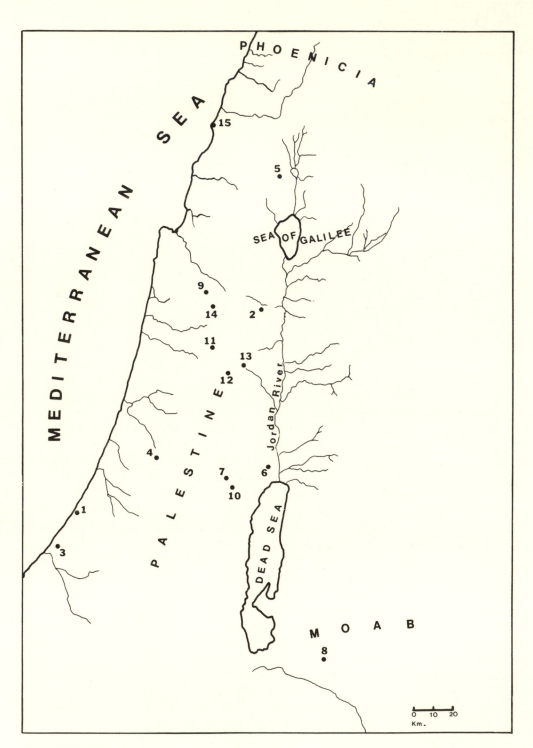

Fig. 4. Map of Palestine:
1. Ascalon   4. Gezer   7. Jerusalem   10. Ramat Raḥel   13. Tell   15. Tyre
2. Beth-Shan   5. Hazor   8. Medeibîyeh   11. Samaria   el Far'ah
3. Gaza   6. Jericho   9. Megiddo   12. Shechem   14. Tell
                                                                           Ta'annek

28

tum VIII), there was a complete revamping of the fortification system. New walls were added in the east, and a massive citadel (Locus 3090) with several ancillary buildings was built in the west, over the casemate wall. A large public building with two rows of monolithic pillars can also be assigned to this phase. The fortunes of the city may have declined slightly in Stratum VII, but two additional building levels (VI and V) can be identified before the razing of the city by Tiglath-pileser III in 732 B.C. Only a small unfortified settlement was placed on the tell in the next few years.

Two volute capitals (pls. 4–6) were found at Hazor, reused as windbreaks for an oven stratified above a floor from Stratum VII.[3] One of the stones is carved on both front and back; the other has one smooth face. Although the pieces have many points in common with other Palestinian capitals, the examples from Hazor seem to be more fully developed. Their volutes are taller and more gracefully curved than was usual in Palestine, they have no basal triangles, and a small, leaflike design is placed between the volutes. A small eye occurs at the center of each whorl, which has a single turn with marginal borders at the edges of the carving. The blocks have small petals at their corners and a generally rectilinear appearance. As was usual in Palestine, they capped pillars. Their upper and lower surfaces were smooth, and a mason's mark, the letter aleph, was incised into the base of one piece. Along with the limestone capitals was a massive stone lintel about 2.4 m. long.

Since the stones were found near the entrance to the large citadel of Stratum VIII (3090, in Area B), they have been assigned to this structure (pl. 7). Only basement rooms were dis-

covered. The building was rectangular (25 x 21.5 m.), with its longest axis running east and west, and was evidently two stories high. Remains of two bases were found at the entrance to a paved corridor running along the northern side of the structure, between it and an adjacent building. This portal was evidently the main entrance to the complex. The measurements of the bases correspond exactly with the dimensions of the capitals, and the distance between them agrees with the length of the large stone lintel. It would seem that the capital with one carved face capped a pilaster standing against the northern wall of the citadel, while the bifacial block was used with a free-standing pillar in the center of the entrance (see the reconstruction in pl. 6). The entire structure may be dated to the ninth century B.C.

MEGIDDO

One of the natural trade routes along the coast of the Mediterranean must have moved north along the Palestinian coast, avoiding the rugged lands to the east until it turned inland where the Plain of Esdraelon pierces the Lebanon Mountains. Here stood Megiddo (fig. 4), wealthy and flourishing during most periods because of its strategic location, but forced, for the same reason, to be a pawn in the hands of the great powers. This role was especially evident during the Iron Age when the city was attacked and burned repeatedly, always to rise again.

Recent excavations by Yadin have clarified the sequence for the Iron Age, and it is now possible to assess more effectively Megiddo's position in this period.[4] After a twelfth century B.C. level in

[3] Y. Yadin, "Excavations at Hazor, 1958," *IEJ* 9 (1959) 79; "The Fourth Season of Excavations at Hazor," *BA* 22 (1959) 10ff.; *Hazor* III–IV, pls. 48 no. 1, 49 nos. 1–3, 362 and 363.

[4] Y. Yadin, "New Light on Solomon's Megiddo," *BA* 23 (1960) 62–68; "Hazor, Gezer and Megiddo in Solomon's Times," in A. Malamat, ed., *The Kingdoms of Israel and Judah* (Jerusalem, 1961) 66ff. (in Hebrew); "Notes and News; Megiddo,"

IEJ 16 (1966) 178ff.; 17 (1967) 119–121; "Megiddo of the Kings of Israel," *BA* 33 (1970) 66ff.; *Hazor* (London, 1972) 150ff.; Y. Yadin, Y. Shiloh, and A. Eitan, "Notes and News; Archaeology; Excavations; Megiddo," *IEJ* 22 (1972) 161ff. For an argument countering the conclusions of Yadin, see Y. Aharoni, "The Stratification of Israelite Megiddo," *Journal of Near Eastern Studies* 31 (1972) 302ff., with a reply by Yadin in vol. 32 (1973) 330. For

which quantities of early Philistine pottery were used (Stratum VIIA), the city was rebuilt on a much smaller scale. This was City VIB, dating from about the late twelfth to early eleventh century B.C. It, too, was destroyed violently, but it was followed by a greatly expanded settlement. The new city (VIA) had fine houses of brick on stone foundations, and its inhabitants must have been much better off than their predecessors; the city's destruction by fire in the late eleventh century left many metal tools and quantities of pottery in a late Philistine style. Next came Stratum VB, a tiny town without even a circuit wall. It was followed by a lavish rebuilding associated by many scholars with the reign of Solomon (IVB-VA). Large city walls now enclosed fine palaces and other public buildings in addition to domestic architecture, and a monumental gate at Megiddo can be compared with similar structures at Hazor and Gezer, furnishing sure architectural links for the era. The next city (Stratum IVA) has been called a "chariot city" because of a large building complex regarded by the excavators as stables, a view which has recently been challenged for several cogent reasons.[5] The city lasted until its conquest by Tiglath-pileser III of Assyria in 733 B.C. City III was built soon after. It had buildings with central courts in the Assyrian manner, suggesting that Megiddo was now an administrative center for the expanding Assyrian empire.

Architectural capitals with vertical volutes are known from two different contexts at Megiddo. Both groups can be assigned to Stratum IV, but since no piece was found *in situ*, they could belong either to the city usually associated with Solomon (IVB-VA) or to the succeeding period (Stratum IVA). For the first group, the earlier dating is probably to be preferred.

Only two capitals are in the first series (pl. 8). They were found at the southern side of the city near a gate (Locus 1567) in a walled enclosure for a monumental building at Locus 1723.[6] Since the two stones are the same size,[7] they were probably used in the same building, even though only one of them has a carved front face. They are very squat in their proportions, with a ratio of width to height of more than four to one. On the worked example, two volutes rise from the block's flat base, while a triangle lies between them. The details are outlined by moldings, and petals occur at the corners, outside the volutes. The second capital is smooth on both front and back, and only the petals at the sides are carved in relief. Both pieces are of limestone.

There are two types of cuttings in the upper surfaces, carved semicircles and dowel holes. Both capitals have the semicircles sunk into the centers of the blocks. On the worked example there are two dowel holes near the edge on the side of the carved face; the smooth specimen has four holes arranged in pairs, with another hole in the center at the semicircular depression.

Two theories have been advanced to explain the capitals: the first would regard them as part of engaged pilasters or doorjambs in a gateway; the second would place at least one of the blocks atop a free-standing pillar, and it would assign them to the portico of a palace. Both theories agree about the dating because in Stratum IV the only large structures from near where the capitals were found are from Stratum IVB-VA, usually assigned to the tenth century B.C. The carved capitals surely date from the same period.

The first theory places the capitals with Gateway 1567 (fig. 5).[8] They were found near this portal, which was certainly monumental enough to have used carved architectural members. Giv-

---

general bibliography for Megiddo, consult K. M. Kenyon, *Archaeology in the Holy Land* (New York, 1970) 319, 346ff., and the bibliography in this work.

[5] J. B. Pritchard, "The Megiddo Stables: A Reassessment," in *Near Eastern Archaeology in the Twentieth Century* (Essays in Honor of Nelson Glueck, J. A. Sanders, ed., Garden City, 1970)

232ff.

[6] Lamon and Shipton, *Megiddo* I, 14–15, fig. 17. They were reused in Stratum III.

[7] They vary slightly in width only. Carved capital (M 5340): ht. 0.57 m.; length 2.44 m.; thickness 0.57 m. Unworked capital (M 5339): 0.57 x 2.39 x 0.56 m.

[8] *Megiddo* I, 15.

ing access to a large, lime-floored courtyard for Building 1723, the gate projected outward from the enclosure wall and included two pairs of rooms. At the north end of the gateway there were projections extending about 0.35 m. inward from the north-south walls, and the capitals could have been used at this point. The projections were the same width as the northern (east-west) walls of the gateway, a measurement which also coincides with the width of the bases of the capitals (about a meter and a half). If the projections were doorjambs, they might have used capitals to support a lintel across the doorway.

A use of the capitals with engaged pilasters is very possible, but the two unworked faces on one stone pose a problem. Was the piece originally stuccoed or painted, or was it perhaps unfinished? Its grooved semicircles and dowel holes indicate it was designed for use, and Lamon and Shipton suggested the possibility that it was unfinished because when the gate was excavated it was thought the enclosure had been demolished shortly after its construction. More recent excavations, however, have shown that the enclosure probably stood for some time.[9] A second (and more serious) problem is presented by the dowel holes. If the holes helped hold a lintel in place across two doorjambs, why are the two upper surfaces dissimilar?

A new theory has recently been advanced to explain these problems. Suggested by Ussishkin, it supposes that the capitals did not go with the gateway but were instead a part of Building 1723, the main construction within the enclosure (fig. 6).[10] This building has been called both a citadel and a palace, and perhaps it was both. Because its walls were preserved only at a very low level, there is no architectural evidence for doorways, and this has led to different interpretations of the plan. The building included an open courtyard (Area A), and the original excavators thought that the wing on the east was a portico used as an entrance to the building. Ussishkin suggests instead that Area H was the porch.[11] His plan is based on a comparison with the North Syrian *bît hilani*,[12] in which a portico flanked by a tower and a square room acts as the entrance to a large reception chamber arranged with its long axis parallel to the front of the building (fig. 7). In Ussishkin's plan (fig. 6), one or more free-standing pillars between pilasters would have been required in the portico. He suggests that the undecorated capital with its two pairs of dowel holes could have capped one of these pillars.[13] Its dowel holes would have helped secure the beam above the doorway, and both sides of the capital would have been visible. The carved capital has only two holes because it would have been used with an engaged pilaster at the side, and the beam would have rested only on the outer half of the stone. One cannot know the width of the walls with certainty, but the excavators' estimate (based on analogies with other buildings) was about 1.5 m. This is the same as the base of the capitals, reinforcing the possibility of this reconstruction.

The theory is very reasonable, and it offers the best explanation advanced so far to explain the arrangements of the dowels. If the capitals were all placed with their long axes parallel to the jambs of the portico, they would all have had

---

[9] Yadin (supra n. 4, 1970) 72ff. Originally the "stables" were assigned to Solomon's reign, which meant that earlier structures could not have stood for long and were perhaps demolished before they were completed.

[10] D. Ussishkin, "On the Original Position of Two Proto-Ionic Capitals at Megiddo," *IEJ* 20 (1970) 213ff.

[11] D. Ussishkin, "King Solomon's Palace and Building 1723 in Megiddo," *IEJ* 16 (1966) 174–186; "King Solomon's Palaces," *BA* 36 (1973) 78ff.

[12] For the *bît hilani* in general, see H. Frankfort, "The Origin of the Bît Hilani," *Iraq* 14 (1952) 120–131, and, more recently, E. Akurgal, *The Art of Greece: Its Origins in the Mediterranean and Near East* (New York, 1968) 69ff., translation of *Orient und Okzident: Die Geburt der griechischen Kunst* (Baden-Baden, 1966). After Ussishkin's research was published, excavation in the northern part of the city showed that Building 6000 was also a *bît hilani*. See Yadin (supra n. 4, 1970) 73–75.

[13] Ussishkin (supra n. 10) 214–215.

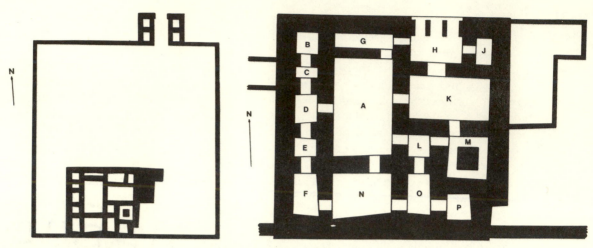

Fig. 5. Building 1723 and its courtyard at Megiddo. Gate 1567 pierces the enclosure's wall at the north. Some very fragmentary foundations (not shown) were between Building 1723 and the west wall of the courtyard, indicating that the doorway was probably in the north or the east. For a state plan see *Megiddo* I, fig. 12.

Fig. 6. Restoration of Building 1723 following the researches of D. Ussishkin. Room H is restored as the main entrance, a portico with two engaged and two free-standing Aeolic pillars.

carved surfaces visible since even the smooth capital is carved on the ends. The number of capitals required for this reconstruction cannot be determined with certainty, but it would seem most likely that there were four.

The second group of limestone capitals from Megiddo may have come from the "chariot city" (IVA) that followed the destruction of Building 1723, but this is not completely certain because again none of the pieces was found *in situ*.[14] Some had been reused as late as Stratum II,[15] but one block may have been found with material from Stratum IVB-V.[16] While such a context could suggest a date in the same period as Building 1723, the stratigraphy of the area is not very clear,[17] and the isolated lower block clearly belongs with the ones found higher up. With this confusion in the available evidence, conclusions concerning the context of these capitals must remain theoretical.

[14] *Megiddo* I, 55ff.; *MRMC*, 4ff. and 10–11.
[15] *MRMC*, pl. III.
[16] *Ibid.*, pl. IV.
[17] The area may have been lower than the surrounding terrain, which would account for the "lower" stratification. See *MRMC*, 8.
[18] One is fragmentary and is kept at the site. The

In their overall form, the blocks (pls. 9–10) are quite different from the first series from Megiddo. They have a ratio of width to height of slightly more than two to one, and their central triangles always cover the bases. The volutes on each specimen rise from the sides of its triangle, not from the base, and the entire design is much more compact. Details, however, prove the close relation: marginal borders are rendered in the same way; the volutes have a single turn; a small eye comes out of the molding, not the turn of the whorl; and petals are added above and below each volute. On one piece there are three small vertical lines above the triangle.

Three of the capitals were carved on both front and back,[18] while several others were carved on the front only. All were carved on the sides. An irregular hole in the back of one example (pl. 10) may have had some function,[19]

other is in the Israel Museum, Jerusalem, no. 36.2189. The third is not fully published. For discussion see Shiloh, *BASOR* 122 (1976) 67ff.

[19] If the hole was a deliberate cutting, it is curious that similar features do not occur in other capitals from the same series, but only in the example in the Oriental Institute, Chicago, no. 3657.

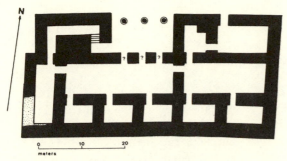

Fig. 7. Plan of the *bît hilani* at Tell Tainat, dating from about 800 B.C. Adapted from C. W. McEwan, "The Syrian Expedition of the Oriental Institute of the University of Chicago," *AJA* 41 (1937) 9, fig. 4.

but its use is not clear.[20] The tops are rough but have no cuttings.

The series of capitals has been tentatively assigned to the nearby building at Locus 338 (pls. 11–12.[21] Perhaps used both as a residence and as a religious center in City IVA, this edifice was part of the "chariot city" built over the ruins of Solomonic Megiddo. Its construction techniques, with walls of alternating ashlar piers and rubble, are typical of this era at the city.[22] The building was set within an enclosure wall, and it had a lime-floored courtyard on the north and west. There were many rooms, some surely functioning as cult places. Doorways were not indicated in the surviving masonry.

Except for the fact that the series of capitals

was found in its vicinity, direct evidence for the use of volute capitals in Building 338 is rather meager. One corroboration for the possibility comes from a comparison with certain terracotta shrines, also found nearby. Fragments of at least two shrines were found at Megiddo.[23] Roughly comparable models are known from sites stretching all the way from Mesopotamia to Cyprus,[24] but the pieces from Megiddo are remarkable for their use of vertical volutes.[25] On one model Aeolic-like whorls (complete with petal-like ornaments like those on the stone blocks) were placed at the upper part of the model's corners above engaged female figures (pl. 13). Engaged pilasters or columns, somewhat more amorphous in form, decorated the corners of the second shrine. From the evidence of the shrines, some writers have reconstructed Building 338 with engaged Aeolic pilasters on the exterior facade.[26] This requires the theory that the worked "back faces" of some of the capitals represent unsuccessful preliminary attempts by the masons,[27] a suggestion which has been weakened by the discovery of Palestinian capitals with both faces worked at Hazor[28] and Ramat Raḥel.[29] While one must still suppose most volute capitals in Palestine crowned engaged pilasters, the possibility of an occasional free-standing pillar seems very strong. Perhaps some of the doorways in Building 338 were wide enough to require a central support for the lintel, or perhaps the building included a portico. Only with such a recon-

[20] The cavity is extremely eroded. No tool marks are visible, and the original purpose (if there was one) can no longer be ascertained from the cutting itself. In the opinion of the present writer, the hole is accidental.

[21] *Megiddo* I, 55–56 and fig. 68; *MRMC*, 4ff.

[22] K. M. Kenyon, "Megiddo, Hazor, Samaria and Chronology," *BIA* 4 (1964) 149–150.

[23] For a discussion, consult *MRMC*, 13ff.

[24] See the lists compiled by V. Müller, "Die Zierradel aus dem III. mykenischen Schachtgrab," *AthMitt* 43 (1918) 160 and by May, *MRMC*, 14–15.

[25] A pottery shrine with added volutes at the corners was also found at the site of Tell Ta'annek, located about five miles to the southeast of Megiddo. Its volutes, however, seem to be more decorative than architectural. See E. Sellin, "Tell Ta'an-

nek," *Denkschriften der kaiserlichen Akademie der Wissenschaften, philosophisch-historische Klasse* 5 (1904) 75, figs. 102, 104–105, and pl. 12. Other shrines with volute capitals come from an unknown site "in Transjordan," discussed below, and from a tomb at Amathos on Cyprus (P. P. Betancourt, "An Aeolic Shrine in Philadelphia," *AJA* 75 [1971] 427–428, pls. 91–92). There are also additional unpublished examples in the Israel Museum (Y. Shiloh, personal communication).

[26] *MRMC*, pl. VI.

[27] *Ibid.*, 11.

[28] Y. Yadin, "Excavations at Hazor, 1958," *IEJ* 9 (1959) 79; *Hazor* III–IV, pl. 362 (illustrated here in pl. 5).

[29] Y. Aharoni *et al.*, *Ramat Raḥel 1959–60*, 14–15, fig. 13 no. 1, pl. 11 no. 1.

struction can the bifacial capitals be explained satisfactorily (provided the bifacial capitals are architectural).[30]

In addition to the clearly architectural pieces, the excavations at Megiddo uncovered a fragment of a limestone capital that seems too small to have been used as the structural part of a building (pl. 14 and fig. 8).[31] Assigned by the excavators to Stratum VB, the small piece (preserved length 0.17 m.) includes a portion of a volute with petals like its larger counterparts. The loss of its center precludes a really close comparison, however, since the stylistic arrangement of the central triangle cannot be ascertained. The fragment may have been used with furniture, or it may have been a votive or a small architectural ornament; its importance comes not from its conjectural use but from what it can tell us about the painted decoration of the Palestinian volute capitals.

Stratified beneath a courtyard, the fragment was protected so that its paint was relatively intact. A number of colors, with red and blue predominating, had been used to enhance its appearance. The front had red petals and borders for the volute, while the background of the volute itself was blue. On the side were small squares in red, white, and gray (originally black or blue?) between red and reddish brown borders. The top and bottom were solid red.

One cannot really know how extensive the practice of painting was in Palestinian architecture, but it was probably a regular one.[32] For the decorative pilasters, the painted capital may furnish some guidelines about the style's outlines. It implies a bright and colorful tradition in which individual elements were picked out in contrast-ing hues.[33] One may perhaps imagine a similar style for the larger architectural members.

SAMARIA

After the dissolution of the Israelite united monarchy, the capital of the newly independent northern kingdom of Israel was placed first at Shechem and then at Tirzah (Tell el Far'ah). A permanent capital was not established until about 880 to 870 B.C. when Omri founded the city of Samaria.[34] The new capital,[35] set atop an easily defensible hill, flourished as a rival of the southern capital at Jerusalem until it was captured by Assyria in the late eighth century B.C. (fig. 4).

Archaeologically, this era can be divided into six building periods, with Period I beginning at the founding of the city. From the first, the summit of Samaria was laid out as a royal precinct, and buildings were set within spacious courts. The city's masonry techniques (with fine walls of flat-dressed blocks and rougher walls and foundations of blocks with rough bosses in the center and finely dressed margins on two or three sides) have been called "Phoenician" because they can be traced to Ugarit where they occur in the thirteenth century B.C.[36] A small enclosure wall set off the royal quarter in Period I, and in Period II the wall was rebuilt as a defensive fortification. Period III ushered in a new era in which the "Phoenician style" masonry was not used. Many new buildings were added to the city, limiting the size of the courts. The courtyards were further reduced in Period IV when many small rooms were built, even up against the fortification wall. Two additional building

---

[30] A. Ciasca has suggested that some of the bifacial examples might have been used to support basins, altars, or the like, which is a very plausible theory. See her "I capitelli a volute in Palestina," *Rivista degli studi orientali* 36 (1961) 193.

[31] *Megiddo* I, 55 n. 37; *Megiddo* II, pl. 270 no. 1.

[32] The practice was in all likelihood inherited from the Bronze Age. Compare the painted columns from the Theban tombs, figs. 1–3, and the reliefs from Medinet Habu, pl. 3.

[33] It is worth noting that the Aeolic style at this

period was applied primarily as a decorative embellishment for buildings of mud brick covered with plaster. Color must have been a vital part of the ornament since it could be used on parts of the buildings where the techniques of construction permitted little variation in structural form.

[34] 1 Kings 16:23–24.

[35] For a brief discussion, see G. E. Wright, "Samaria," *BA* 22 (1959) 67ff.

[36] *Samaria-Sebaste* I, 5ff.

periods (V and VI) can be recognized before the city was captured by Sargon in 722–721 B.C.

Except for fixed dates at the beginning and end of this broad period, the dates of Iron Age Samaria are unfortunately rather flexible. While Kenyon and others have placed Periods I and II in the reigns of Omri and Ahab (c. 870–840 B.C.),[37] Wright has extended them to about 810 B.C.[38] Kenyon would place Period III in the time of Jehu (c. 841–813 B.C.), while Wright would prefer the end of the ninth and the first half of the eighth century B.C., causing similar shifts in the succeeding periods. Even the correlation with other sites is not agreed upon, although as far as the architectural phases are concerned, the collations of Kenyon appear to be the most convincing.[39] She associates Samaria's Period III with Megiddo's Stratum IVA (the period of the "stables" at Megiddo), which could make Solomonic Megiddo (Stratum IVB-V) a long period, coinciding in its later stages with Samaria's Periods I and II. Certainly the "Phoenician-style" masonry at Megiddo (reused in Stratum IVA) and Samaria (I and II) is very comparable.

Seven pilaster capitals with vertical volutes were found at Samaria, built into Hellenistic and Roman walls and foundations.[40] As different sizes were found, the limestone blocks may have been used originally in more than one context. Three complete specimens and fragments of two others were found in the smaller size, which was about a half meter high by a little over one meter long (pl. 15). The larger size, represented only by a half-capital measuring 0.65 x 1.30 x 0.42 m., to be reconstructed as 2.5 m. long, and by a fragment from a piece once 1.4 m. long, was not given details on the front. All others were carved only on the front and sides in a design very obviously related to the second group of capitals from Megiddo (pls. 9–10). As at Megiddo, a central triangle covers the base of each piece. Small petals complete the corners, and marginal borders outline the carved features. The volutes have a single turn, with small eyes at the centers of the whorls.

Since the capitals were all found at the east end of the terraced summit, where the entrance to the royal enclosure was located, it has been suggested they were used to line the walls of a monumental forecourt leading to the main royal precinct.[41] Unfortunately, the early remains at Samaria are extremely fragmentary, and none of the stones were found in their original positions. The suggestion of engaged pilasters on opposite sides of a courtyard is a good one. That the volute capital was sometimes used with this type of continuous facade is suggested by the series of columns depicted in glazed brick on the exterior of a building in Babylon, from the early sixth century B.C. (pl. 16). The larger capitals, however, must have had a different use. For the date, it is likely the blocks should be assigned to one of the fine masonry structures in the royal quarter, within Periods I–II. The close comparison with the second group of capitals from Megiddo places both groups within the same tradition, which must have flourished about the ninth to early eighth century B.C.[42]

SHECHEM

Shechem is located in the plain of Askar, southeast of Samaria (fig. 4).[43] After the earlier city was destroyed at the beginning of the Iron

---

[37] The dates are those adopted by the excavators of Samaria. See K. Kenyon, *Royal Cities of the Old Testament* (New York, 1971) 92.

[38] G. E. Wright, "Israelite Samaria and Iron Age Chronology," *BASOR* 155 (1959) 13–29; (supra n. 35) 67–78.

[39] Kenyon (supra n. 22) 149ff.; (supra n. 4) 269ff. and 347–348; (supra n. 37) 93. For other views see Wright (supra n. 35 and n. 38); Y. Aharoni and R. Amiran, "A New Scheme for the Sub-Division of the Iron Age in Palestine,"

IEJ 8 (1958) 171ff.

[40] For bibliography see pp. 135–136.

[41] *Ibid.*, 14–15. For a discussion of the glazed brick facade from Babylon, see R. Koldewey, *The Excavations at Babylon* (London, 1914) 104ff.

[42] The series cannot be dated closely, and the earlier miniature block from Megiddo (discussed above) could push the series back a little in time.

[43] G. E. Wright, *Shechem: The Biography of a Biblical City* (New York and Toronto, 1965).

Age, the site saw little occupation for several years. Rebuilt again as an Israelite settlement, it was expanded during the tenth century B.C. (Strata XII and XI); the destruction of Stratum XI can perhaps be associated with the invasion of the Pharaoh Shishak in the last third of the century. Stratum X, a hasty rebuilding, was followed by three successive Israelite levels (IXB, IXA, and VIII) culminating in Stratum VIII. The latter marks a prosperous time in the life of the city, a period of long stability when "Samarian Ware" was used.[44] The excavators placed its destruction in the middle of the eighth century B.C. Stratum VII, the last level before the area was invaded by Assyria, marked a slight decline in the fortunes of the city. Historically, Shechem was probably a provincial capital in the tenth century B.C.[45] It became the capital of Israel for a brief time at the dissolution of the united monarchy,[46] and it must have remained an important center even after the seat of government was moved to Samaria.[47]

A fragment of carved stone from this site seems to have come from a capital with vertical volutes (pl. 17). It was found built into a later structure[48] in the vicinity of the Bronze Age sacred precinct,[49] and its original context is not known. It would appear to be the lower half of a capital, broken just below the whorls. While the lower parts of the volutes are plainly visible, the central motif poses some questions. It is surely the base of a palmette or some more simple dividing element, but its slight cant, suggesting the block was not bilaterally symmetrical, is a highly unusual feature. The piece is much more cylindrical than the rectilinear blocks that are usual in Palestine, and it seems to have come from a free-standing column.

The difficulty in dating this capital has already been discussed (see chap. 1). Its best parallels are the two capitals from Hazor (pls. 4–5) which also lack the central triangle. They may suggest something about the missing upper part of the capital from the more southern city, but the comparison is not exact; besides the cylindric aspect of the broken fragment, its volutes were clearly higher and more vertically arranged; a much smaller resting surface is also obvious; and the simple incisions for details create an entirely different overall impression. An Iron Age date is to be preferred,[50] but too little is known of the Palestinian series to reach more than a tentative conclusion.

UNKNOWN SITE, SAID TO BE "IN TRANSJORDAN"

A small pottery shrine, reportedly found "in Transjordan," is now in the Israel Museum in Jerusalem (pl. 18).[51] It was purchased along with two pieces of Palestinian pottery allegedly from the same find, and these can be dated to the first half of the Palestinian Iron Age II period, about the tenth to ninth century B.C. The model is probably from the same era. It was made to resemble a building, with a front that includes columns with volute capitals of an elaborate type. Since the capitals cannot be paralleled from Palestinian architecture but do occur elsewhere, the shrine becomes an important piece of evidence for the history of the volute capital in the early part of the first millennium B.C.

Made to resemble a barrel-shaped jug at the back, the model has an architectural facade at the front only. It includes a small porch sup-

[44] Wright (supra n. 38) 23.

[45] See the discussion in Wright (supra n. 43) 144.

[46] 1 Kings 12:25.

[47] 1 Kings 16:23–24.

[48] E. Sellin, "Die Ausgrabung von Sichem," *Zeitschrift des Deutschen Palästina-Vereins* 49 (1926) 311. Its exact find spot was not reported.

[49] For a possible Bronze Age dating, see above, chapter 1.

[50] An eighth century B.C. date was suggested by G. Welter, "Stand der Ausgrabungen in Sichem," *AA* (1932) col. 313. This was accepted by Ciasca (supra n. 30) 191–192. According to the archaeological record, the eighth century B.C. was a high point in the city's history and a time of much building activity.

[51] J. H. Iliffe, "A Model Shrine of Phoenician Style," *QDAP* 11 (1944) 99–100 and pl. 21.

ported by two columns, with a single room beyond the portico, approached through an open doorway. The roof is flat on the facade, but the upper part of the main room takes its shape from the form of the vase. A plastic bird is above the doorway, immediately beneath the horizontal lintel.

While the piece is carefully made, its architectural elements are rather ambiguous. The columns appear to be arranged prostyle, but small struts join them to the building about halfway up their length, and the capitals are completely engaged. The lintel also forms the cornice, but it is placed very high with respect to the back of the shrine, completely above the level of the "ceiling." The bird projects out from between the capitals. It is difficult to see how it would be supported on an actual building, and unless the figure is a sculpture attached to the wall above the doorway, it may be best to think of it as an actual bird, perhaps a sacred dove flying out from a dovecote beneath the eaves. The spread wings seem to reinforce this possibility.

The columns are very amorphous. They have no abrupt transitions between any of their elements, and details are schematized or missing altogether. It is impossible to tell if bases are intended because the clay spreads slightly at the bottom of each shaft. The capitals, with two sets of whorls, are modeled only on the front. Their lower volutes flow smoothly out of the shafts, a technique that also occurs on one of the pottery shrines from Megiddo, but the example from Megiddo has only one set of whorls.[52] The upper half of each capital forms a stylized floral pattern. The design is a common Bronze Age motif (pl. 1) also familiar from many later examples in the minor arts (pl. 19).[53] Additional whorls

of this type do not occur on any of the stone capitals from Palestine, although they do appear in stone elsewhere, especially in regions like Cyprus that seem to have been under strong Phoenician influence (fig. 9 and pl. 20). The prevalence of this design in the Phoenician minor arts, especially the carved ivories, suggests the shrine was manufactured either by a Phoenician craftsman or under strong Phoenician influence. It must reflect a tradition of wooden architecture distinct from that preserved in the Palestinian stone capitals since these were usually used with pilasters, and their morphology is entirely different.

JERUSALEM

Before its conquest by David in the early tenth century B.C., Jerusalem had been inhabited by the Jebusites, who had held the city as a fortified stronghold. Since the place had never been under the jurisdiction of any individual Israelite tribe, it was a natural choice as the capital of the newly united Israelite monarchy. David had little opportunity to develop the city, but his son Solomon expanded it, revamped its fortification system, and embellished it with magnificent public buildings. Jerusalem flourished under the monarchy, and it became the capital of Judah when the kingdom was divided in the last third of the tenth century B.C.

Although its relevant archaeological remains have almost all passed away, the city's literary records provide important testimony for the early history of the volute capital in Palestine. These written records, in fact, help considerably in the interpretation of the archaeological evi-

[52] MRMC, 17 and pl. 15 (Cat. no. 5 in the present work). A shrine from Tell el Far'ah includes the upper volutes but not the lower (Aeolic) ones (S. Yeivin, "Jachin and Boaz," PEQ 91 [1959] pl. 1, no. 3). Yeivin suggests that these are double capitals, with the upper set upside down. The Bronze Age antecedents of the motif seem to rule out this theory (compare the Egyptian bronze stand, pl. 1).

[53] Numerous examples were collected by H. Danthine, Le Palmier-Dattier et les arbres sacrés (Paris, 1937) pls. 38–49 and passim. A good discussion, especially as it concerns the ivories, is in R. D. Barnett, Nimrud Ivories, 85ff. and 141. While the motif had a rather wide distribution in the Near East, it seems to have been especially popular in the area of North Syria and Phoenicia.

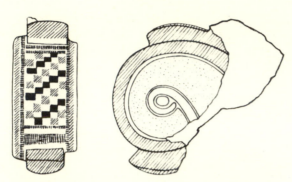

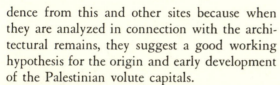

Fig. 8. Fragment of a miniature stone capital from Megiddo, showing the painted designs. After *Megiddo* II, pl. 270 no. 1.

Fig. 9. Capital from a grave stele, from Golgoi, Cyprus, now in the Louvre. After Perrot and Chipiez, *Histoire de l'art* III (1885) fig. 52.

dence from this and other sites because when they are analyzed in connection with the architectural remains, they suggest a good working hypothesis for the origin and early development of the Palestinian volute capitals.

Only one stone capital with vertically rising volutes has been discovered from Jerusalem (pl. 21). It was found[54] with a tumble of fine masonry blocks at the eastern side of the city, stratified beneath a fifth- to third-century B.C. level. The blocks had evidently been used near their findspot, some distance south of the area Solomon used for his royal quarter. The limestone capital has whorls with only one turn each, well-developed eyes at the centers of the volutes, and a large basal triangle. A horizontal weight-bearing element lies across the top. Petals are placed at the corners above and below each volute, and circles decorate the flat areas between triangle and whorls. The capital has a rather rectilinear overall form, and it was used with a pilaster. Its original context is not known.

The block cannot be dated with precision. Kenyon has suggested it may be Solomonic,[55]

but a tenth-century B.C. date is not at all certain. The blocks found with the capital can be closely compared with ninth-century stonework from Samaria,[56] and a comparison with the Samarian volute capitals could suggest the same conclusion. A better parallel, however, can be found from the well-dated site at Ramat Raḥel. Volute capitals from this small citadel (pl. 22) bear a striking resemblance to the example from Jerusalem since all have small decorative circles in the background fields, triple lines to delineate the triangles, and similar proportions. The capitals from Ramat Raḥel decorated a large building complex built about the middle of the seventh century B.C.,[57] which would seem to point toward the latter part of the Iron Age for the example from Jerusalem as well. The exact use of the block from Jerusalem will probably never be known.

The city offers one additional piece of evidence for the early history of the volute capital. The literary account of the temple of Solomon adds several points to our knowledge of the architectural tradition. This building was the

[54] K. M. Kenyon, "Excavation at Jerusalem, 1962," *PEQ* 95 (1963) 16 and pl. VIII B; *Jerusalem; Excavating 3000 Years of History* (London, 1967) 59, pl. 20; (supra n. 37) 49.

[55] Kenyon (supra n. 54, 1967) 59.

[56] *Ibid.*

[57] *Ramat Raḥel 1961–62*, 120.

crowning glory of the Iron Age city. It was constructed in the tenth century B.C. as one part of a vast building program that extended to Hazor, Megiddo, and Gezer.[58] The structure survived until the capture of Judah by Babylon in 587 B.C., but because of later rebuilding on the site,[59] all traces of the stonework have disappeared. We are left with only the literary account, best preserved in the first book of Kings[60] and the second book of Chronicles.[61]

An analysis of the written tradition poses several difficulties.[62] In addition to the problems caused by the various translations, the original terminology is for laymen often applied to an unusual context, and the descriptions are sometimes ambiguous or abbreviated. In addition, the recensions differ among themselves, and there has obviously been a certain amount of editing to reconcile varying traditions.

Most authorities agree that the temple was a rectangular tripartite building with a portico on the eastern end. Behind the portico was a room with a nave flanked by small chambers three stories high, and behind this room was an inner compartment, the Holy of Holies. The building was of stone masonry, with its interior finished in cedar. It was sumptuously decorated with carvings of winged cherubim, flowers, palm trees, and other motifs, and portions of the decoration were overlaid with gold. Similar motifs are well known from Phoenician art, and it seems likely that the artists and craftsmen Solomon imported from Tyre imparted a Phoenician flavor to the Hebrew temple. The tripartite

ground plan had been used for temples in this general area for some time,[63] and a nearly contemporary example from Tell Tainat offers a good comparison. Here, as at Jerusalem, the temple was adjacent to a much larger royal residence.

There is no evidence at all for the design of the capitals in the temple's portico (or in the portico to Solomon's palace), but two bronze columns erected before the temple are described at length: Hiram, a man skilled in working bronze, was brought to Jerusalem from Tyre to work on Solomon's projects. He cast a series of basins and other ceremonial objects for the area in front of the temple, including two colossal columns named Jachin and Boaz. The columns,[64] eighteen cubits high by one account and thirty-five cubits high by another,[65] were capped by bronze capitals rising an additional five cubits (one cubit equals about a half of a meter). The description of the capitals is not completely clear, but they seem to have included a succession of different elements. The texts mention two bowl-like pieces with "checker work" and rows of "pomegranates," as well as a member with "lily work." Since the passages usually describe the shafts of the columns first, then the bowl-like members, and finally the "lily work," these latter components were probably the upper elements. They were certainly the largest sections since they were four cubits high, and the rest of the capital was only one cubit high.

Comparisons with extant architecture have occasionally suggested analogies from many

[58] 1 Kings 9:15.

[59] For a good summary of the Herodian building, with bibliography, consult Kenyon (supra n. 54, 1967) 138ff.

[60] 1 Kings 6–7.

[61] 2 Chronicles 2–5.

[62] For commentary and additional bibliography see J. L. Myres, "King Solomon's Temple and Other Buildings and Works of Art," *PEQ* (1948–1949) 14ff.; J. A. Montgomery, *A Critical and Exegetical Commentary on the Book of Kings* (Edinburgh, 1951) 162ff.; Ussishkin (supra n. 11, 1966) 174ff.

[63] For a list see Kenyon (supra n. 54, 1967) 59–60. The Canaanite tradition is discussed by G. R. H. Wright, "Pre-Israelite Temples in the Land of Canaan," *PEQ* (1971) 17ff.

[64] For discussion and bibliography, see S. Yeivin (supra n. 52) 6ff.; Th. A. Busink, *Der Tempel von Jerusalem* (Leiden, 1970) 299ff.

[65] Eighteen cubits high according to 1 Kings 7:15; thirty-five cubits high according to 2 Chronicles 3:15. There are differences also in reports of the height of the capitals: it is given as five cubits in 1 Kings 7:16, and as three cubits in 2 Kings 25:17.

Near Eastern and even Minoan contexts, but given the known Phoenician influence on the temple, parallels from this area probably rest on a much firmer historical foundation. One possibility, that the "lily work"[66] was related to the vertically spreading volutes of the Aeolic capital,[67] must be seriously considered. In this reconstruction the bowllike elements could be compared with the transitions that often appear between floral capitals and their shafts, as on the balustrade capitals from Ramat Raḥel[68] and the architectural facades of certain Phoenician ivories (pl. 23 and app. A); they also occur elsewhere (pl. 24). The "lily work" which rises above these designs would thus form the main portion of the volute capitals. The columns were probably not structural members for the temple itself but were placed at its front as ceremonial objects.[69]

The description of the columns leaves several questions unanswered, but it is clear on some points: it was from Tyre in Phoenicia that the Israelites imported artists and craftsmen to decorate their major buildings, and among their Phoenician designs were floral capitals that reminded the viewer of the petals of a flower. Taken in conjunction with the "Phoenician style" masonry evident from this period at several Palestinian sites, one can only conclude that Phoenicia played an important early role in the Iron Age architecture of Palestine.

RAMAT RAḤEL

About four kilometers south of Jerusalem is Ramat Raḥel (fig. 4), where a small citadel surrounded by terraced gardens was built in the late ninth to eighth century B.C. (Stratum VB).[70] The settlement was greatly expanded about the middle of the seventh century (Stratum VA), completely transforming the site. There were now inner and outer fortification walls with a large open space between them (perhaps for the marshalling of troops), and the inner wall enclosed splendid new buildings of the finest ashlar masonry. The construction of these rooms is comparable to the best work at the royal precinct of Samaria. The citadel had been in existence for only a brief time when it was destroyed at about the beginning of the sixth century B.C. It was then temporarily abandoned, and no new buildings were erected for several centuries.

Several capitals for Aeolic pilasters were found in the excavation of the stronghold (fig. 10). While most of these had been reused in later structures, an occasional piece was found on the paved court where it had fallen at the destruction of the Judaean fortress. There can thus be no doubt that the pillars were used in the main construction period at Ramat Raḥel, in the seventh century B.C., though the possibility exists that they were originally designed for some earlier building. Three types of capital are preserved. Two of the series differ only in their size and in the fact that one is bifacial; the third series, used for window balustrades, is small and has a slightly different design.

Four complete or nearly complete volute capitals and fragments of at least two others in the same design have been found at Ramat Raḥel (pl. 22). All were made of a soft gray limestone. They have volutes that rise from triangles, with

---

[66] On the assumption that the texts refer to the lily and not to some other flower, which is not absolutely certain. The word is *shushan*, from the Egyptian *sšn*.

[67] For a recent discussion of the evidence, see Busink (supra n. 64) who concludes that the capitals were not related to the Aeolic volutes. In any case, a surface decoration is probably to be preferred over a three-dimensional representation. One should probably think in terms of a succession of cast bronze elements with their decoration raised in relief.

[68] See discussion below.

[69] For arguments that the columns were not structural, see Montgomery (supra n. 62). Against this view, see Myres (supra n. 62) 28–29.

[70] The ancient name is uncertain (G. Garbini, "Sul nome antico di Ramat Rahel," *Rivista degli studi orientali* 36 [1961] 199–205), but the site has been tentatively identified with ancient Beth ha-Kerem. See *Ramath Raḥel 1954*, 152–155; *Ramat Raḥel 1959–60*, 50–51; *Ramat Raḥel 1961–62*, 122ff. For the clearest picture of the stratigraphy, see *Ramat Raḥel 1961–62*, 119ff.

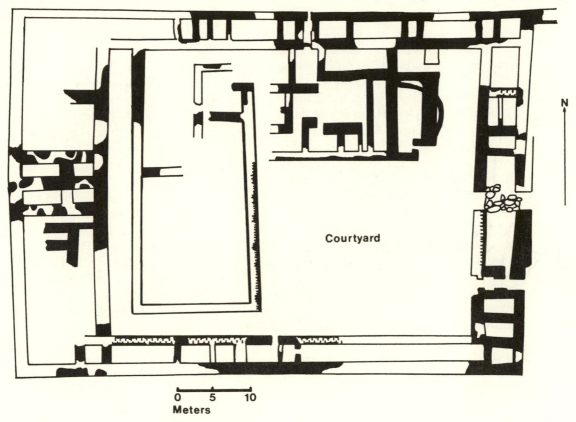

Courtyard

N

0   5   10
Meters

Fig. 10. Plan of the citadel at Ramat Raḥel, based on
the excavations through 1962. By courtesy of the Isti-
tuto di Studi del Vicino Oriente, Università di Roma.
After Aharoni, *Ramat Raḥel 1961–62*, fig. 6.

small circles in the flat fields between triangles
and whorls. Petals occur at the corners, and a
horizontal weight-bearing member with a long
cutting (see pl. 22, at top center) completes
each block at the top. The pieces, which are all
smooth on the back, were used with pilasters.

The closest artistic parallels for these capitals
come from sites in southern and eastern Palestine. Their design approximates that of the
broken capital found at nearby Jerusalem (pl.
21), as both include the small circles in the background fields and three lines at the edges of the
triangles. These features also occur on a capital
from Medeibîyeh, in Moab (pl. 25), but they do
not appear on any of the known capitals from
northern Palestine. In the north, the closest par-

allels are the capitals from Samaria (pl. 15) and
the second series of blocks from Megiddo (pls.
9–10), where the proportions and general appearance seem to be related.

The exact use of the capitals is not known.
The piece found *in situ* was on the paved courtyard, next to the casemate wall that surrounded
the precinct. Important buildings faced this
court on three sides, while the wall occupied the
fourth side. One may imagine a series of engaged Aeolic pilasters on the inner face of the
wall and perhaps on some of the buildings that
fronted on the court as well. Because of the
large number of capitals in one design, a single
coherent scheme seems likely.

A fragment of a somewhat smaller capital

was also found.[71] Although only one corner of the stone remains, it seems to have come from a capital shaped like the larger ones. Both the front and back were carved, indicating it was not engaged. The piece was not found in its original locale, and its use is not known, but the similarity of style between it and the larger series suggests an attribution to Stratum VA.

Also from Stratum VA come two types of carved stones—crenelations and small Aeolic columns. The crenelations,[72] which may have been placed on the roofs of some of the important buildings as an ornamental imitation of defense work, are cut in the form of stepped pyramids (compare the examples shown in fig. 21). Carved from limestone, they would have risen 0.425 m. above the height of the roof.

The small columns were evidently used as balustrades for windows (pl. 26). Each piece consists of a squat shaft with a series of moldings, a girdle of pendant leaves (a leaf drum), and a volute capital with a central oval instead of the usual triangle. The volutes and the remainder of the column were carved from separate limestone blocks which were then doweled together and painted. (Traces of red paint were found, and other colors can be conjectured.) The columns were placed next to each other in a contiguous series, and each group was finished with a horizontal lintel at the top and smaller horizontal bars set into the sides of the columns at the level of the moldings. All of the capitals in each row were carved from a single long, narrow block. That there were three columns in each group is suggested by the upper dowel holes; it would appear that the lintel above the capitals was attached to the outer two columns but not to the center one.

The height (0.365 m. for capital and shaft) and the grouping into threes suggests a use as window balustrades, and there are parallels for this use from several contexts. A bas-relief from Ramat Raḥel itself seems to show a balustrade of this type (pl. 27);[73] the feature also occurs among fragments from the palace of Sennacherib at Kuyunjik (fig. 11),[74] from Tell Halaf,[75] and from a number of sites where plaques with the "Woman at the Window" have been found (pl. 23 and app. A). The "Woman at the Window"[76] has been admirably discussed by Barnett, who concluded that the design is most likely a Phoenician one.[77] Occasionally, as in examples from Cyprus,[78] the female figure was omitted, and only the balustraded window was represented.

While the "Woman at the Window" scene undoubtedly illustrates a temple, the stonework from Ramat Raḥel need not have been used in a completely religious context. Scenes like the one from the palace of Sennacherib show the detail was applied to secular structures as well, and the main buildings within the Palestinian citadel should probably be regarded as a palace rather than a temple. Since the balustrades from this site are the first complete examples to be found in stone, they contribute considerably to the interpretation of the representations in carved stone and ivory. They confirm the design as an actual architectural detail, and they shed light on the construction of several of its important elements. Even the capitals, which are too schematized on the small carvings to identify with certainty, now emerge as true Aeolic columns, with pendant girdles of leaves like those that would later appear in the architecture of the Aeolian Greeks.

[71] *Ramat Raḥel 1959–60*, fig. 13 no. 1, pl. 11 no. 1.

[72] *Ramat Raḥel 1961–62*, 55–56.

[73] B. Maisler, "Ramat Raḥel ve-Hirbet Tselaḥ (Giv'at Eliahu)," *Kovets* (Jerusalem, 1934) 14; M. Stekelis, "Me'arat Kevarim Yehudim be-Ramat-Raḥel," *Kovets* (Jerusalem, 1934) 27–29, fig. 3; M. Kon, "The Stone Capitals from Ramat Rahel," *Bulletin of the Jewish Palestine Exploration Society* 13 (1947) 83–86 (in Hebrew).

[74] Barnett, *Nimrud Ivories*, fig. 53, with accompanying discussion.

[75] R. Naumann, *Tell Halaf* II (Berlin, 1950) fig. 9; "Das Hausmodell vom Tell Halaf und die nach Unten verjüngten Säulen Nordsyriens," *Jahrbuch für kleinasiatische Forschung* 2 (1951–1953) 246ff.

[76] For more complete discussion, see appendix A.

[77] Barnett, *Nimrud Ivories*, 145ff.

[78] *Ibid.*, figs. 55–56.

Most of the fragments of balustrades were not found near the paved courtyard, and one cannot infer that they were all used on the principal facade. On the other hand, they must have belonged to the main palace, the building that occupied the center of the citadel. This structure must have had a number of balustraded windows, some fronting on the court and others facing a street at its back. The stone pilasters suggest an ornamental facade as well, and the bifacial capital may mean that it also had a wide doorway. With elaborate floral capitals capping its pillars and stone crenelations on top of its roof, the palace must have been an impressive civic monument.

MEDEIBÎYEH

Eastern Palestine has a number of square or rectangular Iron Age fortresses. One of these is located at Medeibîyeh, a small site in Moab (fig. 4).[79] Set atop a small knoll, the square enclosure was probably built as a border fortress or defensive strong point, although it has not yet been associated with any historic situation. The construction (fig. 12) included a complete perimeter wall with a square tower at each corner and additional towers at the centers of the southern and northern sides. There were two gates, one in the east and one in the west.

Two building phases can be recognized.[80] In the main phase, the walls were built of roughly dressed basalt blocks, while the gates were added in limestone, with the stones laid as alternating headers and stretchers. At a later date, the walls were repaired with small stones and large undressed blocks of basalt.

The fort can be compared with a whole series of Iron Age citadels in Moab,[81] where the tradition of rectangular walled enclosures strengthened by towers goes well back into the Bronze

Fig. 11. Assyrian relief from the palace of Sennacherib at Nineveh (ancient Kuyunjik), illustrating a building with balustraded windows. After Perrot and Chipiez, *Histoire de l'art* II (1884) fig. 76.

Age. The building techniques can be favorably compared with those of ninth- and eighth-century Palestine (as at Megiddo and Samaria), and it is likely that the construction at Medeibîyeh dates from this period, or slightly later.

One Aeolic pilaster capital was found just inside the eastern gateway (pl. 25). Carved in low relief from the same limestone used for the gate itself, the block has rudimentary whorls and a very large triangle. Details are outlined by molded rims, and small circles flank the apex of

---

[79] N. Glueck, "Further Explorations in Eastern Palestine," *BASOR* 51 (1933) 13 and fig. 2; "Explorations in Eastern Palestine I," *AASOR* 14 (1933–1934) 66ff. and pl. 11; "The Civilization of the Moabites," *AJA* 38 (1934) 216, fig. 5.

[80] Glueck (supra n. 79, 1933–1934) 66–67. For the possibility of an even earlier level, see Glueck (supra n. 79, 1933) 13.

[81] Glueck (supra n. 79, 1933–1934) 67.

the triangle. The large size of the triangle gives the piece a very blocky appearance.

While the capital can be generally compared with examples from more western sites in Palestine, it has a few unique features. The circles in the field at the top of the stone occur also at Jerusalem (pl. 21) and Ramat Raḥel (pl. 22), and the outlining of the triangle can also be compared with the pieces from these sites. The enlargement of the triangle and the concomitant diminution of the whorls, however, are entirely new features. These details and the squat appearance move away from the original floral aspect of the motif toward a more schematic rendition. Because of this, the example from Medeibîyeh is not likely to represent an intermediate step midway between the other Palestinian capitals and their prototypes. Instead, it must be regarded as a related form, perhaps derived from sources that looked much like the extant capitals from Ramat Raḥel and Jerusalem.

Architecturally, the block was probably used with the eastern gateway. Towers four meters wide flanked this entrance, projecting about two meters out from the citadel's walls, but defensive considerations eliminate the possibility that the capital was used with one of the towers—carved architectural members do not normally decorate the exposed outer surfaces of fortifications. There are no constructions at the inner faces of the walls which could accommodate an engaged pilaster since these were kept clear of obstructions (presumably for the movement of troops). While the capital could have been used with one of the fort's buildings, later additions within the citadel (and the absence of modern excavation) preclude a knowledge of the Iron Age constructions at the center of the compound. This leaves only the gateway itself. Since the width of the capital (1.90 m.) conforms to the thickness of the walls, it is very possible that the block was used at the top of a doorjamb, to help support a lintel across the entrance. It would have formed an impressive architectural note at the main access to the citadel.

HISTORICAL DEVELOPMENT

Stone volute capitals have been noted from enough cities to suggest they were a regular characteristic of Palestinian architecture in the first third of the first millennium B.C. They occur in a variety of contexts, usually in connection with the region's finer architectural monuments. Their first occurrence seems to coincide with the extensive building program of the time of Solomon, and their use continues until the seventh century B.C. They do not usually appear at non-Palestinian sites in this region, although Medeibîyeh (which cannot be associated with a historic people) may be an exception.

The stone capitals from Palestine fall easily into four groups:

Group I. The first series from Megiddo
Group II. The second series from Megiddo and all of the examples from Samaria
Group III. The capitals from Hazor and Shechem
Group IV. The specimens from Jerusalem, Ramat Raḥel, and Medeibîyeh

Excluded from these four groups are the designs which are not preserved in stone architectural examples. Of these, the most notable are the columns for balustrades from Ramat Raḥel and those on the small shrine said to be from Transjordan. Other capitals from the Palestinian minor arts (as in the building models from Megiddo) are so simplified and schematized they cannot be fitted into their correct place in the tradition.

The earliest series seems to be *Group I*, which includes the two large capitals from Megiddo (pl. 8). The date may be as early as the tenth century B.C., and it is possible the stones were associated with the Solomonic building programs at Megiddo. They are very low in comparison with their width, so that the volutes are exceptionally far apart and rise from the base of the capital instead of from the central triangle. Their low profile is somewhat surprising in view of what is known about earlier floral capitals (e.g.

from Egypt, figs. 1–3), and it may be that they represent an early stage of the lithic tradition, only recently translated from wood to stone. Their squat dimensions could have resulted from the conservatism of the Iron Age stonemasons, who might have been reluctant to use tall, graceful forms because of the stresses on the supporting members in heavy stone architecture. Opinions differ about the use of the capitals, with some researchers regarding them as the upper parts of door jambs while others prefer a use with pillars in the portico of a *bît hilani*. Either view is possible, but the theory of the *bît hilani* seems to fit better with the cuttings on the blocks.

The second stylistic group includes the smaller capitals from Megiddo (pls. 9–10) and the series from Samaria (pl. 15). The date of the Samarian specimens cannot be earlier than the foundation of the city in the ninth century B.C., and they can probably be assigned to the first major construction on the site. The ones from Megiddo may be from about the same time. In this group the volutes rise from the sides of the central triangle. A single marginal border delineates the features, and there is no decoration in the background field. The proportion of width to height is a little more than 2 to 1, so that the carved features fill the front face of the block. As with the first group, they were used with pillars rather than columns. Neither the series from Megiddo nor the one from Samaria was found in its original context, and their use is problematical. The best suggestion so far advanced restores them atop rows of pilasters lining the walls of major courtyards in the two cities. The theory is quite feasible, since most of the blocks are carved only on the front and sides. The bifacial capitals from Megiddo may have had another use.

Group III includes the two capitals from Hazor (pls. 4–5). They can be placed with Stratum VIII at the northern Israelite city, a level that dates from the ninth century B.C. The capitals are quite different from the other Palestinian pieces. They lack the central triangle, they have much taller and more graceful volutes, and they

also include a small leaflike design (a rudimentary palmette?) between the whorls. Like the other Palestinian examples, they include small petals at the corners. They have been restored as the crowning members of a pair of pillars supporting a lintel at the entrance to a corridor. The fragment from Shechem (pl. 17), from an unknown architectural context, may also be placed in this group. It seems to have come from a free-standing column, not from a pilaster.

In the fourth group are the capitals from Ramat Raḥel (pl. 22), Jerusalem (pl. 21) and Medeibîyeh (pl. 25). The only dating evidence for this group comes from Ramat Raḥel, where the blocks can most likely be placed in the seventh century B.C. The architecture at Medeibîyeh could date the specimen from that site slightly earlier, as could the style of the masonry blocks found with the capital from Jerusalem. The capitals from the three sites have much in common, at least on the stylistic level. They differ from *Group II* in three principal ways: in the addition of an abacus at the top; in the use of two or three marginal borders for the triangle; and in the inclusion of small circles in the background fields. At Medeibîyeh, the size of the triangle is greatly expanded. The use seems to have varied from site to site. The blocks from Ramat Raḥel fronted on a large, paved courtyard, and perhaps they formed an ornamental facade. One bifacial capital from this citadel probably had both faces exposed. The context at Medeibîyeh, where the block was part of the citadel's gateway, is fairly secure; it probably capped a decorative doorjamb. At Jerusalem the use is not known.

The four Palestinian groups form a loosely connected tradition. The capitals are rather blocky in appearance, actually little more than modified rectangular blocks. With the exception of the piece from Shechem, they were all used with pillars, although there was evidently some difference in use between one series and another. From differences at the sides, Y. Shiloh has shown (*BASOR* 222 [1976] 67ff.) that some (but not all) of the capitals were set partly into the walls. It would seem that the volute capital was the standard capital for stone architecture, and it was used for whatever context was needed at the time.

To the tradition of the stone pillars must be added the separate designs that seem to imitate wood. In this class are the balustrades from Ramat Rahel and the small pottery shrine "from Transjordan." Both of these have cylindrical columns with relatively high capitals betraying their wooden ancestry. Neither uses a central triangle as a base for the volutes. Obviously, these columns cannot have developed from the stone pillars. Since they show traits that never occur in contemporary stone buildings from Palestine but do occur in Egyptian and Near Eastern designs from as early as the Late Bronze Age, they must be part of distinct traditions that developed along independent lines. Palestine can thus be seen as the recipient of a number of separate foreign influences in the use of floral decoration for architecture. Since the examples from Ramat Raḥel and "Transjordan" are far more suited to wood than to stone or baked clay, it would seem highly unlikely that the styles reached Palestine in the media that have been preserved. Instead, one should postulate a lost tradition in wood, with occasional columns like those preserved in the shrine and the balustrades.

No stone prototypes are known for the Palestinian styles, but since the Israelites were a nomadic people with no stone architectural tradition of their own, a foreign inspiration seems highly likely. The settlement of the Israelites in Palestine gradually created a need for splendid public buildings, and several pieces of evidence point in the same direction as the source for their architectural styles and technology. The literary evidence is very explicit in its statements about Phoenician influence on the Israelite building projects, and it would seem that Tyre and the other Phoenician cities must be regarded as the immediate inspiration for at least part of the Israelite architecture. The archaeological evidence partially confirms this picture. Certain Palestinian building techniques, like the use of masonry with well-dressed margins on two or three sides of a central boss, have been securely traced to Ugarit. It is likely that the literary tradition is correct, at least for the royal precincts, and it is in these precincts that the volute capitals can be found.

The Phoenician predecessors of the Palestinian pillars have not yet come to light.[82] Perhaps most examples were of wood, but one might still expect the future appearance of an occasional piece in stone. In later times, one can find the style near Tyre and Byblos in Phoenicia itself,[83] as well as at many of the Phoenician colonies in the western Mediterranean (pl. 28).[84] The tradition also appears in Cyprus, where it has a vigorous development in the late Archaic (pl. 20 and figs. 9 and 13). The later Phoenician forms (compare pl. 28) often have a triangle at the base from which the volutes rise, as is commonly found on the Palestinian capitals. Both

[82] The absence of Phoenician examples has occasionally been cited as evidence that the origins of the Palestinian series must lie elsewhere (D. Auscher, "Les Relations entre la Grèce et la Palestine avant la conquête d'Alexandre," *Vetus Testamentum* 17 [1967] 28–29), but the many examples of the Phoenician "Woman at the Window" motif (now known to represent Aeolic columns because of the discovery of actual examples from Ramat Raḥel) prove that the style was well known in Phoenicia, at least as a carpentry motif.

[83] H. Seyrig, "Antiquités Syriennes. Les bas-reliefs, prétendus d'Adonis, aux environs de Byblos," *Syria* 21 (1940) pl. 18; M. Dunand and R. Duru,

Oumm ed-'Amed. Une ville de l'epoque hellénistique aux échelles de Tyr (Paris, 1962) 147ff. and pls. 28, 2, and 29, 1. For even later examples from this area, see *Capitello Eolico*, 18–19.

[84] For the stelai in general, see A. M. Bisi, *Le Stele puniche* (*Studi semitici* 27, Rome, 1967). For Carthage, see also M. Hours-Miedan, "Les Representations figurées sur les stèles de Carthage," in *Cahiers de Byrsa* 1 (Paris, 1951) 43–44; C. Picard, "Thèmes hellénistiques sur les stèles de Carthage," *Antiquités africaines* 1 (1967) 9ff.; For Spain, see A. García y Bellido, "Materiales de Arqueología hispano-púnica: Jarros de bronce," *Archívo español de arqueología* 29 (1956) 100–102, figs. 26–27.

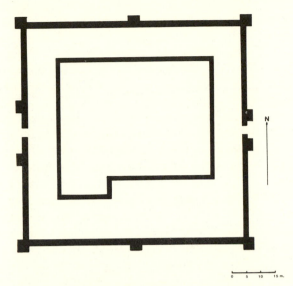

Fig. 12. Plan of the fortifications around the site at Medeibîyeh. The interior wall is from a later period, and the Iron Age remains within the enclosure have not been investigated. No state plan has been published. By courtesy of the American Schools of Oriental Research, after N. Glueck, "Explorations in Eastern Palestine, I," *AASOR* 14 (1933–1934) pl. 11.

Fig. 13. Capital from a grave stele, from Trapeza, Cyprus, now in the Louvre. After Perrot and Chipiez, *Histoire de l'art* III (1885) fig. 51.

styles also use half-capitals (in Palestine they occur on pottery shrine models from Megiddo and Ta'nnek), and an occasional piece without the basal triangle also occurs in both contexts. Individual details like the extra petals or the lines at the triangles and at the edges of the whorls are also comparable. Thus, the morphology of the known Phoenician examples seems to reinforce the theory suggested by the literary and the archaeological testimony; the origins of the Palestinian development almost certainly lie in Phoenicia. The capital with vertical volutes must have traveled to the Israelite cities along with a whole series of new construction techniques which resulted in splendid citadels and royal precincts built of "Phoenician style" masonry, with buildings laid out and decorated in the Phoenician manner.

[85] The fullest recent discussions are those of O. Masson, "Kypriaka I, Recherches sur les antiquités de Tamassos," *BCH* 88 (1964) 199–238, and H.-G.

Some of the best indications of what this Phoenician style may have been like come from the so-called "Royal Tombs" at Tamassos, dating from the late seventh to early sixth century B.C.[85] Plate 65 illustrates the most elaborate tomb in the group (Tomb 2 in the system of Masson, Tomb V in Section IV by the early nomenclature of Ohnefalsch-Richter), a large and well-preserved sepulcher with two chambers dating from the sixth century B.C. It is approached by a descending flight of steps which terminate at a small rectangular space flanked by Aeolic pilasters. Above the pilasters is a beam, which in turn supports a row of dentils. Beyond the porchlike space, a door leads to two chambers with gabled roofs, arranged in line. The sarcophagus was placed in the inner room, presumably leaving the antechamber for offerings. False windows were above both the first door and the door leading to the burial vault, suggesting the tomb copied building practices in

Buchholz, "Tamassos, Zypern, 1970–1972," *AA* (1973) 295ff. Earlier bibliography is listed in these publications.

wood. The same conclusion may be inferred from the gabled roofs, the dentils, and other details of the carving.

Phoenician influence in the style seems certain. The sills of the windows are carved with elaborate "sacred trees," a motif familiar from both Phoenician and Cypriote art, and the Aeolic capitals themselves are of the type found at the western Phoenician colonies as well as in Phoenicia itself in much later times. Here each capital has only one volute and the start of another, plus the central triangle. The corner is adorned with a small petal, and the whorls are given a single turn around a tiny eye. They are quite shallow, protruding only slightly from the stone behind them. Yet, the structural arrangement is clear, with a tall shaft to each pilaster and a separate capital which acts as the supporting element. The use of the plant forms is thus quite different from that found at Medinet Habu (pl. 3), where the edges of the panels extend beyond the carving and make the reliefs simple surface ornaments; here, it is blocks carved in the form of volutes which support the lintel.

The structural system used at Tamassos is repeated in a small building model from Amathos,[86] and it is also compatible with the evidence from other Phoenician areas where the style was regularly used with architectural facades consisting of engaged columns or pillars flanking the entrance of a temple or some other structure. It seems quite likely that the Phoenicians often used wooden Aeolic pilasters at the entrances of important buildings. Whether they are to be taken as decorations on the inner facings of antae or as simple doorjambs is not clear from the nature of the evidence. Either use is possible, since the structural origins would be the same—a wooden facing to strengthen and protect the ends of mud-brick walls and give needed support for a heavy wooden beam. The ceiling beams, visible in plate 65 as dentils,

would then be laid across this horizontal member. Most of the surviving examples of the system used gabled roofs, but the date at which this feature was added is not known for certain. It was surely after the style was first transmitted to Palestine.

There is no reason to believe the Palestinian tradition was based on only a single influx of foreign influence. On the contrary, there is widespread evidence for continuous contact between Palestine and Phoenicia during the early first millennium B.C.[87] The architectural styles are simply one of the many results of this interrelationship. One must not think of a single pinpoint source and a straight line of development, but a complex ancestry and a constantly modified tradition, giving rise to a series of related forms.

The growth and development of the Palestinian styles can be closely related to both the political situation and the geography of Iron Age Palestine. The date of *Group I* coincides with the time of the Israelite united monarchy when major architectural innovations were made under the rule of Solomon. By the ninth century, the monarchy had split into two principal segments, and the north and south each went their separate ways. This is precisely what we find in the later capitals where *Group II* is restricted to Megiddo and Samaria in the north, while *Group IV* occurs only in southern and eastern Palestine. *Group III*, occurring only in Hazor and Shechem in the north, forms a separate division and seems to reflect an independent stream of influence.

The Palestinian volute capitals were part of a strong and viable tradition. Beginning at about the time of Solomon, they continued to be used for many years, adding their elegant note to the finer architectural monuments of many cities. The latest Iron Age examples come from the

[86] Betancourt (supra n. 25).

[87] As is perhaps to be expected, after the dissolution of the united monarchy, Phoenician influence was more keenly felt in the northern kingdom of

Israel which was closer to the Phoenician cities. This is especially evident from the reign of Ahab, who was married to the Phoenician princess Jezebel (1 Kings 16:31).

eighth century in the north and the seventh century in the south; the style was apparently

brought to a close by the invasions of Assyria and Babylon.[88]

[88] This picture accords very well with the pattern of widespread destructions at this time, as evidence from both the literary records and the archaeological remains indicate. For a discussion of the chronological problems as they apply to Judah, see A. Malamat, "The Last Kings of Judah and the Fall of Jerusalem," *IEJ* 18 (1968) 150ff. A good review of the situation in general is summarized in S. S. Weinberg, "Post-Exilic Palestine: An Archaeological Report," *Proceedings of the Israel Academy of Sciences and Humanities* 4 (1969) 78ff.

Chapter III

THE HALIKARNASSOS PENINSULA

Greek settlement along the Halikarnassos peninsula seems to have begun during the Late Bronze Age,[1] but there was probably only a small Hellenic population there until the Dorian migrations of the Iron Age, and even then much of the land remained firmly in the hands of Anatolians. The Greeks settled mostly in the west where Halikarnassos became the chief city, and the interior was left to its own development.

The peninsula was a land of fortified hill towns inhabited by the Lelegians and other Carian peoples who had spread to most parts of southwestern Asia Minor by the early Iron Age.[2] The Carians earned a living chiefly through agriculture and animal husbandry, and their land supported a relatively large number of small towns. There is some evidence that these villages were combined into units under central seats of power, foreshadowing the closely knit political divisions established in the first half of the fourth century B.C.[3]

No Aeolic buildings have been discovered in any of the Greek cities of southwestern Anatolia,[4] but this situation may well change with additional excavation. Only at the Carian site of

[1] G. F. Bass, "Mycenaean and Protogeometric Tombs in the Halicarnassus Peninsula," *AJA* 67 (1963) 353ff.

[2] There is great difficulty in distinguishing a Lelegian culture, if such existed apart from that of the Carians in general, and the ancient sources show some uncertainty in the use of the two names. Herodotos (1. 171) repeated a Cretan story that said the Lelegians had originally inhabited the Aegean islands, and that they were called Carians after they were forced to move to Anatolia in the time of King Minos. Homer distinguished between Carians and Lelegians (*Il.* 2. 867–868; 10. 428–429), while Pausanias said that Cretans had united with Carians who were already in Anatolia (7. 2. 5). Strabo (14. 2. 27) agreed with the story that the Carians were known as Lelegians when they lived in the islands, but he reported that other Lelegians had lived in Anatolia. According to Herodotos (1. 171) the Carians themselves said they were completely indigenous. Strabo (13. 1. 59) wrote that the identity of the Lelegians was gradually lost as they were absorbed by the Carians. The Carian language is still undeciphered, and its affinities are not known. Only the culture from the Iron Age and later has been investigated, and its origins remain obscure.

[3] On this, see G. E. Bean and J. M. Cook, "The Carian Coast III," *BSA* 52 (1957) 143–144.

[4] An Archaic block with floral designs, either a capital from a pilaster or a piece from a grave stele, was built into a mosque near Körmen. Reported by G. E. Bean and J. M. Cook, "The Cnidia," *BSA* 47 (1952) 178–179, fig. 4 and pl. 38e, it

Alâzeytin have volute capitals with vertically rising whorls appeared. Their exact origin is not known, but close comparisons with Greek designs suggest a connection of some type between these floral capitals and the motifs used by the Hellenic regions to the west.

ALÂZEYTIN

On the peninsula of Halikarnassos, about ten kilometers east of modern Bodrum, is Alâzeytin,[5] the site of an ancient city whose original name is not known.[6] The Carian settlement was surrounded by a circuit wall of rough limestone masonry, and its inner space was crowded with stone buildings, some of which remain preserved above ground into modern times. Little is known of the town's early history, but it was already settled by the seventh century B.C.[7] A destruction in the 540s B.C. seems likely, since the entire area was conquered by Persia at this time, but the city was not abandoned until somewhat later. Since its population seems to have left rather suddenly in the fourth century B.C., the place may have been one of the small Lelegian communities Maussolos moved to Halikarnassos at that time.[8]

The city occupied an oval hilltop. Its religious center, and apparently its civic center as well, was a terraced area on the eastern side of the hill. Up the slope from the terrace (on the west) were several steps, perhaps from an early theatral area; a large square building stood nearby. Along the other side of the terrace were additional public buildings, the largest of which (Building 30) has been tentatively identified as a heroon. Immediately to its north were two

structures which were also of large dimensions (Buildings 31 and 26). Two of the buildings at the east of the terrace (Buildings 30 and 31) used stone capitals with vertically rising volutes.

Building 30 was built on the slope of the hill and consisted of both an upper and a lower building. The two stories were not bonded together, and they were of completely different construction. The building was one of the few projects in the city to be built as a true rectangle instead of as an informal quadrangle.

The lower part, with two vaulted rooms beneath the foundations of the upper story, was partially built of gigantic boulders. It had doorways on the downhill side, so that one could enter the rooms from a lower terrace to the east. The chambers were roofed by corbeled arches, and they were interconnected. Their purpose is unknown.

That the upper story of Building 30 was an important public building is assured by its size and the excellence of its architecture (fig. 15). Radt has suggested it was used as a sanctuary, perhaps a heroon,[9] and this is quite plausible. Its foundations were placed over the walls of the lower chambers, except that a spur wall at the southeast corner of the lower foundations had no superstructure—it was used merely as a terrace wall for a small court in front of the entrance to the upper building (the slope of the hill allowed a separate entrance for the upper story).

Enough finely worked blocks of local dark gray limestone were found to reconstruct the building's appearance. Among these were fragments of two Aeolic pilaster capitals, carved from the same stone as the remainder of the building. The structure was a simple rectangle.

---

is not an Aeolic capital, although its design may be related to the Aeolic tradition, as suggested by J. Boardman, "Chian and Early Ionic Architecture," *AntJ* 39 (1959) 209.

[5] W. Radt, *Siedlungen und Bauten auf der Halbinsel von Halikarnassos* (*IstMitt*, Beiheft 3, Tübingen, 1970) 17–71 and 237–258, with earlier bibliography.

[6] Suggestions include Sibde, Euranion, Amynan-

da and Syangela, but no inscriptional evidence has come to light. For a discussion see Radt (supra n. 5) 17.

[7] For Greek sherds of the eighth or seventh century B.C., see G. E. Bean and J. M. Cook, "The Halicarnassus Peninsula," *BSA* 50 (1955) 125.

[8] Strabo, 13. 1. 59. See especially the discussion of Bean and Cook (supra n. 7) 143ff. and 169.

[9] Radt (supra n. 5) 39ff.

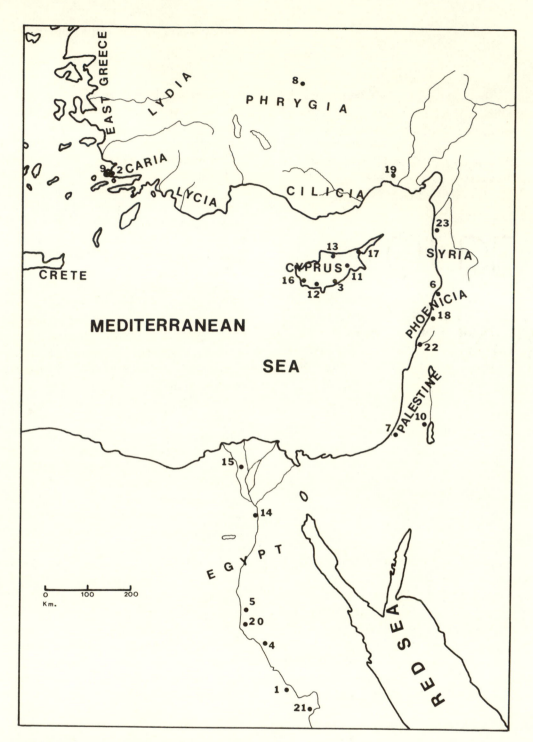

Fig. 14. Map of Egypt and the Eastern Mediterranean:

1. Abydos	6. Byblos	11. Kition	16. Paphos	21. Thebes
2. Alâzeytin	7. Gaza	12. Kourion	17. Salamis	22. Tyre
3. Amathos	8. Gordion	13. Lapithos	18. Sidon	23. Ugarit
4. Badari	9. Halikarnassos	14. Memphis	19. Tarsus	
5. Beni Hasan	10. Jerusalem	15. Naukratis	20. Tell el Amarna	

Its outer dimensions were 11.9 m. x 6.4 m., and its doorway was in the southern end. The capitals could only have been used with the doorjambs so that their volutes would project slightly both inside and outside the building. Two painted moldings (an egg-and-dart above a bead-and-reel) were placed immediately below the geison, but the structure was otherwise rather austere in its architectural embellishment. Its date, based on the style of the moldings and the capitals, should be the second half of the sixth century B.C.

The two capitals (pls. 29–31 and figs. 16–17) are of considerable interest. They are carved in the same low relief, and they are of the same height,[10] but surprisingly (and in spite of the fact that they seem to be a matched set), they are of somewhat different design. Both have vertically rising volutes on the front while on the back the center of each block is plain,[11] and only the volutes are shown in relief. The whorls rise from horizontal bands, and they have two turns. On one stone (pl. 29 and fig. 16) they are separated by a five-petaled palmette. On the other (pl. 30 and fig. 17) the central space is filled with a heart-shaped figure with spirals and a pendant palmette inside it. The volutes of the palmette capital have no eyes, while those of the piece with the heart-shaped figure have eyes on the front only.

Building 31 was built immediately to the north of Building 30, and it, too, had upper and lower rooms which were not bonded together. Its lower section faced downhill (to the east) and consisted of two rooms with an interconnecting doorway (fig. 18). These lower chambers, roofed with a barrel vault of the corbeled type (like Building 30), were of about the same size and opened onto a small terrace.

The upper building, which faced uphill, was a rectangular construction 9.45 m. x 4.25 m. in size with one open side (fig. 19a). It was built of dark gray limestone. Within the rectangle

were five stone steps, with the third step forming a one-meter-wide platform. The lowest step was at the open (western) side.

Among the ruins of Building 31 were the fragments of two stone capitals (pls. 32–35 and fig. 19b). Made of the same gray limestone used for most building operations at Alâzeytin, they were carved on both front and back. Their lower portions are no longer preserved, but one of the blocks was in a more complete state in the nineteenth century, and at that time one could see that capital and pillar were carved from the same slab.[12] The upper surfaces are smooth. Rising from horizontal bands placed on the same level as the centers of the whorls, the volutes on these capitals curve to make two and one-half turns before they terminate in large eyes. A rudimentary palmette with three leaves divides the whorls at the upper center.

Although the building is now in an extremely ruined state, it was in better condition in the late nineteenth century when it was examined and described by Paton and Myres.[13] A comparison between this description and the present evidence[14] suggests the structure was a covered hall, open on the long side facing up the hill, with the roof supported on pillars between antae. Paton and Myres supposed that the two Aeolic pillars stood on what is now recognized as the wide stone step. One socket was visible on the step at that time, but it is no longer extant. The fact that the entire floor was filled with the steps was not recognizable in the nineteenth century, and it is more likely that the supports were at the front of the building. According to Paton and Myres, the pillars supported an architrave, and above this were stone beams to support the roof (perhaps visible as dentils at the front of the building?). These blocks are no longer preserved. Although the purpose of the building is unknown, one must suppose a series of objects (perhaps of a dedicatory nature) was placed on the enlarged middle step.

[10] Height 0.53 m.; width of palmette capital 0.975 m.; width of heart capital 1.055 m.

[11] Where the stone would be against the doorjamb.

[12] W. R. Paton, and J. L. Myres, "Karian Sites and Inscriptions," *JHS* 16 (1896) 199–200, fig. 2.

[13] *Ibid.*, 200.

[14] Radt (supra n. 5) 6off.

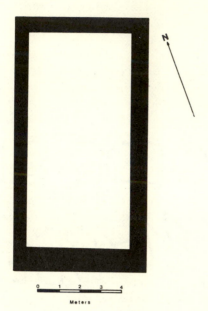

Fig. 15. Building 30 at Alâzeytin (upper building).
The door was in the south. For a state plan see W.
Radt, *Siedlungen und Bauten auf der Halbinsel von
Halikarnassos*, fig. 2.

Fig. 16. Pilaster capital with palmette between the
volutes, from Building 30 at Alâzeytin. The carved
portion of the back is shown at the top. After W. Radt,
*Siedlungen und Bauten auf der Halbinsel von Halikar-
nassos* (1970) figs. 22 and 24 no. 1.

Fig. 17. Pilaster capital with heart-shaped form between the volutes, from Building 30 at Alâzeytin. The
carved portion of the back is shown at the top. After
W. Radt, *Siedlungen und Bauten auf der Halbinsel
von Halikarnassos* (1970) figs. 23 and 24 no. 2.

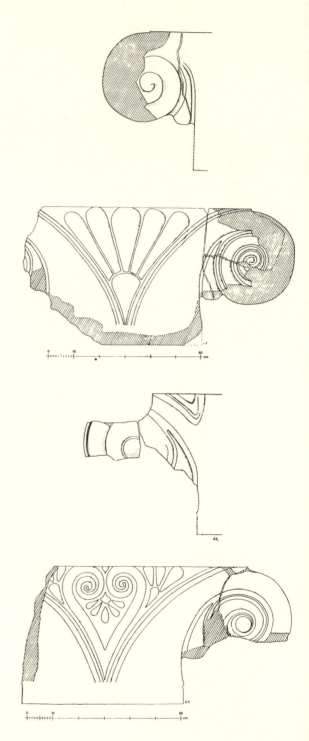

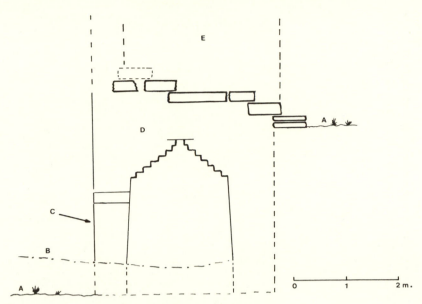

A. Original ground level
B. Ground level in 1970
C. Entrance to room at lower level
D. Vaulted roof of room at lower level
E. Room at upper level

Fig. 18. Cross section of Building 31 at Alâzeytin. Adapted from W. Radt, *Siedlungen und Bauten auf der Halbinsel von Halikarnassos* (1970) fig. 6 no. 3.

The capitals from this building have a form that is well known from Greek grave stelai.[15] The design was also used occasionally with architecture, and a good parallel comes from the Athenian Akropolis (pls. 56–59). In Athens the pattern was used for columns rather than pillars, and details were painted rather than carved, but the designs from the two cities are very similar. Both have well-curved whorls with round eyes, horizontal bands at the centers of the designs, and small three-petaled palmettes. Their overall forms seem closely related, in spite of the fact that the Athenian variation used a heavy abacus at the top. The architectural use at Athens is not clear, but it was certainly used to support an entablature,[16] as was the case at Alâzeytin.

While there is no stratigraphic evidence for the dating of Building 31, several stylistic points suggest the second half of the sixth century B.C. for its Aeolic capitals. Among these are the ratio

of height to width, the curvature of the whorls (with their two and one-half turns), the presence of the large round eyes, and the form of the palmette. The lower structure, with its corbeled vaulting, should perhaps be assigned to an earlier period. Perhaps the upper building was rebuilt sometime after about 550/540 B.C., following the destruction of the Persians in the Halikarnassos peninsula,[17] over a lower structure of somewhat earlier design. It still stood when Alâzeytin was abandoned in the fourth century B.C.

HISTORICAL DEVELOPMENT

Almost nothing is known of Lelegian history in the sixth century B.C. Living in small isolated towns, the inland people played a very minor role in the dynamic events that swept the Anatolian subcontinent in this period. They gradually absorbed some measure of Greek culture,

[15] From several of the Greek cities. See the discussion of the style by E. Buschor, "Altsamische Grabstelen," *AthMitt* 58 (1933) 22ff., fig. 8, pls. 15

no. 2 and 16 nos. 1–2.

[16] See the discussion in chapter v.

[17] As suggested by Radt (supra n. 5) 259.

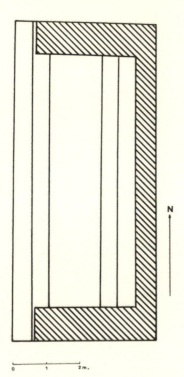

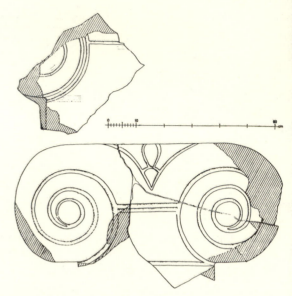

Fig. 19. A. Ground plan of the upper level of Building 31 at Alâzeytin. Adapted from the state plan of W. Radt, *Siedlungen und Bauten auf der Halbinsel von Halikarnassos* (1970) fig. 6 no. 2.

B. Two fragmentary pilaster capitals from Building 31 at Alâzeytin. After W. Radt, *Siedlungen und Bauten auf der Halbinsel von Halikarnassos* (1970) fig. 24 nos. 3 and 4.

but their development seems to have been largely an independent one. By the second half of the century, when the buildings with Aeolic capitals were probably built at Alâzeytin, the entire region had become a part of the Persian empire, which must have led to increased traffic with both east and west. The Aeolic designs may be a tangible result of these increased foreign relations, but the exact source of the new tradition is difficult to discover.

Only three possibilities exist for the origin of the style as it appears at Alâzeytin: it could be a local invention derived from earlier Carian floral motifs; it could have been imported from the Greek areas to the west; or it could have reached the small town from some inland region to the east. No final decision can be reached on the matter, but there are indications that militate against the first and third possibilities,

leaving the second as the most likely explanation.

It is unlikely that the Aeolic capitals represent the end of a long local series. They are isolated examples, apparently contemporary in date, in a region that has no earlier tradition in the carving of floral motifs in stone for stelai or architectural decoration. On the other hand, generally similar motifs are known from sixth-century contexts elsewhere, and very close parallels can be found from the stonework of Greek Asia Minor.

The second possibility, that the style was imported from East Greece, seems very strong at first glance. Good parallels for the capitals from Building 31 occur from East Greek floral decorations, and the capitals from Building 30 are also similar to Hellenic examples in some of their essential decorations.[18] East Greece is

[18] For the heart-shaped figure, compare the extra designs on the capital from Larisa, pl. 42. A relation

with Greek examples exists in the use of a palmette between the volutes, in the use of whorls with more

the only common denominator which links Caria with Archaic Athens where a capital resembling the ones from Building 31 was found on the Akropolis. The painted moldings on Building 30[19] are also Greek, and this may be the deciding factor. One problem is that the building types at Alâzeytin have no exact parallels from Greek lands. The lower sections, with their corbeled vaulting, may be compared somewhat with the "Dragon Houses" from Euboea and elsewhere;[20] however, the upper buildings are not so easily paralleled. The most curious construction is the shedlike room filled with steps. It is not exactly like the Greek altars,[21] and it may have been used to hold dedications. If the idea of the capitals came from East Greece, it may have been applied under strong local influence.

The third possibility, that the Lelegian designs reached Alâzeytin from some non-Greek area in the Near East, cannot be confirmed or denied. As our corpus of information stands now, there are no earlier stone examples of Archaic pillar capitals with central palmettes and with horizontal lines instead of central triangles. One possible parallel for the palmette capital from Building 30 can be found in a somewhat later architectural relief from the vicinity of Byblos,[22] and another possibility is suggested by the Assyrian reliefs. A panel from the palace of Assurbanipal at Nineveh (ancient Kuyunjik) furnishes an excellent example of the latter (fig. 21). It shows a building which seems to have a porch with two columns *in antis*. Both the columns and the antae have volute capitals which might be of the correct type, although the examples on the relief are double tiered. The problem of the origin must remain open, at least for the present. No eastern parallels exist for the buildings themselves, especially the open-sided construction with the series of steps.

Based on the currently available evidence, the second of the three possibilities appears to be the most likely. The Aeolic buildings may best be regarded as local variations of an East Greek style which has left us stone examples only in the grave stelai. Perhaps wooden antecedents may be conjectured for the capitals, but there are no exact parallels for the open-sided building filled with steps. The style seems to have been a short-lived one at Alâzeytin, where there was little tradition of carved architectural decoration.

---

than one turn, and in the completion of the whorls with large central eyes.

[19] Radt (supra n. 5) fig. 4.

[20] A parallel noted by F. P. Johnson, "The 'Dragon-Houses' of Southern Euboea," *AJA* 29 (1925) 409. For additional references and discussion, see Radt (supra n. 5) 196–197.

[21] Only slightly similar are open-sided altars like the one at Perachora (H. Payne, *Perachora* 1 [Oxford, 1940] 89ff., pls. 6 and 130).

[22] H. Seyrig, "Antiquités syriennes: Les bas-reliefs, prétendus d'Adonis, aux environs de Byblos," *Syria* 21 (1940) 113ff., pl. 18a and 18b.

Chapter IV

AEOLIS, NORTHERN IONIA, AND THE
NORTH AEGEAN

The first capital with vertically rising volutes to be rediscovered in modern times was found at the Aeolic city of Neandria on September 24, 1882.[1] Subsequent finds have confirmed the theory that the northern cities of East Greece played a major role in the history of this style, and several sites now provide testimony for the Aeolic tradition in Aeolis. While many details about the development are still unclear, some of its most significant aspects have already emerged. For one thing, we now know the style was more widely spread than was once supposed—its Greek development was certainly not limited to areas that spoke the Aeolic dialect. Aeolis, however, played such a strong and individual role in this tradition that it is fitting the style should be called Aeolic, just as the Doric and Ionic styles owe their names to the other major dialect groups of Classical Greece.

A new feeling appeared in the Aeolic buildings of the Archaic Greek cities, contrasting markedly with the employment of Aeolic columns in the Near East. For the first time, vertical volutes were applied to architecture as one part of an on-going system of architectural design. Stone columns were set up in monumental peristyles along with a specific group of fictile revetments and decorative moldings, producing an external architectural facade of an entirely new type. While local schools produced several individual variations in building styles, enough general stylistic traits can be recognized to justify the designation of the system as a nascent architectural order.

OLD SMYRNA

South of Aeolis, near the modern city of Bayrakli, stands the site of Old Smyrna (so called to distinguish it from Smyrna, the Hellenistic city on the slopes of Mt. Pagos). According to Herodotos and other ancient writers,[2] the city's first Greek settlers were Aeolians. The new polis prospered, and at some point in its early history, it joined with eleven other Aeolic cities to form a league of twelve, mirroring the Ionic dodecapolis. The city, however, was located somewhat to the south of natural Aeolic territory, and it was captured by Ionians (presum-

---

[1] J. T. Clarke, "A Proto-Ionic Capital from the Site of Neandreia," *AJA* 2 (1886) 1–20, 136–148.

[2] Hdt., 1. 149–150. For other ancient references, see *PW*, ser. 2, vol. 3, pt. 1, cols. 728ff.

ably in the early seventh century B.C.), reducing the Aeolic league to eleven. By common agreement the city's population was distributed among the remaining Aeolic cities, and Old Smyrna became Ionic. It continued to thrive until it was destroyed by King Alyattes of Lydia at the end of the century.

The archaeological evidence[3] agrees with the literary texts in suggesting that the seventh century was a period of great prosperity. Following a destruction level of about 700 B.C. (to be equated with the expulsion of the Aeolians?), the city was extensively remodeled. A large temple was now begun on an artificial terrace at the north edge of the city. Successive building levels on the platform may suggest the work was done in several phases, until by the end of the century or slightly later, when the site was destroyed by the Lydians, the still unfinished temple was being constructed of stone. A visitor entering the sacred precinct at this time would have approached it from a residential area to the south. Beginning at ground level, he would have to pass through a monumental stone pylon and walk along an inclined passageway before he could gain access to the temple atop its large platform. The terrace was large enough to allow an open walkway beside the building at the south; on the north, the platform seems to have been extended all the way to the city wall.

The excavation of the temple[4] has yielded numerous fragments of stone architecture—carved capitals, both unfinished and fluted column drums with sharp arrises (32 flutes), and carved drums once called bases but now known to be part of the capitals, since their diameter matches that of the top, not the bottom of the shafts (pl. 36). The temple seems to have been incomplete at the time of its destruction. The excavators have suggested that it was a single long cella, with an exterior peristyle of 6 x 11 columns. The entrance was on the east. While the main building material was tufa, the stone columns were probably to have supported an entablature of wood. An inscribed bronze bar found in the debris suggests the building was dedicated to Athena.

As restored by the excavators from many fragments,[5] the capitals have a tall, graceful form (fig. 20). Their volutes spring vertically and then spread slightly, terminating at decorative rosettes. They are divided by a palmette, and an abacus completes each specimen at the top. The whorls are not as tightly rolled as in most of the more northern examples (as those from Neandria, Larisa, Klopedi, and Mytilene), and their design more nearly approaches that of several volute capitals from the Near East and the Etruscan west.[6] The capitals from Hazor, for example (pls. 4–5), have several comparable points, although the Greek specimens were elaborated somewhat differently from the Palestinian ones. The eyes, quite small at Hazor, are stylized into flowerlike forms at Old Smyrna. In addition, the extra petals that characterize all Palestinian capitals are not present, and the Greek design includes a more carefully formed palmette and abacus. Details, however, may imply a connection: an identical turn in the spirals; a similarity in the spiral's edging; and a relationship in the rectilinear appearance and the overall form of the blocks. The Etruscan examples (all from much later in time) are also very similar. The usual Etruscan capital had volutes with only a

---

[3] J. M. Cook, "Archaeology in Greece, 1951," *JHS* 72 (1952) 104–106; *The Greeks in Ionia and the East* (New York, 1963) 71–74, 81, and 83–84; E. Akurgal, *Kunst Anatoliens*, 182ff.; *Ancient Civilizations and Ruins of Turkey*, 2nd ed., trans. by J. Whybrow and M. Emre (Istanbul, 1970) 119ff.; 3rd ed. (1973) 119ff.; M. J. Mellink, "Archaeology in Asia Minor," *AJA* 71 (1967) 169; 72 (1968) 141; 73 (1969) 221; 74 (1970) 172; 75 (1971) 176; 76 (1972) 183.

[4] Excavations from 1948 to 1951 conducted jointly by Ankara University and the British School of Archaeology at Athens, by J. M. Cook and Ekrem Akurgal, resumed in 1966 by Professor Akurgal for the Turkish Historical Society, the General Directorate of Turkish Museums, and the Universities of Ege and Ankara.

[5] Akurgal (supra n. 3, 1970) fig. 41.

[6] *Capitello Eolico*, pls. 10–12 and 16.

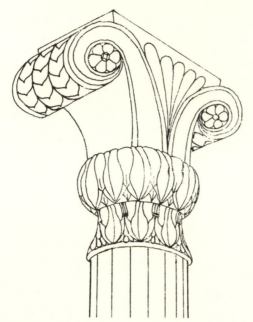

Fig. 20. Restoration of the capitals from the Temple of Athena at Old Smyrna. After E. Akurgal, *Ancient Civilizations and Ruins of Turkey* (1970) fig. 41.

ing constructed. Their application to free-standing stone columns arranged in series as exterior supports is a purely Greek notion, though it may grow out of the Near Eastern practice of using free-standing supports in a portico.

Along with the fragments of shafts and capitals from Old Smyrna were found complete and fragmentary semicylindrical blocks, each divided into a convex and a concave element and decorated with two tiers of floral ornament (pl. 36). The decoration, of an oriental character, is the lotus-buds-and-flowers motif that had once been Egyptian but was now spread through much of the Near East. Generally similar leaf-decorated elements (see figs. 27–28) were found at the Aeolic temple at Neandria,[7] and a similar block from Thasos (pl. 37) must also have come from an Aeolic building.[8] Another example (pl. 42) was found at Larisa,[9] a site that also included stone Aeolic structures, but additional pieces come from Aigai[10] (fig. 23) and Phokaia[11] (pl. 38) where no Aeolic remains have yet been found.

The leaf drums from Old Smyrna (pl. 36) must have been used just below the volutes; their diameter corresponds to the upper diameter of the shaft rather than to the bottom of the column (since there was some tapering to the shafts). They may thus be compared with the balusters from Ramat Raḥel (pl. 26), the relief from Tell Tainat (pl. 24), or (possibly) the relief from the palace of Assurbanipal at Nineveh (fig. 21). In Aeolis, one may note the elements below the volutes on a terracotta building model from Larisa (pls. 39–40), which has been dated to the sixth century B.C.[12] Suggestions that the blocks were bases,[13] made by Wesenberg and

single turn, no eye, and a generally rectilinear appearance. The palace reliefs from Assyria preserve the same type (fig. 21), suggesting that generally similar capitals were probably present in a number of Near Eastern regions by the seventh century B.C.

The many similarities in detail, however, seem to emphasize the different mood of the Greek columns. In the non-Greek areas, volute capitals were used in a variety of ways, for both columns and pillars. They were employed most commonly with wooden architecture where they were given different uses based on the desires of the architects and the style of the building be-

[7] *Neandria*, pls. 60–62. See the discussion below.

[8] F. Salviat, "Chronique des fouilles en 1955: Thasos VI, Architecture," *BCH* 80 (1956) 421; Martin, *Problème des ordres*, 125, pl. 26 no. 3.

[9] *Larisa* I, pl. 19a.

[10] R. Bohn, *Altertümer von Aegae* (*JdI*, sup. I, vol. 2, Berlin, 1889) 32, fig. 31, occasionally considered a much later monument (A. von Gerkan, "Zum Tempel von Neandreia," *Neue Beiträge zur klassischen Altertumswissenschaft* [Festschrift B.

Schweitzer, Stuttgart, 1954] 75).

[11] E. Akurgal, "Les Fouilles de Phocée et les sondages de Kymé," *Anatolia* I (1956) 3ff.; R. Martin, "Bulletin archéologique," *REG* 72 (1959) 324; Akurgal, *Kunst Anatoliens*, 287, 328, n. 16, and pl. 252.

[12] *Äolische Kapitell*, 43ff.

[13] For the reconstruction as a base, see especially *Kapitelle und Basen*, 111 no. 1 and 112ff.

Fig. 21. Assyrian relief from the palace of Assurbanipal at Nineveh, illustrating a building with volute columns set within a park. After Perrot and Chipiez, *Histoire* *de l'art* II (1884) fig. 42. For photographs of this relief, see R. D. Barnett, *Assyrian Palace Reliefs*, pls. 133–134.

others before the lower diameter of the shafts was known, may now be abandoned.

The exact origins of the Aeolic style at Old Smyrna are not readily apparent. Although the capitals from Hazor (pls. 4–5) seem related to the Greek treatment of the volutes,[14] one would prefer a prototype from a column, not a pillar. In addition, the absence of the leaf drum and the palmette from the Palestinian series surely rules out any close connection. The volute capitals illustrated in the Assyrian palace relief (fig. 21) may be more closely comparable. They are too small and too generalized to offer any help with details like the palmette, but the eyeless volutes are curved in a similar way. Unless the Assyrian

capitals are meant to be double-tiered like those of the decorative facade of glazed bricks from Babylon (pl. 16) or the relief from Tell Tainat (pl. 24), they include leaf drums immediately below the volutes. A problem, however, is that the Assyrian relief may show a North Syrian rather than a local architectural style. Another possible correlation is offered by the Aeolic balusters from Ramat Raḥel (pl. 26) and elsewhere (see app. A). They have leaf drums, tall, eyeless helices, and a division between the volutes (though it is not a palmette). Most important, the balusters are columns, not pillars, and they occur in series to support a higher, horizontal element. As can be seen from appendix A, the

[14] One of the capitals from Hazor was bifacial, suggesting that its two faces were visible; the other is carved only on the front. Their use must have

been completely unrelated to the use of the capitals at Old Smyrna.

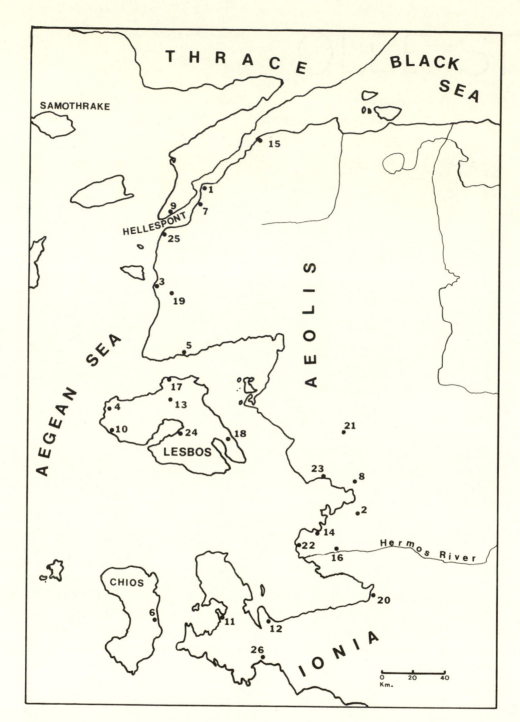

Fig. 22. Map of Aeolis and northern Ionia:

1. Abydos	6. Chios	12. Klazomenai	18. Mytilene	24. Pyrrha
2. Aigai	7. Dardanos	13. Klopedi	19. Neandria	25. Sigeion
3. Alexandria	8. Elaia	14. Kyme	20. Old Smyrna	26. Teos
Troas	9. Elaious	15. Lampsakos	21. Pergamon	
4. Antissa	10. Eressos	16. Larisa	22. Phokaia	
5. Assos	11. Erythrai	17. Methymna	23. Pitane	

Fig. 23. Leaf drum from an unknown context, found at Aigai. After Perrot and Chipiez, *Histoire de l'art* VII (1898) fig. 278.

baluster tradition survives most often from Phoenician-related areas, but there is no way to localize the architectural style very precisely. One can be sure the Greek tradition was borrowed from some nearby region in the Near East, but an exact source cannot be identified from our present evidence.

The similarities between the Aeolic style at Old Smyrna and the style of Etruria can offer some interesting conclusions. The Etruscan examples are all later than the ones from Old Smyrna, but the shape of their volute elements seems closely related. This is a crucial point because by the next generation the Greek style had changed to a stage where it was very unlike the Etruscan examples. This suggests that if there is any Greek influence in the Etruscan Aeolic style, it must have traveled westward before the time of the Aeolic capital with well-pronounced eyes and more than one turn to the volutes, developments from about the second quarter of the sixth century B.C. The eyed volute is extremely rare as a capital type in Etruria, and the dominant form almost invariably has helices like the examples from Old Smyrna. While an occasional piece without the large eyes exists from Greece

in later times, it is inconceivable that later Greek influence could result in the extensive Etruscan development without transmitting more examples of the later capital. Only a few theories can explain the situation: the Etruscan tradition was derived from Greek sources no later than the beginning of the sixth century B.C.; it was derived from non-Greek sources; it was derived from a conservative Greek style we know nothing about. Since the Etruscan fashion was evidently used primarily with carpentry, its origins may remain obscure, but at least some possibilities can now be eliminated. If the earliest Etruscan examples can be definitely shown to postdate the beginning of the sixth century B.C., as now appears to be the case, it is highly unlikely that they were inspired from East Greece. A non-Greek origin would also explain the absence of the leaf drum from Etruria as well as the Etruscan preference for pillars and pilasters over free-standing columns used in the Hellenic manner.

NEANDRIA

Neandria[15] was built on a rocky hill that rose to a sufficient height to command the surrounding territory. Located approximately thirteen kilometers in from the Anatolian coast and about midway between Assos and Ilion, the city's livelihood was probably based largely on the wool trade. It enjoyed a period of early prosperity that lasted until its citizens were taken away at the founding of Alexandria Troas at the end of the fourth century B.C. The city's major Archaic monument was an Aeolic temple of local stone, built at about the middle of the sixth century B.C.

The construction of this temple has caused a considerable amount of controversy. There is disagreement on several of the most basic issues in the building's design including the reconstruction of its capitals, the function of a podiumlike platform around the cella, and the presence or absence of a peristyle. All of these

[15] For literary references, see *PW*, vol. 16, cols. 2106–2107.

problems are interrelated since they involve two interpretations of the same pieces of evidence. Good points can be raised on each side, and the answers revolve around which arguments should take priority over the others.

The temple[16] was oriented northwest and southeast, conforming to the alignment of the hill itself rather than to the cardinal directions (fig. 24). It included a rectangular foundation 12.87 m. wide by 25.71 m. long, which may or may not have supported a peristyle, and a central cella built of tufa blocks with a door in its northwest end. The inner dimensions of the cella were 8.04 x 19.82 m., a ratio of a little less than 2½ to 1. Seven stone columns formed a "spine" down the center of the building in line with its centrally located doorway.

An outer foundation acted at least partially as a terrace, giving added support to the cella's foundations. It was built by outlining the cella and the outer dimensions with roughly cut blocks and then filling the space between these courses with additional blocks, smaller rough stones of various sizes, and even earth. The foundations were sunk all the way to bedrock. When completed, the front at the northwest end would have been about even with the original ground level, while the back would have been raised slightly above the slope of the hill.

The foundations of the cella, about .60 to .65 m. wide, were regular only on their inner sides. An opening 1.27 m. wide was left for the entrance, and at the center of the back was a small channel for drainage, laid through the wall. One unique feature of the building was the floor of the cella, which was slightly lower than the doorway.

Outside the building about five meters from the back were two additional rectangular foundations. They were placed at an angle to the temple and were oriented generally (but not exactly) with each other. Since large quantities

of ash were found in the larger one,[17] as well as throughout this area, it seems certain these were the precinct's altars, even though it is highly unusual to have an altar behind its temple. Presumably the only partially preserved smaller one was the earlier of the two, but there is no evidence for their chronology.

Within the cella and in the vicinity of the temple were fragments of stone capitals and unfluted column drums carved from local volcanic tufa. The exact height of the columns could not be reconstructed, but fragments of cylindrical drums with a diameter of c. 0.53 m. were still in place within the cella set upon granite foundation blocks. The excavators believed these fragments to be parts of the lower drums of the interior columns, but the possibility that they were simple cylindrical bases has also been raised.[18] A rectangular paved platform bordered by stone slabs, perhaps used as a hearth[19] or a bench for offerings, was at the end of one of the temple's two aisles; the cult image was undoubtedly placed at the end of the other.

Three different capital elements were found at Neandria (pl. 41 and figs. 25-28):

1. Blocks with vertically rising volutes
2. Leaf drums decorated with leaves in low relief
3. Larger leaf drums, also with carved leaves (sometimes called *Blattkränze*)

The volute elements (figs. 25-26) are more developed than their counterparts from Old Smyrna, since the whorls are tightly rolled, with well-carved edgings at their margins. The volutes have circular eyes, bored partially in some cases and completely through the stone in others for the insertion of some other material (perhaps bronze rosettes like the carved stone ones from Old Smyrna[20]). Besides delineating the volutes, the marginal borders continue onto the trunk

[16] Clarke (supra n. 1) 1-20, 136-148; *Neandria*, 23ff.

[17] Its size was 4.80 x 4.10 m. The smaller one was too fragmentary for clear measurements.

[18] *Kapitelle und Basen*, 133.

[19] C. G. Yavis, *Greek Altars: Origins and Typol-*

ogy (St. Louis, 1949) 66.

[20] That the entire scheme recalls metalwork has been suggested by H. Drerup, "Architektur und Toreutik in der griechischen Frühzeit," *MdI* 5 (1952) 13ff.

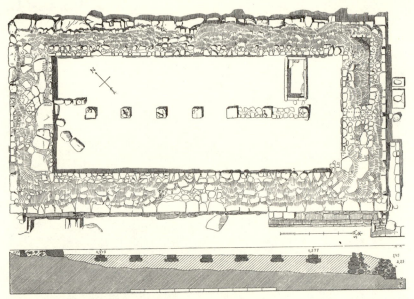

Fig. 24. State plan of the temple at Neandria. After Koldewey, *Neandria*, fig. 52.

of each capital where they form decorative lines. At the upper center of each block is a seven-petaled palmette which rises from a triangular shape with an inverted teardrop within it. Only the central part of each capital (with five of the palmette's petals) rises to form the weight-bearing surface. The blocks are usually about 1.20 m. wide, but one smaller piece (fig. 26) measures only 0.95 m.[21] The columns were conceived in a two-sided way, with rather carelessly carved backs.

Fragments of the smaller leaf drums were found at scattered locations both inside and outside the temple. The style varied somewhat from piece to piece, and two principal subvarieties were present: examples with a single plain molding above a leaf-decorated element (fig. 27, upper two drums); and pieces with two plain moldings above the carved portion (fig. 27, lower drum). From a study of the fragments, the excavators concluded that at least three and perhaps four leaf drums were represented in the finds. At the top their diameter was about 0.40

m., the same as the diameter of the shafts and the lower part of the volute elements.

The third element from Neandria was a large leaf drum, often called a *Blattkranz* in both German and English publications (fig. 28). Again, fragments of several examples were found (certainly five, perhaps as many as seven). All were carved with leaves in low relief, varying slightly from piece to piece. In some cases the leaves were made straight, while in others they were curved to form a more elegant profile.

One of the most hotly contested problems about Neandria involves the reconstruction of these three elements. In the excavation report,[22] Koldewey suggested a three-tiered arrangement with two pendant girdles of leaves below each volute member (pl. 41 and fig. 29). His view, accepted by a number of later writers,[23] has been most effectively defended in this century by Armin von Gerkan.[24] On the other side is the theory that there were two separate colonnades. This opinion goes back to the researches of Dörpfeld[25] and has also found a number of ad-

---

[21] *Neandria*, fig. 63.   [22] *Ibid.*, 33ff.

[23] A list through 1938 is given by H. Johannes, in *Larisa* I, 66–67. See also Robertson, *Greek and Roman Architecture*, 58; Dinsmoor, *Architecture of Ancient Greece*, 63; Lawrence, *Greek Architec-*

ture, 130–131; Cook (supra n. 3, 1963) 83 fig. 26, and 84; A. Mallwitz, "Der alte Athena-Tempel von Milet," *IstMitt* 18 (1968) 135ff.

[24] Von Gerkan (supra n. 10) 71–76.

[25] *Histoire de l'art*, vol. III, 624, fig. 277.

Fig. 25. Volute elements from the temple at Neandria. After Koldewey, *Neandria*, figs. 60–62.

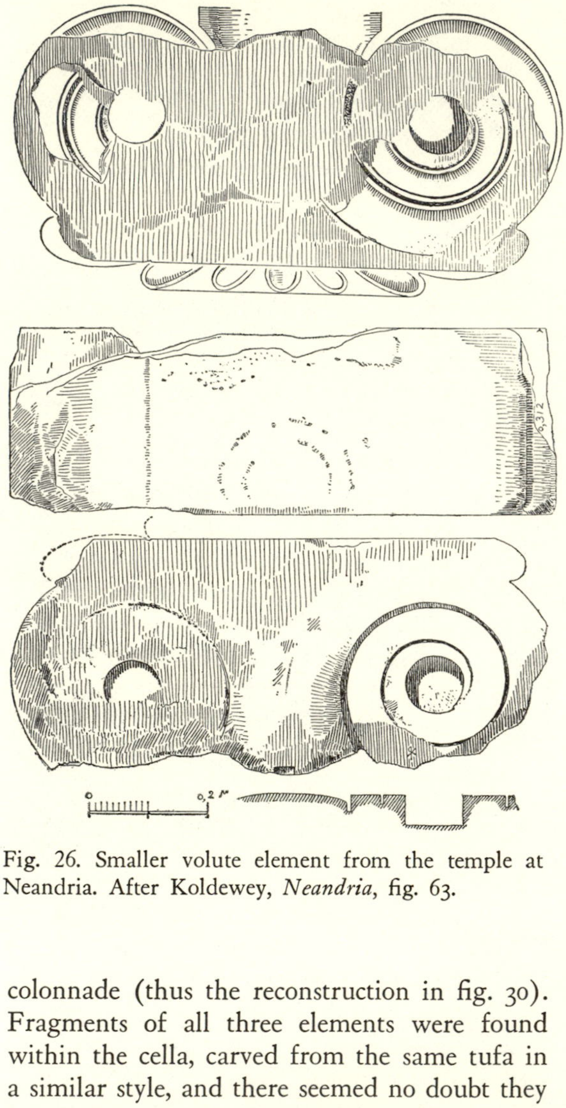

Fig. 26. Smaller volute element from the temple at Neandria. After Koldewey, *Neandria*, fig. 63.

herents.[26] The definitive arguments on this side were raised by Schefold[27] and Martin.[28]

Koldewey first suggested a three-tiered reconstruction because he had discovered a temple of early date, with secure evidence for a central "spine" of columns and no trace of any other

colonnade (thus the reconstruction in fig. 30). Fragments of all three elements were found within the cella, carved from the same tufa in a similar style, and there seemed no doubt they were contemporary. Yet even if one leaves aside considerations which presuppose a knowledge

[26] H. Riemann, *Zum griechischen Peripteraltempel* (Frankfurt, 1935) 124ff.; *Äolische Kapitell*, 48; F. Krischen, "Werden und Wesen der jonischen Formensprache," *Antike und Abendland* 2 (1946) 81, figs. 4 no. 4, and 7; *Weltwunder der Baukunst in Babylonien und Jonien* (Tübingen, 1956) 54–55;

Drerup (supra n. 20) 10; E. Akurgal, "Vom äolischen zum ionischen Kapitell," *Anatolia* 5 (1960) 4; *Kunst Anatoliens*, 287–289.

[27] *Äolische Kapitell*, 48.

[28] *Problème des ordres*, 122ff.

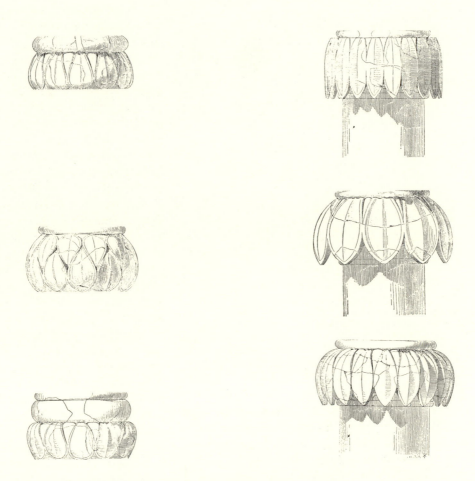

Fig. 27. The smaller leaf drums from the temple at Neandria. After Koldewey, *Neandria*, figs. 60–62.

Fig. 28. The larger leaf drums from Neandria, set upon shafts as capitals. After Koldewey, *Neandria*, figs. 60–62.

of Archaic aesthetics (i.e. that the rougher backs of the volute members mean they would not be visible, that the Aeolic capital is "two-sided" for exterior use while the leaf drum is circular as befits an interior capital, etc.), there are sound structural reasons for refuting Koldewey's the-

ory. The principal problem arises from the fact that the upper surfaces of the larger leaf drums have no dowel holes, while the lower surfaces of the volute members do.[29] This suggests the elements were joined together by dowels, and

[29] *Äolische Kapitell*, 48. The upper surface of only one large leaf drum survives. The lower surfaces of two volute members are preserved. Noth-

ing is known of the upper and lower surfaces of the small leaf drums because of the fragmentary condition of all extant specimens.

Fig. 29. Three-tiered reconstruction of the capitals from Neandria (almost surely incorrect). After Koldewey, *Neandria*, fig. 62.

the upper surfaces of the large leaf drums were finished in the same way as the tops of the volute elements because they had a similar function— they supported the building's superstructure.

Additional problems, however, complicate the situation. Koldewey's publication of his excavation made it clear that the interior of the cella was still fairly intact when the building was uncovered.[30] There were fragments of volute members within the cella, which suggested to him (as it has to many writers since that time) that these blocks belonged with the interior colonnade. It can be noted, however, that in several cases pieces of the same block were found at several different points on the site. Koldewey's publication is a remarkably scientific document for its time, but it is possible that some mixing of the deposit could have occurred, since the site had been used as a source for building stone over a

long period of time. Because of this, the discovery of some of the fragments within the building cannot be regarded as definitive evidence.[31]

Since placing the volute members with one column type and the larger leaf drums with another requires the presence of a second set of columns, the evidence for and against this possibility must also be considered. A single row of supports inside the temple itself seems assured since the original floor was still nearly intact when the cult place was excavated, and there was only one set of foundations which could have held columns. A prostyle arrangement can also be ruled out because of the regular width of the stone platform around the building. Whatever the structure's purpose may have been, it clearly surrounds the main chamber. If columns had been intended at the front only, the podium would have been significantly wider at this point, and it is not. Two stages of construction, with one capital type being replaced by another at a later date, seem to be impossible because of the stratigraphy. The floor of the cella was immediately overlaid by a single burned layer, above which was an accumulation of humus. Most of the architectural fragments were found in the humus, where no element was stratified above or below the others. Since there was no trace of more than one building period, the only tenable conclusion is that if two colonnades were present, one must have been a peristyle, supported by the platform around the cella.

Could this foundation have been a stylobate for an exterior colonnade? Several arguments against this possibility have been raised, beginning with its construction. The stonework consisted not of set courses, but of an outer edge of strong blocks backed by a fill. In addition, the width varies from 1.55 m. to 1.98 m., so that with a peristyle the distance between columns and cella would have been rather uneven. If the builders had tried to compensate for this irregularity in the foundation by placing the columns

---

[30] The floor was relatively undisturbed because it was slightly lower than the surrounding land. Portions of the columns (or, as some have said, column bases) were still *in situ* on some of the foundations

along the central "spine."

[31] On this, see most recently the discussion of Wesenberg, *Kapitelle und Basen*, 133–134 n. 694.

at a uniform distance from the wall of the cella, some of the shafts would have been above the fill, not above the largest supporting blocks. Because of these inconsistencies, von Gerkan has suggested the platform was neither a podium nor a foundation for a peristyle but a simple terrace, designed to provide a level area for the temple.[32] This seems unlikely because such terracing would not have been necessary along the front, where the land slopes upward.

Structurally, there is no reason to assume the platform could not have supported a colonnade. One must think in terms of a wooden superstructure, not a heavy stone one, and the dimensions at Neandria are not especially large. At the back, where bedrock lies the deepest, the foundation is a well-built wall along part of its course; it is strengthened with large boulders along the remainder. In addition, the weight of the roof could have been shared by the cella walls, as well as by the central colonnade. It can be noted that the foundations for the central "spine" were simple blocks not even sunk to bedrock, indicating the builders did not feel a deep and sturdy foundation was absolutely necessary. And finally, since the foundations for the cella were also built by laying a single line of stones (on the interior side) and filling in behind them, it should cause little surprise that a similar technique was used twice in the same building. We now know this technique was not unique to Neandria. It had a long history in East Greece going back to "Temple A" at Ephesos,[33] and it was also used for the Archaic temple at Larisa (described below).

The irregularity of the pteroma would be unusual by later standards, but it may be proper to ask if fifth-century B.C. aesthetics should be extended to earlier eras. There was often very little regularity in the sacred precincts of Archaic

Greece, and their informality only gave way gradually in favor of more studied proportions and arrangements.[34] Marked differences between individual capitals, irregularities in sizes and spacings, and an altar at the back that was not aligned with the temple would not have been tolerated in later times either, but they all occur at Neandria. Perhaps informality can be as strong a virtue as regularity, and one should not reject an architectural possibility because it does not conform to the right canon.

An additional argument against the existence of a peristyle has been raised by Johannes.[35] Clarke once argued that the small weight-bearing surfaces of the volute elements might have been designed to lower the whorls so a sagging wooden beam would not damage them,[36] but this seems to be denied by the design at Klopedi and in the Old Palace at Larisa where the whorls helped in the support. Johannes suggested the small upper surfaces of the Neandrian capitals seem better suited to a ridge beam than an exterior colonnade, although he pointed out that the differences could be based on chronological development instead of architectural usage. The fact is that too little is known of Aeolic temple construction to reach a conclusion based on this aspect of the remains.

The definitive evidence remains the dowel holes. As the volute members clearly indicate, they were attached with dowels to the pieces below them. Since the larger leaf drums have no cuttings in their upper surfaces, they must be assigned to another set of columns, even if this means the builders at Neandria put up an irregular temple on rather poor foundations. The conclusion that the temple was peripteral seems almost inescapable.

That the large leaf drum was a separate capital is not as great a cause for surprise as it was

---

[32] Von Gerkan (supra n. 10) 73.

[33] D. G. Hogarth, *Excavations at Ephesus: The Archaic Artemisia* (London, 1908) 54.

[34] See especially B. Bergquist, *The Archaic Greek Temenos* (Lund, 1967) 135–136. For the theory that site planning and the organization of space in sacred precincts emerged during the sixth century

B.C., see C. A. Doxiadis, *Architectural Space in Ancient Greece* (Cambridge, Mass., and London, 1972) 21 and *passim*.

[35] *Larisa* i, 67–68. See also Cook (supra n. 3, 1963) 84–86.

[36] Clarke (supra n. 1) 6.

some years ago because generally similar leaf elements are now known from a number of sites.[37] Their origins may be traced to the Neo-Hittite styles of North Syria where they were obviously used as capitals,[38] and they may represent a loosely connected tradition of floral capitals used at a few Greek cities in Archaic times.[39] Almost every example shows individual characteristics, but all are semicylindrical or barrel-shaped drums with carved decoration. Yet there are strong reasons for questioning the use of the examples from Neandria as the crowning members of columns. As Mallwitz has pointed out,[40] these pieces do not serve the structural purpose which makes capitals necessary in the first place. Their upper surfaces are circular, not rectangular, and they are merely continuations of the shafts, so that if they were used as capitals, they could not adequately transfer the weight of the superstructure to the supporting shafts. At the minimum, one would like to see a rectangular abacus upon each block.

The position of the smaller leaf drum, Koldewey's middle element, also raises questions. Eliminating the larger leaf drums from the volute capitals need not mean the smaller ones should also be eliminated, and it has been suggested they could still have served as pendant girdles of leaves, placed below the volute members;[41] an alternate theory, advanced by Wesenberg, restores them as bases.[42] This latter theory supposes that the large leaf drums were placed atop the columns within the cella, and it explains the presence of the extra set of carved elements as bases for the exterior colonnade. Carved bases

had a rich history in the Near East, especially in the Neo-Hittite cities of North Syria, and several parallels can be found which are quite similar to the Greek specimens with the large carved element (fig. 27, upper drum).[43] For the drums with a sizeable plain molding above the carved portion (fig. 27, middle and lower drums), the only parallels are from later times.[44] The reconstruction is a tempting one, even though it may imply the presence of some unkown and as yet undiscovered element which was placed between the shafts and the volute members.[45] The question of the transition between shaft and capital is the largest problem in the reconstruction of the small leaf drums in this way, because the rather full archaeological record may perhaps have been expected to yield fragments of this piece, if it were present. There is a good deal of evidence to suggest transitional elements were usual between volute capitals and their shafts, and a large corpus of vases, ivories, bronzes, and other objects could be assembled from both Greece and the Near East to illustrate this point (see pls. 2, 16, 23–24, 26–28, and fig. 21). Some of these transitional elements seem very much like the pieces from Neandria (pl. 43).[46] An example from Aeolis itself is a small clay building-model from Larisa (pls. 39–40) with a good illustration of the superstructure of an Archaic Aeolic building.[47] The model includes a torus below the capital which may well represent an element like the small leaf drums from Neandria, although this is not certain. Architectural evidence pointing to the same conclusion comes from Thasos,[48] where a leaf drum with a cutting

---

[37] For Aigai, see above, n. 10 and fig. 23; for Phokaia, see above, n. 11 and pl. 38; for Larisa, see above, n. 9, and pl. 42.

[38] E. Akurgal, *The Art of Greece: Its Origins in the Mediterranean and Near East* (New York, 1968) pls. 49–50, 54–57, translation of *Orient und Okzident: Die Geburt der griechischen Kunst* (Baden-Baden, 1966).

[39] They must be distinguished from the palm capitals which led to the "Pergamene" capitals of the Hellenistic Athenian stoas and elsewhere. This group is ultimately of Egyptian inspiration.

[40] Mallwitz (supra n. 23) 135ff.

[41] L. Curtius, *Die antike Kunst* (Potsdam, 1938) fig. 167.

[42] *Kapitelle und Basen*, 77ff., 132ff., fig. 164.

[43] *Ibid.*, 87–89, figs. 179–182.

[44] Especially from Achaemenid contexts. See *Kapitelle und Basen*, 132–133.

[45] Wesenberg restored a torus between two moldings on the analogy of Klopedi.

[46] E. Buschor, "Altsamische Grabstelen," *Ath Mitt* 58 (1933) pl. on p. 22.

[47] Published by Schefold, *Äolische Kapitell*, 43ff.

[48] For bibliography, see above, n. 8. Wesenberg, *Kapitelle und Basen*, 135, has suggested this block

and a circular trace on its upper surface was found (see pl. 37), as well as from Old Smyrna, discussed above. An additional difficulty in Wesenberg's reconstruction is the absence of contemporary (or earlier) parallels for the base system with a large plain molding over a carved element. One could perhaps solve the problem by supposing some of the leaf drums were bases while others were neckings below the volute capitals, but the issue must be left open for the present—there is simply not enough available information.

Given the ambiguous and conflicting nature of the evidence, it should be clear that no single reconstruction is totally satisfactory. How, then, should the building be best reconstructed? The evidence of the dowel cuttings seems definitive, and one must suppose both an exterior and an interior colonnade (fig. 31). Since fragments of stone were *in situ* on the foundation blocks forming the "spine," extra bases cannot be added here; the larger leaf drums should be restored as capitals for the columns within the cella. Because of the structural difficulty arising from using these blocks as complete capitals, it seems best to restore a missing abacus of wood or stone above each member—a simple rectangular block would suffice. The volute elements may be placed in an exterior peristyle of rather irregular dimensions. An analogy with the spacing of the interior "spine" would imply 6 x 11 or 6 x 12 columns, but a more likely arrangement can be based on structural considerations. Extending the lines of the front and back walls gives an intercolumniation on the sides that works well with twelve columns. For the two ends, centrally placed supports would continue the line of the "spine" and help hold the ridge beam, a common practice in other Archaic buildings (like the temple of Apollo at Thermon). An equal spacing on the ends requires seven columns, allowing an alignment with the side-walls also. Thus one arrives at 7 x 12 columns as the most

probable reconstruction for the peristyle. With the volute elements, the smaller leaf drums should be assigned to this exterior colonnade. They were either bases or transitions between shafts and capitals, with the latter possibility appearing to be far more likely (fig. 32).

While this reconstruction leaves some questions open, it seems to provide the best interpretation of the evidence as we now know it. One difficulty would have been the arrangement at the corners. Since Aeolic capitals were two-sided, one wonders if the corner columns faced toward the ends or if some other solution was devised. No evidence survives from any Aeolic building to shed light on the problem. While it may seem unusual for a sixth-century B.C. Greek temple to add a peristyle to a closed single room with neither pronaos nor opisthodomos, this was evidently a regular practice in Archaic Aeolis; examples from Larisa and Klopedi will be discussed below.

Several problems still cloud the issues at Neandria. Our picture could easily be altered with new investigations, but what is needed is more evidence. Apparently additional excavation is necessary.

For the date of the temple, the best evidence comes from the terracotta decorations and the roof tiles. The roof tile system, of an early design, used flat pan tiles[49] with turned up lateral edges; half cylinders covered the joints. At the roof's edges, the pan tiles terminated in spouts, while ornamental antefixes decorated with facing panthers concealed the semicircular ends of the cover tiles. The exact design of the tiles from the ridge could not be determined from the few fragments found, but there was a terracotta disc akroterion at the front of the building. A sima with running animals, also of terracotta, completed the scheme.

As Koldewey noted,[50] the terracottas are more advanced than those of the Heraion at Olympia (early sixth century B.C.) so that a date before

---

was a base, but the expansion in the diameter from 0.22 m. at the bottom to 0.316 m. at the top and the presence of dowel holes in both the upper and lower surfaces are not consistent with this usage.

[49] 0.53 m. wide by 0.84 m. long.
[50] *Neandria*, 49. See also the discussion of Dinsmoor, *Architecture of Ancient Greece*, 62 n. 2.

71

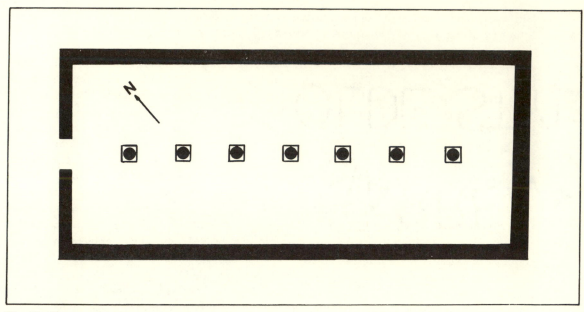

Fig. 30. The temple at Neandria restored as a simple cella with a central "spine" of columns.

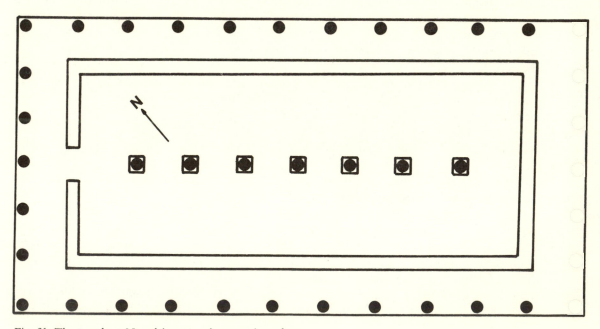

Fig. 31. The temple at Neandria restored as a peripteral building.

Fig. 32. Restoration of the elements from Neandria with a single leaf drum below the volutes.

about 580 B.C. is not possible. At the other extreme, a date of 540–530 B.C. has been suggested for the temple based on the stylistic development of the volute motif in the sixth century B.C.[51] The latter date seems to be a little too late,[52] because the molding at the top of the sima at Neandria is more primitive than comparable moldings from Larisa dated to the middle of the sixth century.[53] A date in the second half of the century has been proposed for the architectural terracottas, which also appears to be a little late,[54] while the style of the painted animals points toward the middle of the century. These pieces of evidence seem to converge around the

period from c. 560–550 B.C., so that a date around the second quarter of the century seems likely.

LARISA ON THE HERMOS

According to the archaeological evidence,[55] Aeolians settled in Larisa about 700 B.C.,[56] replacing an Anatolian people who used gray, undecorated pottery. The site had much to recommend it to the newcomers. Its location in the valley of the Hermos River was a strategic one since the valley would have been an important route to the interior of Anatolia, and the north-south road connecting Aeolis with the other Greek cities to the south would also have passed nearby. While the city was always rather small during the Archaic period, the impressive architecture that crowned its summit testifies to the wealth of its inhabitants.

By the sixth century B.C. the akropolis at Larisa was a fortified citadel (fig. 33). Within the confines of its massive walls, there gradually arose two major groups of buildings, one religious and one secular. These two precincts—the official residence of the city-state's ruler and the sacred temenos of a major deity—stood until their destruction at the time of the Persian wars. At least a few of the Larisan buildings used columns with vertically rising volutes, and there were also isolated Aeolic columns set up in the sacred precinct.

The earliest extant Aeolic capital from Larisa (pl. 42 and fig. 34) is an elegantly carved tufa

---

[51] *Larisa* I, 147.

[52] It was based largely on the development of the volute motif as worked out by Buschor for the East Greek funerary stelai. For some very cogent arguments that some of Buschor's dates are a quarter of a century too late, consult J. Boardman, "Chian and Early Ionic Architecture," *AntJ* 39 (1959) 202.

[53] Compare Frieze VIII, a sima assigned to the Old Palace (c. 550 B.C.), *Larisa* I, pl. 27; *Larisa* II, pls. 34–42.

[54] Åkerström, Å., *Die architektonischen Terrakotten Kleinasiens* (Lund, 1966) 13. For comments

on the late dating, see N. Bookidis, "Review of *Die architektonischen Terrakotten Kleinasiens* by Åke Åkerström," *AJA* 72 (1968) 81–82, and C. Le Roy, "Les Terres-cuites architecturales et la diffusion de l'hellénisme en Anatolie," *Revue Archéologique* (1967) 127ff.

[55] J. Boehlau, K. Schefold, and L. Kjellberg, *Larisa am Hermos* I–III (Berlin and Stockholm, 1940–1942).

[56] A circumstance which has caused some scholars to doubt the identification because the literary evidence suggests a much earlier settlement.

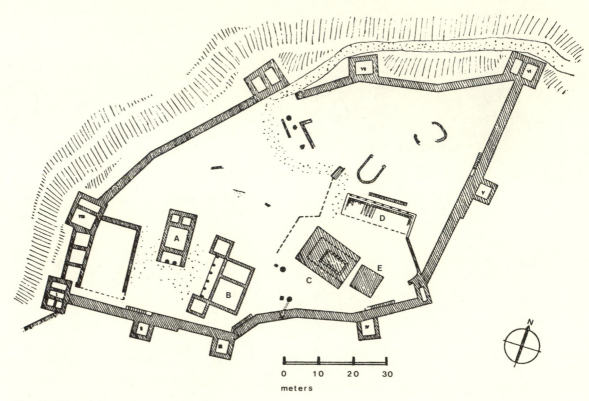

Fig. 33. Plan of the major buildings on the akropolis of Larisa on the Hermos, about 500 B.C.

A. Megaron, B. Old Palace, C. Temple, D. Stoa, E. Altar. For state plans see *Larisa* I, pls. 32–36. By courtesy of Walter de Gruyter and Co., Berlin, adapted from Boehlau and Schefold, *Larisa* I, fig. 4.

block of large proportions, 1.308 m. across its greatest width.[57] The whorls, delineated by incised grooves, move upward from a heart-shaped central form from which also spring subsidiary tendrils. A palmette fills the upper center of the capital. The volutes have two and a half turns, but they do not terminate in eyes. Their form is echoed by the smaller whorls and by similar turns within the heart-shaped nucleus.

The date of the capital must be based on stylistic analysis: Kjellberg placed it at c. 570 B.C.;[58]

Schefold preferred the end of the previous century;[59] and other writers have placed it variously within these limits. The exuberance of the floral decoration, the linear style, and the absence of eyes at the centers of the volutes clearly indicate an early date; the block must come from before the second quarter of the sixth century, but one cannot really be precise.

Several writers have tried to complete the capital by placing it atop a leaf drum with a shallow cyma reversa profile from the same site,

dating was based largely on the style of the leaf drum, which he joined to the capital, subtracting this element places the capital much earlier.

[59] *Larisa* I, 147.

[57] Mendel, *Catalogue*, 37ff., no. 277; L. Kjellberg, "Das äolische Kapitell von Larisa," *Corolla Archaeologica . . . Gustavo Adolpho dedicata* (Lund, 1932) 238ff.; *Larisa* I, 142–143, pls. 19a, 29, and 40.

[58] Kjellberg (supra n. 57) 245. Since the late

74

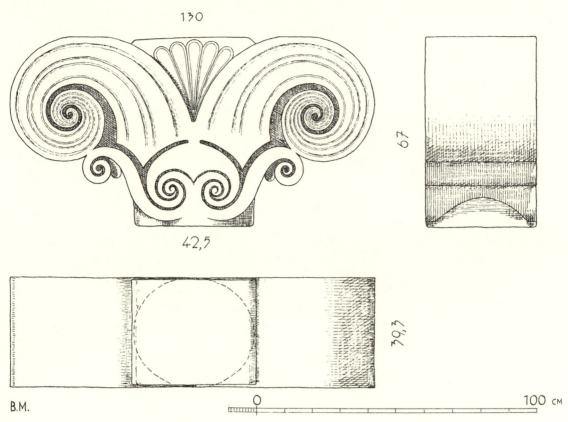

Fig. 34. The large Aeolic capital from Larisa. By courtesy of Walter de Gruyter and Co., Berlin, after Boehlau and Schefold, *Larisa* 1, pl. 40.

following Koldewey's reconstruction of the capitals from Neandria (see pl. 42)[60] and examples in the minor arts (pl. 43). Others have completely rejected this reconstruction, maintaining that the leaf drum belongs with a separate column, probably of somewhat later date.[61] The find spots of the two pieces offer no help in this matter since both were found in a later context. The internal evidence, however, is in favor of assigning the piece with the carved leaves to another monument. The upper diameter of the leaf drum is only 0.36 m., while the lower diameter of the capital varies from 0.40 m. to 0.425 m. The system of dowel holes also may not match; a circular socket is in the capital's resting surface (0.063 m. in diameter), while the upper surface of the leaf drum may have no ancient cuttings.[62] To compensate for these differences, it has been suggested that a third element, a block with a bead-and-reel decoration (a small fragment of

[60] The main study is Kjellberg (supra n. 57). For additional arguments see also Dinsmoor, *Architecture of Ancient Greece*, 62.

[61] The definitive research is by Schefold, *Äolische Kapitell*, 50; *Larisa* 1, 142.

[62] There are cuttings in both the upper and lower surfaces, made to aid in the display of the piece at

the turn of the century. Mendel, *Catalogue*, 37 no. 277, was unable to decide if they were made from ancient cuttings. Kjellberg (supra n. 57), 239, thought an ancient cutting was in the upper surface. Schefold, *Äolische Kapitell*, 50, considered a cutting in the lower surface to be original.

which was found at a different point on the site), was inserted between the two elements. As Schefold has pointed out,[63] however, the volutes and the leaf drum are of different colored stone, and the bead-and-reel has too large a diameter. The final argument against the double-tiered construction is the problem of style. The plastic rendering of the leaf drum, with relatively solid, three-dimensional leaves, is very different from the linear treatment of the capital itself. If this difference is taken as an indication of chronology, the carved piece should be placed more than half a century after the time of the volutes, well into the third quarter of the sixth century B.C.[64] The only possible conclusion is that the volute element could not have used this particular stone as a pendant girdle of leaves.

The original location of the Aeolic capital also presents problems. The earliest known structure large enough to accommodate this size of column was a megaron[65] built in the southwest corner of the akropolis (fig. 33 A). This building, probably the home of the ruling family, was built around the second quarter of the sixth century B.C. Since this date seems too late for the linear style of the capital, it is possible the block does not come from a building at all. With this in mind, Schefold has considered it a part of an isolated votive monument, reconstructing it as the capital for a large column whose fragments were found on the ancient site (pl. 44).[66] The style would thus have been first used at Larisa with a free-standing column, a situation with possible parallels from the early stages of Ionic architecture.[67] Problems arise from this reconstruction because the capital has no cutting in the top to help hold a piece of statuary, and its central ornament and volutes are flattened as if

they supported a higher member. Since the absence of a cutting usually suggests a use with architecture, and since the flat upper edges of the volutes and central filling ornament make no sense unless the block was designed to support something else, it may be necessary to give a later date to the capital so that it can be assigned to the megaron.

A second Aeolic monument from Larisa dates from somewhat later. In the southwest corner of the citadel, the megaron was replaced about the middle of the sixth century B.C. by a building usually called the Old Palace (fig. 33 B).[68] Extensive remains of the foundations, along with architectural terracottas, fragments of Aeolic capitals, and other stone architectural details, permit at least a tentative reconstruction of this impressive structure (pl. 45).

The palace faced an open area which could have been used as a courtyard. At its front was an open porch supported by columns, flanked by slightly projecting square towers (fig. 35). Beyond the colonnade were the main two rooms of the building, arranged side by side with the larger one on the right. As was the custom at Larisa, the principal room was square. Access within the palace was somewhat limited. From the porch, one could enter either the principal compartments or the towers, but there was no access between towers and royal chamber. The thickness of the foundations indicates a second story, perhaps to accommodate bedrooms.

Aeolic capitals from the portico's columns (pls. 46–47) recall the earlier Aeolic monument from the city in such matters as the overall proportions, but the later specimens eliminated the exotic floral ornament, leaving simple pairs of volutes with a palmette between them. Unlike

[63] *Äolische Kapitell*, 50. See also Akurgal (supra n. 26, 1960) 4–5.

[64] *Äolische Kapitell*, 50. Even if this difference could be regarded as a contemporary stylistic variance (which is highly unlikely), one would not like to place the two styles within the same column.

[65] The foundations were fragmentary, but a megaron-type ground plan seems likely.

[66] *Larisa* I, pl. 29.

[67] The possibility that Ionic capitals were first used with isolated columns has been suggested by G. Gruben, "Die Sphinx-säule von Aigina," *AthMitt* 80 (1965) 207.

[68] Since it was excavated in 1902, the building was not dated stratigraphically, but several pieces of evidence (including the terracottas) suggest the c. 550 B.C. date.

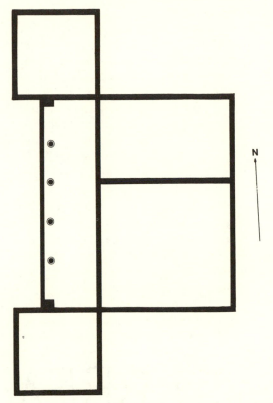

Fig. 35. Plan of the Old Palace at Larisa, restored with two symmetrical towers and four columns in the portico (the form of the northern tower is not absolutely certain). No complete state plan has been published.

the specimens from Neandria, the Larisan blocks have broad weight-bearing surfaces composed of the upper parts of the volutes as well as the central palmettes. The best preserved piece (pl. 46) has small eyes at the center of each whorl. Small holes suggest the blocks were sheathed with bronze.

The capitals were supported by unfluted stone columns, and there were also low stone bases of a simple design (the excavators suggested an undecorated torus over a spira). Four supports are likely, but a central placement of the door

[69] *Greek Architecture*, 239.

[70] *Larisa* 1, 84–85.

[71] For its appearance on a tablet from Mari, see G. Dossin, *Archives royales de Mari I: Correspondance de Šamši-Addu* (Paris, 1950) no. 3, rev. 10.

to the palace is not absolutely certain, and three columns have also been proposed.[69] Since no remains of the superstructure were uncovered, it is presumed this portion was of wood.

Several different types of architectural terracottas were found in the vicinity of the Old Palace. Since they can be dated to about the same period, they must have formed an integrated decorative scheme. A large disc, used as an akroterion, suggests a gabled roof at the center of the building. Akroteria with volutes were also used, while a figured frieze was employed for the geison. The building must have had an impressive facade (pl. 45).

Because of the placement of the towers at the sides of the porch, a single roof for both towers and central rectangle is not possible. One must suppose instead a tectonic construction in which towers, porch, and central rectangle were roofed separately. A very similar arrangement was preserved in the facades of scene buildings for the later Greek theater. Here, too, there was often a central room flanked by towers, and it is possible the scene buildings preserved some memory of early Near Eastern or East Greek palaces.

Since the Old Palace replaced a megaron, its style does not seem to have been a local inheritance. There are no Greek antecedents for the ground plan, and one must suppose either that the palace was an innovation or that sources must be sought somewhere in the Near East. In seeking these sources, both the *bît hilani* and the Achaemenid palaces have been proposed as possible prototypes.[70]

The *bît hilani*, an architectural form with early antecedents on the upper Euphrates,[71] was especially popular in the Neo-Hittite cities of North Syria in the centuries following the end of the Bronze Age.[72] Its standard form included a columned portico approached by steps leading to a rectangular throne room (fig. 7). The throne room, with its long axis parallel to the

[72] For excellent surveys of the *bît hilani*, see H. Frankfort, "The Origin of the *Bît Hilani*," *Iraq* 14 (1952) 120–131: Akurgal (supra n. 38) 69ff. For its possible presence in Palestine see the discussion in chapter II.

portico, was joined by one or more accessory rooms at the side or back. A staircase for the upper story was usually placed in the end of the porch. The columns in the portico were of wood, but they were regularly given sturdy stone bases —an early manifestation of the articulated column built from base, shaft, and capital in strict contrast with the Doric style of the Greek mainland.

Using the evidence of a carved relief from Tell Tainat (pl. 24), some writers have suggested the Syrian *bît hilani* occasionally used Aeolic capitals for the columns in the portico.[73] This remains a strong possibility, but more clearly architectural reliefs are unfortunately somewhat ambiguous in the design of the columns.[74] Since these were regularly of wood, the matter cannot be decided with finality.

It was probably the Assyrians who were most responsible for the spread of the *bît hilani* throughout the Near East. As the Assyrian king Sargon recorded at Khorsabad, it was he who had

> erected palaces of ivory, maple, boxwood, mulberry, cedar, cypress, juniper, pine, and pistachio wood, as his royal dwelling therein; who roofed them with great cedar timbers, covered door leaves of cypress and mulberry with a sheathing of shining bronze and set them up in their entrances; who built a portico, patterned after a Hittite palace, which in the tongue of Amurru they call a *bît-hilani*, in front of its gates (doors); who set up as posts to support their doors eight lions in pairs, weighing 4,610 talents of shining bronze ... [and] upon [which] lion-colossi he placed four cedar columns, exceedingly high, each 1 GAR in thickness.[75]

The word Hittite in the Khorsabad inscriptions most likely refers to North Syria, where the use of "lion-colossi" as column bases is known from several sites. Yet even with the possibility of Aeolic capitals in the Syrian *bît hilani*, and assuming a strong Assyrian tradition which could have spread the style throughout the Near East (as an alternative to direct Syrian-Aeolic contacts), the *bît hilani* still does not offer a truly convincing parallel. A comparison between the ground plan of the Larisan palace and any typical North Syrian *bît hilani* (as at Tell Tainat, fig. 7, where the Aeolic capital was found carved on the relief) serves to point out the many basic differences. The only major similarity is in the facades; both would have presented the viewer with a columned porch flanked by towers, with major reception rooms beyond the portico. Aside from this, the ground plans are quite unrelated.

A very similar picture emerges when one considers the Achaemenid palaces of Persia. The date of the palace at Larisa suggests comparisons with Pasargadae rather than Persepolis, and a strong case can be made for East Greek influence in the architecture of the city of Cyrus.[76] Yet, the ground plans of the most relevant palaces from Pasargadae (fig. 36) have a completely different overall plan. Again, the only close correspondence is in the facade, a columned portico flanked by towers. In the absence of comparable architecture from areas where one might expect a closer relation (for example, the palace of Croesus at Sardis), the origins of the Old Palace must remain open. One can only note that similar facades were in current use at many points in the Near East, and that one of these probably influenced the Greek city. The plan itself was certainly foreign to Aeolis, even though

[73] C. W. McEwan, "The Syrian Expedition of the Oriental Institute of the University of Chicago," *AJA* 41 (1937) 16, fig. 12; S. Lloyd, *Early Anatolia* (Baltimore, 1956) 164–165.

[74] R. Naumann, *Tell Halaf* II (Berlin, 1950) fig. 9; "Das Hausmodell vom Tell Halaf und die nach Unten verjüngten Säulen Nordsyriens," *Jahrbuch für kleinasiatische Forschung* 2 (1951–1953) 246ff.

[75] D. D. Luckenbill, *Ancient Records of Assyria and Babylonia* (Chicago, 1927) II, 49.

[76] See C. Nylander, *Ionians in Pasargadae* (Uppsala, 1970). In contrast with Schefold (*Larisa* 1, 84–85), Nylander suggests that any lines of influence in connection with the palaces probably moved from Greece to Persia, not the other way.

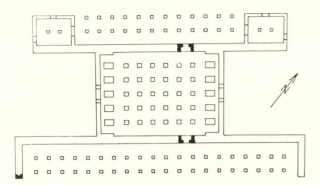

Fig. 36. Palace P at Pasargadae. Date uncertain, perhaps c. 546–530 B.C., within the reign of Cyrus. Some would place the structure slightly later, based on the style of the sculpture. After C. Nylander, *Ionians in Pasargadae* (1970) fig. 34b.

the individual architectural details were well within the local Greek tradition.

A few years after the completion of the Aeolic palace, the inhabitants of Larisa rebuilt their temple, transforming it into a major piece of architecture. Their most sacred temenos was on the akropolis (fig. 33), at a spot sanctified by the early existence of a pre-Greek cult place. On the basis of inscriptions and other evidence, the deity who was worshiped here by the Greeks can be identified as Athena.[77] Few remains attest to the earliest days of the Olympian cult, but by the first half of the sixth century B.C., a small temple (fig. 33 c), an altar (fig. 33 e), and a stoa (fig. 33 d) had been erected, and the temenos was marked off from the rest of the akropolis. The early temple was a simple rectangle with foundations 3.25 m. x 6.25 m. on the inside,[78] oriented northwest and southeast (fig. 37). No trace remains of the doorway, but the exterior altar was at the southeastern end. The building was placed atop a small terrace.

Because of its small size, columns would have been unnecessary.

When the early temple was replaced about 530 B.C.,[79] the terrace was enlarged considerably until it became a U-shaped podium extending from the higher bedrock at the southeast to well beyond the end of the temple at the northwest (fig. 38). A much larger altar was built in the same period, on the site of the earlier one. The new cella kept the 2:1 ratio of length to width used by its predecessor, but it was much larger. Its interior measurements seem to have been very close to the 5.775 m. x 11.55 m. resulting from counting 17.5 and 35 local feet, each .330 m. long.[80]

Only scanty remains were found within the cella. There was no evidence for the location of the door, and the excavators were divided about its location.[81] No remains of a base for a cult statue were found, but a rectangular pit, discovered near the center of the building, was perhaps used for sacrifices during this period. Although no bases were found, fragments of stone shafts suggest a series of interior supports for the roof.

Two possibilities exist for the capitals of the inner columns. The first is the leaf drum often placed below the largest Aeolic capital from Larisa (pl. 42). The piece was not found at the temple's site, but the style of the carving accords well with the date of the temple, and some writers have theorized that it could have capped one of the supports for the building's roof.[82] The second possibility is that the temple used Aeolic capitals. Several votives (see pl. 48 and others listed in the catalogue), including a building model with Aeolic columns, suggest

---

[77] For an attempt to identify the goddess as Cybele, see Johannes, *Larisa* I, 60, 66. The arguments of Schefold (in favor of Athena) are more convincing (*ibid.*, 22, 156–157).

[78] The measurements were given as 3.25 x 6.25 m. in a preliminary report by K. Schefold, "Ausgrabungen in Larisa am Hermos im Frühjahr 1934." *AA* (1934) col. 372, but were given as 3.30 x 6.60 m. in the final publication, *Larisa* I, 65.

[79] Dated by the pottery as well as the terracotta ornaments. See *Larisa* I, 61.

[80] For the computation of this foot at Neandria, see Riemann (supra n. 26) appendix. For the computations at Larisa, see *Larisa* I, 65.

[81] Johannes placed it in the northwest end (*Larisa* I, 59ff.), while Schefold suggested the southeast (*ibid.*, 156–157).

[82] *Äolische Kapitell*, 42ff.; *Larisa* I, 157.

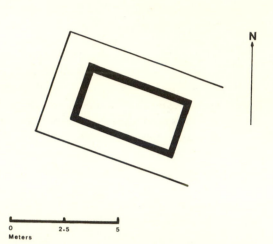

Fig. 37. Plan of the early temple at Larisa, showing the small cella and its podium. For a state plan see *Larisa* I, pl. 36.

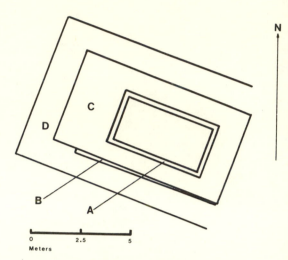

Fig. 38. Plan of the Archaic temples at Larisa.

A. The early temple, B. Podium for the early temple, C. Foundation for the later temple, built in the third quarter of the sixth century B.C., D. Podium for the later temple. For a state plan see *Larisa* I, pl. 36.

this theory, but no archaeological proof has come to light to substantiate it.[83]

The conclusion that the temple at Neandria had a peristyle raises the same question for Larisa. Is there any evidence that it also had an exterior colonnade? Preliminary reports of the excavations restored the c. 530 B.C. temple as peripteral,[84] assuming a new peristyle had been added around a small, original cella in a later remodeling; by the time of the final publication, the excavators had concluded this was not a likely possibility, and the outer foundations were restored as a new cella. The original view, of course, would produce a very coherent view for Aeolic architecture in general: all three major Aeolic temples (Larisa, Neandria, and Klopedi) would have been peripteral; both Neandria and Larisa could have used Aeolic columns on the exterior with leaf capitals within the cella; the construction techniques for the peristyles of the two buildings would have used an outer rim of blocks with a fill behind because they were built

in the same style; the small building model discussed below could be interpreted as a reflection of the temple at which it was dedicated, a situation paralleled at other Greek sanctuaries; the door at Larisa could be placed in the northwest end, the end away from the altar, as at Neandria.[85] In short, the similarities between Neandria and Larisa would be explained by the fact that the two buildings were a part of the same architectural order. There are clearly strong external reasons for restoring both Neandria and Larisa as similar structures.

Yet, there is no internal architectural evidence for this view. The theory was abandoned by Larisa's excavators because of the difference in orientation between the small inner cella and the outer foundations whose axis deviates about 1.5 degrees from the axis of the earlier construction.[86] This argument is still valid, and although this amount of variation could easily be tolerated

[83] Pl. 48 is in the correct style for the period of the temple, but it seems too small to have been used with architecture. See *Larisa* I, 142.

[84] H. Johannes, in K. Schefold, *AA* (1934) cols. 371ff.

[85] At Larisa the altar is at the highest point, and at Neandria it is at the lowest point, so topography plays no role.

[86] *Larisa* I, 61.

in an Archaic building, there remains no clear evidence to restore the building with a peristyle. Certainly the enlarged podium cannot have been used in this way because it does not extend all the way around the building. Unless further information should be forthcoming, the Larisan temple must be regarded as a simple cella without peristyle, with capitals of an unknown design. To do otherwise could result in premature and possibly highly incorrect assumptions about the Aeolic style in general.

Additional details of the temple's construction are furnished by the associated terracotta ornaments. Besides akroteria and fragments of a facing terracotta quadriga which must have stood in the pediment, friezes of several types were found in the vicinity of the temple. Their style agrees with the c. 530 dating, and it seems certain they should be assigned to the same building. They would have created a very decorative effect, with a raking sima at the gables with running chariots, a separate sima at the eaves with gorgoneion and leopard heads, and several additional friezes with centaurs, horsemen, banqueting scenes, and floral ornaments. Even though the exact placement of all the decoration is not known, one must imagine a structure of great splendor rising to dominate the temenos from the top of its podium.

Even with so much about the temple in doubt, one fact is certain. The construction techniques, the orientation, the placement of the altar, and many individual details closely associate the building with its counterpart from Neandria. Both must be placed within the same architectural tradition, whether the temple at Larisa had vertically rising volutes on its capitals or not.

An additional piece of evidence must be considered in determining the course of the Aeolic style at Larisa. In the excavations of 1902, two fragments of a small terracotta building model

were uncovered.[87] The piece seems to represent a small oikos with volute columns at the front, arranged prostyle (pls. 39–40). It can be dated to the sixth century B.C. Because of the stylization of such building models, Schefold suggested that a peristyle arrangement might have been represented this way, and that the columns on the model might be either Ionic or Aeolic.[88] It would be very surprising, however, if the model was based on anything except an Aeolic building. The earliest Ionic structures at Larisa can be no earlier than the end of the Archaic period,[89] well after the Ionic order had matured. The element below the capital on the model thus cannot represent an Ionic echinus because only very early Ionic capitals (as, for example, at Naukratis, fig. 57)[90] had a low echinus of this type. In addition, the volutes clearly seem to rise from the center of the capital. The problem, of course, is that none of the known Aeolic buildings at Larisa can be shown to have had either a peristyle or a prostyle arrangement of columns. In spite of this, the model remains one of the few indications for the wooden superstructure of Aeolic buildings.

If the model may be believed, it suggests an architectural member was used as a transition between shaft and capital. On this model, at least, the member is too small to be a large pendant girdle of leaves like those on the leaf drum of pl. 42. Although the carving is very schematized at this point, a simple torus seems more likely. The volutes are tall and have an abacus over them, and above this is an architrave with either a molding at the top or with two fasciae, the upper one projecting slightly. Above these members is the edge of the roof. There is no frieze above the architrave. The columns on the model seem to have been freestanding, but unfortunately their lower portions are not preserved, so questions regarding bases

[87] I am indebted to N. Dolunay, director of the Archaeological Museum, Istanbul, for kindly examining the piece for me. It has been published incorrectly in previous publications as a stone model.

[88] Äolische Kapitell, 45.

[89] The excavators suggested c. 530 B.C., but a later

dating has been proposed more recently. See J. Boardman (supra n. 52) 209.

[90] W. M. F. Petrie, Naukratis 1 (London, 1886) pl. 3; Robertson, Greek and Roman Architecture, fig. 45.

must remain unanswered. The model is not incompatible with the superstructure suggested by the terracotta fragments from the vicinity of the Old Palace and the Archaic temple, but whether or not it should be allowed to suggest a stone building with exterior Aeolic columns at Larisa is not certain; the alternative, that wooden Aeolic buildings existed in the city, is also possible.

KLOPEDI

Greek contact with Lesbos can be traced during the Mycenaean period,[91] but the date at which the first permanent Hellenic colonists came to the island in the north Aegean is not completely clear. While there may have been a few earlier Greek settlers, the Aeolians who went to Lesbos after the end of the Bronze Age were certainly the first Hellenes to reach the island in large numbers. Lesbos' population increased gradually until by about 700 B.C. the Aeolic cities felt the need to send out colonists of their own. Traveling to the neighboring coasts, they ushered in a period of vigorous expansion that brought new wealth to many of the individual cities.[92]

Against this background of brisk economic development, a temple in the Aeolic style was built in the interior of the island, at a small plateau named Klopedi,[93] near the modern village of Ayia Paraskeve (fig. 22). We do not know who was responsible for this building. Koldewey[94] thought it might be the temple of

Apollo Napaios mentioned by Strabo,[95] but there is no real evidence for this identification, and the cult place cannot be associated with any specific ancient city. Judging by the excellence of the architecture, the precinct must have been an important one.

The temenos lay in a picturesque location, in the midst of rolling hills. Excavations carried on in the 1920s[96] and again beginning in 1971[97] have revealed the remains of two temples. The older was largely of perishable materials; the later was of stone, with a peristyle of Aeolic columns supporting a wooden entablature.

In the early days of the precinct, as was the case with many Greek religious centers, there may have been little more than an open-air altar. Early walls can probably be associated with a period before the building of the two temples,[98] but the site has not yet been thoroughly investigated. The earliest sherds found are of a local gray ware (bucchero), dated to the late Geometric or early Archaic period.[99] A bronze fibula is surely as early as the seventh century B.C.[100]

The older of the two temples was completely destroyed, and no worked stones from above the foundations are preserved (fig. 39). It was a peripteral building with both a pronaos and a back room, either an opisthodomos or (more likely) an adyton. The structure was oriented east and west, with the entrance on the east. From the design of the ground plan, a date in the very late seventh or the sixth century B.C. seems indicated.

[91] W. Lamb, Excavations at Thermi in Lesbos (Cambridge, 1936) 212–213. The evidence may indicate only occasional trade.

[92] For a résumé, with bibliography, see A. R. Burn, The Lyric Age of Greece (New York, 1960) 98ff., 145, and 226ff.

[93] In the literature the temple has been referred to by a confusing variety of names: Nape (a temple of Apollo on Lesbos mentioned by Strabo); Klomidados (a Byzantine church where several capitals were found); Kolumdado (error for Klomidados); simply "from Lesbos"; Klopedi, the designation used by the excavators, is the actual name of the locale.

[94] R. Koldewey, Die antiken Baureste der Insel Lesbos (Berlin, 1890) 44.

[95] 9. 426.

[96] D. Evangelides, "12η Ἀρχαιολογικὴ Περιφέρεια 1) Ἀνασκαφαὶ ἐν Λέσβῳ," Deltion, Parartema (1924–1925) 41–44; Ἀνασκαφαὶ ἐν Λέσβῳ," Praktika (1927) 57–59; (1928) 126–137.

[97] D. Hatzi, Εἰδήσεις ἐκ Λέσβου, Κλοπεδή," AAA 5 (1972) 43ff.

[98] Ibid., 43.

[99] Some bear incised or impressed geometric decorations. Hatzi (supra n. 97) 43.

[100] Apparently found in a mixed context. Evangelides (supra n. 96, 1928) fig. 11.

Sometime within the late Archaic period, a nearby reconstruction on a grander scale resulted in a new building with an entirely different ratio of length to width (fig. 40). While the older temple had had a ratio of less than 1:1½,[101] the newer structure had a ratio of almost 1:2⅓, with a width of 16.25 m. and a length of 37.50 m.

Above a leveling course (euthynteria) was the stepped platform for the temple (the krepidoma), composed of three steps. The highest step acted as the stylobate. Circular markings on this feature showed where columns were placed, and two bases with portions of their shafts were still in position at the northwest corner (the only place where the stylobate was preserved). From the spacing of the bases and the circular markings, one can compute that the peristyle consisted of eight by seventeen columns.

Within the peristyle were two additional foundations. One of these must have supported the walls of the cella, while the other, extending all the way around the interior of the building, may have held an interior colonnade. The suggested reconstruction (fig. 40) poses several difficulties. A U-shaped interior colonnade would have left almost no space around the enormous base (4.20 m. square!) at the western end of the room, opposite the door. Perhaps this base was a carry-over from an earlier period, incorporated into a later building as a base for the cult image. The evidence was never completely published, and it is no longer visible at the site; it is to be hoped that new excavations will be able to clarify some of these problems.

Several worked limestone blocks were found at the southern side of the temple, and these could have come from the building's walls. No remains of the superstructure or of interior supports were found, suggesting these portions were of wood. The roof was of tiles.

The capitals for the colonnade, carved in the Aeolic style from a local trachyte, have an advanced form (pl. 49 and fig. 41). They seem closely related to the capitals from Neandria

since both groups use marginal borders at the edges of the whorls and palmettes that rise from inverted teardrop motifs. At Klopedi, however, the weight-bearing surfaces are greatly expanded. This is not accomplished (as in the Old Palace at Larisa) by raising the volutes but by expanding and leveling the central palmette until it spreads evenly across the entire upper part of the stone. One can note that this produces small petals at the upper corners of the volutes, just as in the Iron Age pillar capitals from Palestine (see chap. 11).

The advantages of the new design are self-evident. There is now a broader surface to support the architrave, distributing the stresses much more uniformly. With the basic design of the capital made into an inverted cone, the weight of the superstructure would be transmitted more directly and more evenly to the supporting shaft.

The columns can be completely reconstructed (fig. 42). An undecorated element, consisting of a large convex molding flanked by two smaller ones, was placed immediately below each capital (pl. 49). The shafts were unfluted, and each was supported by a simple base, a small convex molding resting upon a larger one (fig. 41).

Fragments of fictile revetments were found in both temples. They included pieces of akroteria decorated with palmettes, as well as end tiles with several designs—palmettes, heads of gorgons, human figures, lions attacking deer, and other designs. Often the antifixes used palmettes above the figurative work. The evidence is not conclusive with respect to the presence of terracotta friezes on the entablature. Fragments decorated with leaves and palmettes could have come from the raking sima, but it is not impossible that they belonged to the entablature. There are also tiny fragments of human figures drinking and dancing (best described by Åkerström in *Die architektonischen Terrakotten Kleinasiens*) which must also have come from a separate frieze, perhaps placed somewhere above the height of the capitals.

[101] The older temple was not preserved along its entire length. Walls were 26.50 m. long along the

south side and 14 m. long along the east side.

Fig. 39. Conjectural restoration of the smaller temple at Klopedi, from very fragmentary remains. The building was apparently peripteral, with a pronaos on the east and an opisthodomos or adyton on the west, behind the cella.

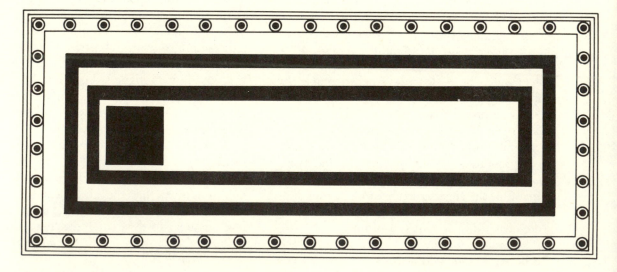

Fig. 40. Restored plan of the Aeolic temple at Klopedi. The door was in the east, since a large base for a cult statue was found at the west end of the cella. The interior foundation probably supported a colonnade of perishable materials. No state plan has been published.

84

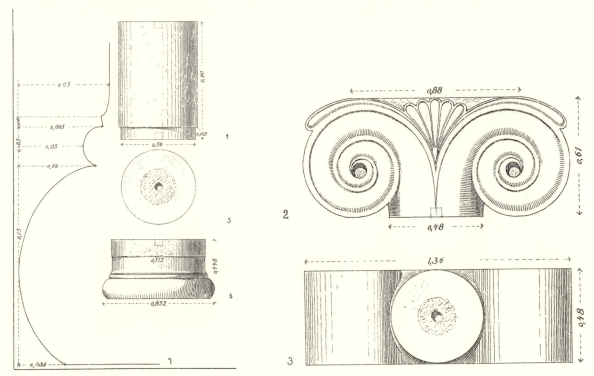

Fig. 41. Elements from the larger temple at Klopedi.

No. 1. Column base and drum, nos. 2–3, Aeolic capital. After Koldewey, *Die antiken Baureste der Insel Lesbos* (1890) pl. 16 nos. 2–7.

The terracottas may be placed in the late Archaic period, but unfortunately they are too fragmentary and ambiguous to provide a precise date for the buildings. The entire area had apparently been disturbed by cultivation and the search for building stones until the deposit was considerably mixed. Terracottas were found in both temples along with material dating from as late as the Hellenistic period. Stylistic comparisons with the Aeolic capitals from the other Greek sites suggest a date for the larger temple in the late Archaic period. The well-dated series from Larisa furnishes especially important guidelines for the style, and the last third of the sixth century seems the earliest tenable date; a slightly later dating is possible since there is

no firm stratigraphic evidence, but the terracottas would fit best with a late sixth-century foundation.

Besides the blocks found at the temple site and in its general vicinity, five Aeolic capitals, two column drums, and a base were found by Koldewey in a Byzantine church at Klomidados,[102] three kilometers away. Another capital was found near Ayia Paraskeve in 1969.[103] Another piece, in the Archaeological Museum in Istanbul (pl. 50), is also sometimes attributed to the temple. All of the capitals are of similar size and style, and they must have all come from the same tradition. There is no doubt that the blocks from Klomidados and Ayia Paraskeve came from Klopedi, but the piece in Istan-

[102] Erroneously called Kolumdado. R. Koldewey (supra n. 94) pl. 16 nos. 1–7.

[103] Hatzi (supra n. 97) 45 n. 8.

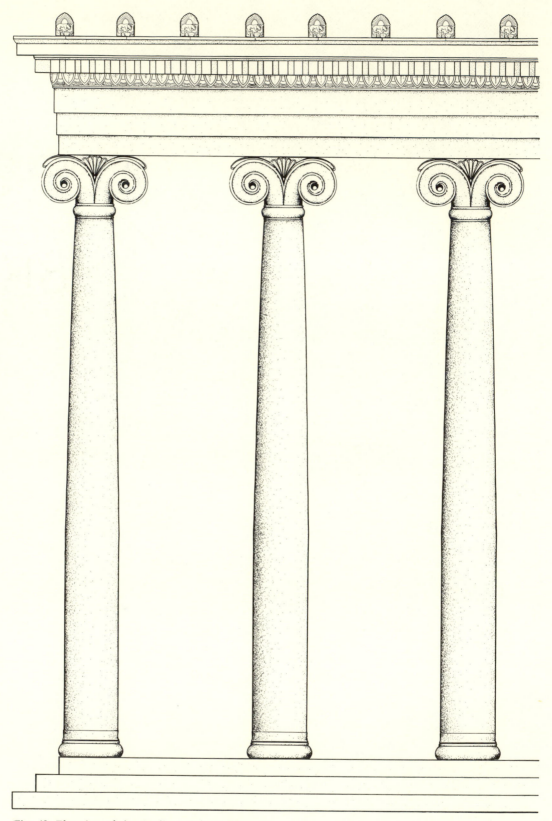

Fig. 42. Elevation of the Aeolic temple at Klopedi.

bul has several distinctive traits. For one thing, its eyes are bored completely through the stone. The others are bored only slightly, for the insertion of some other material.[104] A more serious problem is the difference in the design of the marginal borders, and this has convinced some writers that the specimen in Istanbul must come from a different building.[105] On the capitals from Klopedi, the marginal borders are simple raised lines, while on the other specimen they have a central channel that divides them into two parts. The block in Istanbul was given to the museum many years ago, with the label "found on the akropolis of Mytilene." Since the name has been applied both to the city of Mytilene and to the entire island, the possibility that the capital came originally from the site near Ayia Paraskeve has sometimes been suggested.[106] In this theory, the stone could have traveled to Mytilene in ancient or modern times, or it could simply have been collected at Klopedi and labeled "Mytilene." Except for the single capital in Istanbul, no evidence for an Aeolic-style temple at the main Lesbian city is known, but the possibility cannot be excluded.[107] On the other hand, the measurements of the capital in Istanbul tally very well with those from Klopedi, and the habit of including capitals of slightly different design in the same building was very widespread with this style. The evidence is not all in yet, but since recent excavations have uncovered several new capitals at Klopedi,[108] none of which are like the unique specimen "from Mytilene," the preponderance of evidence seems to favor the theory of two separate temples.

MYTILENE

In spite of a number of political upheavals that often erupted into bloody civil war, My-

tilene remained the largest and most important city on Lesbos during the entire Archaic period. Unfortunately, the city's pertinent archaeological remains have almost all disappeared, and its history during this time must be reconstructed largely from the literary accounts.[109] The home of both Sappho and Alkaios, Mytilene was a thriving cultural center as well as a hub of commerce. It took the lead in the island's colonial efforts, stubbornly resisted Athenian expansion into the north Aegean during the sixth century B.C., and was generally recognized as the foremost city of Lesbos.

A single Aeolic capital from the city is now in the Archaeological Museum in Istanbul, where it has been since the late nineteenth century (pl. 50). The block has been discussed above, in connection with the temple at Klopedi. It bears a striking resemblance to the capitals from that site, and the absence of definitive information about its discovery has led to several writers' associating it with the better known temple. As more and more capitals are excavated from Klopedi, however, it becomes increasingly evident that the example "from Mytilene" is the only piece with double margins around the carved features and eyes bored completely through the stone. From a visual examination, the material also seems different. There could be easy explanations for the similarities that do exist in size and style,[110] and historically there is no reason to assume that Mytilene could not have had an Aeolic temple. In fact, it would be somewhat surprising if the city did not. As the largest polis on the island, it must have tried to assume a leading position in temple building paralleling its preeminence in literature, economics, and political influence. Since the Aeolic order was the leading architectural tradition of Archaic Aeolis, an example from Mytilene comes as no surprise.

---

[104] The same two variations occur at Neandria.

[105] The best discussion is that of J. D. Condis, "Capitello eolico di Eresso," *ASAA*, new series, 8–10 (1946–1948) 29–30.

[106] *Äolische Kapitell*, 46.

[107] Very little remains from the Archaic period of Mytilene. See the fuller discussion below.

[108] Hatzi (supra n. 97).

[109] A good account is that of Burn (supra n. 92) 226ff., with additional bibliography.

[110] The blocks are surely products of the same workshop. There is no reason to assume an architect on Lesbos would be called upon to build only a single temple.

ERESSOS

Eressos,[111] one of the smaller of the principal cities of Lesbos, was located on the west coast of the island. Both lumber and excellent farmland were easily available, and the city prospered. Famous for the quality of its grain,[112] it was overshadowed politically by Mytilene and played only a minor role in the history of the Archaic period.

One Aeolic capital was found reused in a modern house near the ancient city.[113] It is carved from gray granite, with vertical volutes incised into the front face (pl. 51 and fig. 43). While the upper surface is smooth and has no dowel holes, a socket is sunk into the underside. The back is schematic, without volutes.

The capital's highly unusual design is unique in several ways. Its volutes begin at the base of the stone and have no central palmette or other ornament, although it is likely this element was rendered in paint. The manner in which the volutes rise can be compared with this detail on certain other columns (compare the clay model from Larisa, pls. 39–40),[114] and similar designs are known from the minor arts (pl. 43),[115] but it is remarkable for the whorls to rise from such a low point on the stone. They are also separated considerably, creating a vertical empty space at the center of the stone. The back is completely unique. While the slightly convex volutes have a doubled form familiar from a few Ionic capitals,[116] the feature is not otherwise known from Aeolic designs.

[111] *PW*, vol. VI, cols. 420–421.

[112] According to Archestratos, as quoted by Athenaios (*Deipnosophistai* 3. 111), if the gods wished to eat bread they sent Hermes to Eressos to purchase it.

[113] O. Walter, "Archäologische Funde in Griechenland von Frühjahr 1939 bis Frühjahr 1940: Inseln des Aigaion," *AA* (1940) col. 288; J. D. Condis (supra n. 105) 25ff.

[114] For a capital on a relief from Carchemish, see *Capitello Eolico*, pl. 3 no. 1.

[115] Influence from the minor arts cannot be excluded on unique capitals such as this one.

[116] For Ionic capitals with doubled volutes, see

We have no way of ascertaining exactly how the block was used originally. Because of its small size (dia. at base 0.295 m.), a large building can be excluded. The absence of a cutting in the upper surface rules out a support for statuary. Walter has suggested it was part of a constructed tomb,[117] but there is no real evidence.

The dating is also problematical. A date in the sixth century B.C. (presumably in the second half) has been supposed,[118] but an even later time is possible. All the Ionic capitals with doubled whorls are considerably later, and there is no reason to think the Aeolic style on Lesbos need have ended with the end of the Archaic period.

THASOS

It was undoubtedly a desire for mineral wealth that first encouraged Paros to send out colonists to Thasos (fig. 44).[119] In an expedition led by the father of the great poet Archilochos, the Parians established themselves on the northern island off the coast of Thrace a little before 650 B.C.[120] They exploited the deposits of gold here and on the nearby coast, bringing wealth to the colony over a considerable period of time —the mines were still rich enough in the fifth century to tempt the Athenians into seizing some of them for themselves.[121]

At least in its earlier days, the settlement probably had a flavor of the rugged northern outpost about it. Wooded hills rose above the

F. W. Hasluck, "Sculptures from Cyzicus," *BSA* 8 (1901–1902) 195 and pl. 6 no. 5 (perhaps from an altar); W. Lamp, "Excavations at Kato Phana in Chios," *BSA* 35 (1934–1935) 142 and pl. 30 c–d; for a stele see Buschor (supra n. 46) pl. 15.

[117] Walter (supra n. 113) col. 288.

[118] Condis (supra n. 105).

[119] Hdt. 6. 46–47 reports that mines (presumably gold mines) were known at a very early period.

[120] F. Jacoby, "The Date of Archilochos," *CQ* 35 (1941) 97ff.

[121] Thuc. 1. 100. A dispute with Athens over the mines on the mainland led to the city's secession from the Delian League in 465 B.C.

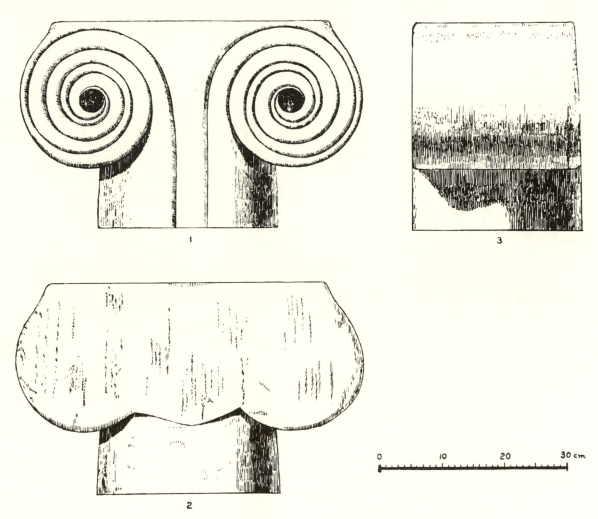

Fig. 43. The Aeolic capital from Eressos. By courtesy of the Italian School of Archaeology in Athens, after J. D. Condis, "Capitello eolico di Eresso," *ASAA*, new series, 8–10 (1946–1948) fig. 2.

city, creating a scene of wild beauty and providing enough lumber for ships and other needs. Fine Thasian wine also contributed to the economy,[122] and archaeological excavations have revealed a prosperous state.[123] Since there was a local school of sculpture, a concomitant development in architecture may be surmised; important public buildings date back to Archaic times.

While the city seems to have been primarily Greek, there were also some oriental ties. Herodotos reported[124] that the Phoenicians had colonized Thasos at an early period and that a sanctuary of the Phoenician Herakles (i.e. Melkart)[125] was an important cult place in his time.

[122] Ath. 1. 29; 1. 31; Xen., *Symp.* 4. 41.

[123] *Etudes thasiennes* (Paris, 1944–), with annual reports in the *BCH*.

[124] Hdt. 2. 44; 6. 47.

[125] For the archaeological remains of this sanctuary see M. Launey, *Le Sanctuaire et le culte d'Héraklès à Thasos, Etudes thasiennes* 1 (Paris, 1944).

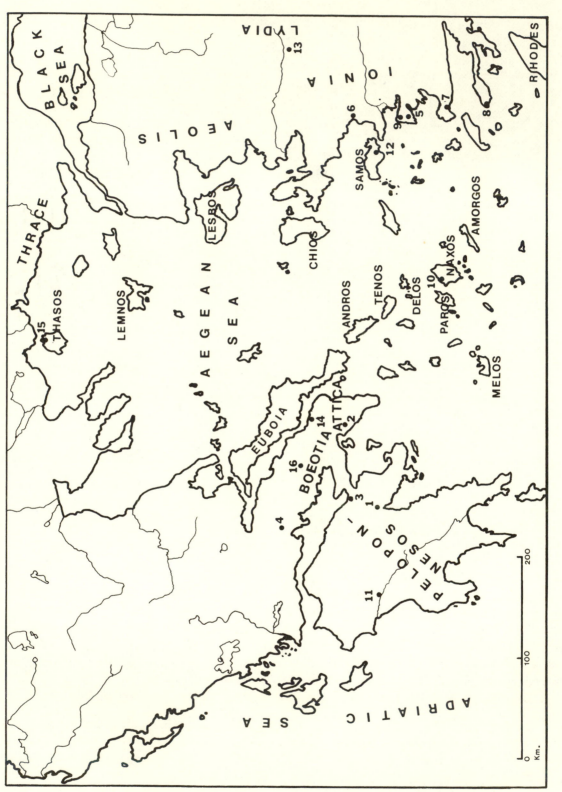

Fig. 44. Map of Greece, the Aegean, and coastal Anatolia:

1. Argos	4. Delphi	7. Halikarnassos	10. Naxos	13. Sardis
2. Athens	5. Didyma	8. Knidos	11. Olympia	14. Sykaminon
3. Corinth	6. Ephesos	9. Miletos	12. Samos	15. Thasos

This oriental presence, still an active tradition in the days of Pausanias,[126] must have been strong enough to be easily noticeable. The culture, however, was clearly Greek; the dominant influences were Parian.

In 1955 a marble leaf drum decorated with leaves was found in the Thasian agora.[127] The block had been built into a later structure, but the early style of the carving places it within the Archaic period, in the sixth century B.C. It is an inverted truncated cone, with a leaf-and-dart in low relief (pl. 37). In the upper surface are a dowel hole and a circular trace from another block, while a second dowel cutting is in the bottom.

Although the circular marking on the upper surface has suggested to Martin that the stone was the leaf drum from a volute capital,[128] Wesenberg has preferred to think of it as a column base.[129] The expansion of the block's diameter from 0.22 m. at the bottom to 0.316 m. at the top seems to militate against the idea that it is a base, and the presence of dowel holes in both surfaces suggests the same conclusion. The piece must surely be the lower half of a two-tiered capital whose upper member had a circular resting surface. Since the separate echinus blocks of early Ionic capitals (as at Naukratis and Samos) are shaped entirely differently, one can only suppose the upper section was an Aeolic volute element, confirming the theory that the Greek Aeolic style sometimes used a leaf-decorated element between shaft and volutes.

Similar drums are known from the Aeolic site of Neandria (pl. 41), and elements which may have had this purpose have been found at Larisa (pl. 42) and several other sites.[130] The complete arrangement is occasionally illustrated in the minor arts.[131] While the Thasian example shows that at least occasionally these drums were placed below another architectural element, one must not infer that all such pieces were used in this way—some were evidently complete capitals.[132] Unfortunately, there is too much individual variation within the series to distinguish between the subordinate elements and the complete leaf capitals from the shape or decoration.

Since Thasos does not seem to have had close ties with Aeolis, one may well ask how widely dispersed the Aeolic style is likely to have been. While this study has shown Aeolic buildings were not limited to regions where Aeolians lived, only a little evidence survives for an island-style with vertically rising volutes. Paros and Delos, however, have yielded Aeolic votive capitals, and a tradition in this region cannot be ruled out.[133] Presumably the building on Thasos was built under Parian influence, but one cannot be sure without additional evidence.

The Phoenician ties on Thasos raise additional questions about the oriental origin of the Aeolic style, but the morphology seems to rule out this possibility for the piece being considered here. The style of the Thasian block is purely Greek, and it cannot be favorably compared with anything Phoenician. If the piece is Aeolic, it is obviously from a mature stage in the style, after the fashion had become completely Hellenized.

DELOS

Famed as the birthplace of Apollo and Artemis, the tiny island of Delos became one of the great Panhellenic centers. Its importance as a cult place increased during the sixth century B.C.,

[126] Paus. 5. 25. 12.

[127] See above, note 8.

[128] *Problème des ordres*, 125.

[129] *Kapitelle und Basen*, 135.

[130] See above, notes 10–11.

[131] Buschor (supra n. 46) pl. on p. 22; *CVA, Taranto, Museo Nazionale*, fasc. 2 (Italia, fasc. 35) pl. 27 no. 2.

[132] This was surely the case at Delos (*Problème des ordres*, pl. 28 no. 1).

[133] The evidence from Delos and Paros is treated more fully below. The exact relation of a hypothetical "Island Style" to the Aeolic tradition in Aeolis itself is difficult to assess on the evidence now available, but the streams of artistic influence would surely have flowed from east to west. No island capitals are as early as the earliest ones from coastal Anatolia.

and both Peisistratos of Athens and Polykrates of Samos showed a keen interest in the island, using its prestige to enhance their own influence across the Cyclades. Even the Persians respected the sanctuary at the beginning of the next century. The site remained important until the disorders of the first century B.C., partly because a wealthy secular community complemented the religious aspects of the island.

An Aeolic votive capital (fig. 45) was found on Delos in the nineteenth century. Its incised volutes, with two and one half turns, are separated by a floral ornament. They have large eyes, as was usual in the second half of the sixth century B.C. The lower part of the capital is unusual in that the design terminates rather abruptly. A cylindrical lower section (actually far more damaged than in fig. 45) would have formed the transition with the shaft, but there was evidently no leaf-carved element at all on this capital.

The absence of the leaf drum or its equivalent has suggested to Martin that the design may be a hold-over from an earlier time when Aeolic capitals had no such members (one may compare the Palestinian and Phoenician styles discussed in chap. II).[134] In this case, however, the large eyes and the central ornamentation seem to suggest an inspiration from one or more Greek sources, probably within the sixth century B.C. While an early survival cannot be ruled out, Archaic votive columns were often much more fanciful than their architectural counterparts. It is also possible that furniture or one of the other minor arts could have played a role in the design.

PAROS

An island with an area of sixty-four square miles, Paros supported several cities in antiquity, of which the most important was named Paros also (at the site of modern Paroikia). Its inhabitants were Ionians, but the colonization of Thasos in the seventh century B.C. must have resulted in lively contacts with the Aeolians to the north and east. Large deposits of fine white marble made the island famous throughout the Aegean, and a well-known school of sculpture flourished during the Archaic period. After the Persian wars Paros became subject to Athens.

A small Aeolic column, now in the Archaeological Museum in Paroikia (fig. 46), was found in an early Christian church east of ancient Paros on the road toward Naoussa.[135] The column had been inverted and the lower surface hollowed out for use as a basin. It was placed near the front door of the church, and an inscription was also added around the edge of the new upper surface.

The monument consists of a base, shaft, and capital, carved from the same block. Above a vertical section (acting as the base) the squat shaft diminishes rapidly with a concave profile. Above this is the low Aeolic capital of the type with large eyes and slightly more than two turns to the whorls. A tiny echinus is tucked between the volutes but protrudes considerably from the surface of the stone. Surprisingly, it is undecorated; perhaps it was once painted. The area between the volutes, where a palmette was usually placed, is also plain. An inordinately large abacus lies above the capital. It was once covered with stucco, since it is roughened, but all traces of plaster or color have now disappeared.

In general, the monument does not suggest the highest standards of design. While the material is fine Parian marble, the finish is not particularly outstanding, and the proportions leave something to be desired. The back is not well carved, and the capital itself has details only on the front.

The stone must have been used as a base for

---

[134] *Problème des ordres*, 127.

[135] An. Orlandos, "Πάρος," Τὸ Ἔργον τῆς Ἀρχαιολογικῆς Ἐταιρείας (1960) 178–179 and fig. 194; (1961) 192–193 and figs. 198–199; G. Daux, "Chronique des fouilles 1960; Paros," *BCH* 85

(1961) 844 and fig. 14; "Chronique des fouilles 1961; Paros," *BCH* 86 (1962) 856ff. and figs. 6-7; G. Gruben, "Naxos und Paros. Dritter vorläufiger Bericht über die Forschungskampagnen 1970 und 1971," *AA* (1972) 379 and fig. 37.

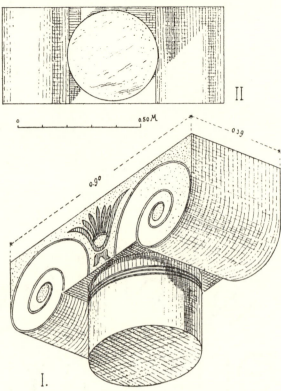

Fig. 45. Capital from an Aeolic votive column, from Delos. After Perrot and Chipiez, *Histoire de l'art* VII (1898) pl. 53 nos. 1–2.

another element, presumably statuary. A small dowel hole is at the center of the upper surface, and a pour channel leads from the back to this cutting. The rough back would suggest the piece was designed to be placed in a niche or against a wall, where only the front would be visible. A use as a grave monument is the most likely possibility.

[136] Gruben (supra n. 135) fig. 35.

[137] While they do not properly form a part of the Aeolic tradition, several pilaster-capitals have been found with three superimposed volutes on each side. The pilasters may have had some peripheral relations to the mainstream of the Aeolic development since the volutes do spring upward, but this relation cannot have been a close one. It is probably best to consider them (like the many stelai with volute-decorations) as one more system of ornamental stonework that grew out of the decorative traditions of Archaic Greece. The largest group of triple-volute pilaster capitals was found at Didy-

The form suggests a late sixth-century B.C. inspiration, but there are questionable points about a strict Archaic dating. The abacus and the low profile of the capital rule out any date before about 550 B.C. The column, however, seems at least one step removed from the architectural usage that guided the Archaic development, since the shaft and the abacus are much heavier than the capital requires. These points should make the column a little later, and the pour channel suggests the same thing. While the monument thus provides evidence for the existence of an Archaic Parian style, its own date could be as early as the late sixth century or as late as the early fifth century B.C.

Another example of the Aeolic style, a large fragment of a marble votive capital, was found in the ruins of a modern house east of the Asklepieion near ancient Paros.[136] While in somewhat broken condition because of the later use, most of the front of the block is still visible. A large echinus separated the whorls, which were given two and one-half turns around large flat eyes. A palmette occupies the center of the stone. The date should be about the last third of the sixth century B.C.

HISTORICAL DEVELOPMENT

The Aeolic style is only one manifestation of a development in floral decoration that had many facets in Archaic Greece. Some aspects of this development, like the Aeolic and Ionic columns, were applied to architecture,[137] while

ma, but examples are also known from Samos and elsewhere. They have been studied in detail by Walter Hahland, "Didyma im 5. Jahrhundert v. Chr.," *JdI* 79 (1964) 142ff., who has shown that they were most often employed to decorate altars. Compare the example on the well-known Caeretan hydria in the Kunsthistorisches Museum, Vienna, showing Herakles in Egypt, M. Robertson, *Greek Painting* (Geneva, 1959) pl. on p. 76. For the occasional use of related blocks in architecture, see E. Buschor, "Altsamischer Bauschmuck," *AthMitt* 72 (1957) 4.

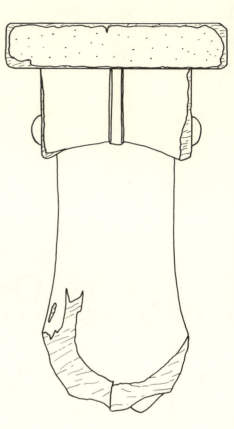

Fig. 46. Large fragment of a marble base in the form of an Aeolic column, from Paros. For a reconstruction of the complete column see G. Daux, *BCH* 86 (1962) 860 fig. 7; A. Orlandos, *To Ergon tes Archaiologikes Etaireias* (1961) 193 fig. 199.

others surfaced in painting, decorative metal-work, woodcarving, or other artistic endeavors. Since these traditions grew up in the same milieu and constantly reinforced each other, it is no surprise that they often existed in different disciplines in a relatively similar form. Occasion-ally, someone advances the suggestion that the Aeolic columns were simply an enlargement to monumental size of motifs developed for furni-ture or other crafts. While the many architectural

antecedents that have come to light in recent years render this theory unnecessary, there must still have been an interrelation within the arts.[138] The Aeolic style did not exist in a vacuum. In-novations using volute motifs in carpentry, metalwork, vase painting, and other crafts pre-ceded the architectural usage in Greece by many years, and they must have exerted a certain amount of influence on the movement as a whole. Within the architectural tradition of the

[138] That Archaic architects in East Greece worked in a variety of media is suggested by several pieces of evidence, such as the traditions that Rhoikos and Theodoros were architects, bronze workers, sculp-tors, and jewelry smiths. Paus., 3. 12. 10; 8. 14. 8; 10. 38. 6; Plin., *HN*, 34. 83; 36. 90; Diod. Sic., 1.

98. 5–9; Hdt., 3. 60; Vitr., 7 *praef.* 12; Diog. Laert., 2. 103. One can note that the capitals of the Old Palace at Larisa were apparently sheathed in bronze, implying close cooperation between stone-cutter and metalsmith.

north Aegean, however, most of the major stylistic changes can be explained as a result of internal development.

We lack many of the intermediate steps in the stylistic advancement of the Aeolic buildings. The style's course can perhaps be best understood by considering the monuments we do have, and these suggest three stages of development. In the earliest known examples of the Hellenic tradition, the large capital from Larisa (pl. 42) and the temple from Old Smyrna (fig. 20), the form of the Aeolic capital differs little from its shape in many parts of the Near East. In the second and third stages of the style, dating from the middle and the end of the sixth century B.C., the tradition departed considerably from this mode. The Greek buildings and votive monuments suggest a coherent and relatively smooth artistic progression, characterized by repeated experiments to achieve better solutions for both structural and visual problems.

In the earliest Greek capitals, the volutes rise vertically from the base of the block and spread slightly at the top, curving but forming no circular eye. Similarly shaped volutes are found at Sippar as early as the ninth century B.C. (pl. 2). They continue to appear in Asia in subsequent years (pl. 24 and fig. 21), and they were also used in the Italian west. In Greece the extant examples are very tall in comparison with their width, and they often have elegant floral embellishments of a highly individual nature. Both of these features would disappear in subsequent years, as the style turned toward architectural function as opposed to elegant floral decoration for its own sake. Little is known of the Aeolic buildings themselves at this point in their development, which can be dated to the late seventh and early sixth centuries B.C. The context of the early Larisan capital is not really certain. More is known from Old Smyrna, but the temple was very much destroyed. It seems to have had a peristyle, but it did not employ many subsidiary details (like terracotta revetments and specific decorative moldings) that would be so typical of Greek buildings in later times. We may probably imagine a considerable amount of local variation in the construction of individual monuments.

By the second quarter of the sixth century, the style had matured considerably. The temple at Neandria (figs. 31–32) and the Old Palace at Larisa (pls. 45–47 and fig. 35) serve as examples of this second stage. We have more information about the buildings themselves during this period, and it is obvious the style had already abandoned its reliance on Near Eastern forms in favor of an internal development of its own. The Greek temple—a home for the sacred image of the deity set within a more or less clearly defined temenos with an exterior altar for sacrifices—represented a specific tradition in worship, and the architecture associated with that tradition came to be part of the visible reflection of the Olympian religion. At Neandria the Aeolic system was already completely joined to the Greek temple style. The building was most likely a peripteral structure with a single long cella for the cult image. Stone columns with volute capitals were probably placed in the peristyle, and leaf capitals may have crowned the supports in the central "spine." While we have little evidence for the wooden superstructure of the building, its decorated sima may be an early step toward the elaborate system of terracotta friezes that decorated the temple at Larisa, constructed in the next generation.

The Old Palace at Larisa shows the style was applied to secular architecture as well as to temples. Built on a plan that was new to the city, the palace had a broad porch flanked by towers, with major rooms at the back. Its moldings and the details of its construction were entirely Greek. The columns, articulated with base, shaft, and capital, supported an entablature with a decorated geison containing a continuous frieze. The capitals had raised whorls to aid in the support of the entablature, but because they survive merely as cores for bronze sheathing, we can learn little of their outward form; the slightly earlier examples from Neandria give a better view of the design during this time.

At Neandria the capitals were tall and finely carved, with a relatively small weight-bearing surface. The most likely reconstruction suggests no more than a single leaf drum decorated with leaves below each volute element (fig. 32). Additional ornament is minimized, and large eyes at the centers of the whorls create an entirely different appearance from that of all earlier volute capitals.

Since the large, well-formed eye appears neither in the earliest Hellenic examples nor their antecedents, it may be regarded as a purely Greek innovation. It does not develop until about the second quarter of the century (the earliest examples in architecture are from Ephesos and Neandria).[139] The feature is a significant detail because it seems to arise from the methods of manufacture. Capitals without eyes can be laid out by beginning the volute at the base and drawing a line up and out, curving it to form the whorl. Probably only one side would be made on a pattern which would then be reversed to insure symmetry. In the Near Eastern capitals with eyes (see especially the series from Palestine), the eye is always a very tiny dot that does not grow directly out of the helix. It looks as if these Near Eastern capitals were laid out by drawing a pair of diagonal lines from the base up to the small dots; the volutes might then be added around these ribs, but they never connect with the eyes. With the Greek design, the technique was evidently completely changed. The first step was probably to inscribe a circle for the eye. By then setting a string-wrapped cylinder of the same diameter on the eye and slowly unwinding the string with a marker or graver attached to its end, a perfect volute could be achieved easily. This different technology causes the new appearance since the whorls have more than one turn before they "terminate" in the large eye at the center. The new conception, which may be traced most easily in the sixth-century B.C. grave stelai, seems to have been first applied to architecture in East Greece. By the third quarter of the sixth century, it was fairly

well distributed in Hellenic areas, and it was especialy popular in Athens.

The final stage in the Archaic Aeolic style can be best observed in the fine stone temple at Klopedi (figs. 40–42 and pl. 49). The building dates from the end of the sixth century B.C. or perhaps even slightly later and includes several new architectural features. Founded on a better foundation than its predecessors at the same site and at Larisa and Neandria, it was built of carefully joined masonry. The informality which resulted in the use of several variations of capitals and an irregular podium at Neandria was replaced by a more careful attention to uniformity of detail. A peristyle of 8 x 17 columns was set on a platform of three steps, with the top step acting as the stylobate. There was a wooden entablature, although the walls of the cella were of stone.

In its ground plan, the temple at Klopedi shows that a successful solution to the problems of proportion could be found along lines that depended on neither Doric nor Ionic predecessors. Its peristyle conforms to the double-plus-one-unit ratio of length to width that would become canonical in Classical times, but the interior arrangement of the building makes no use of the megaron-type plan with pronaos, naos, and opisthodomos. Instead, it draws on local traditions (compare Larisa, figs. 37–38 and Neandria, figs. 30–31) and uses a long, narrow cella, with the interior supports forming a colonnaded hall down the center of the building and focusing attention on the cult statue.

The columns at Klopedi also have an advanced design. Their capitals show the effects of a concern for the heavier superstructure necessitated by tile roofs, in that both the upper and lower surfaces were expanded considerably. Since the height of the capital was constricted at the same time, the end result seems very compact when it is compared with previous examples. What is probably a related change appears in the

[139] For a general discussion of the appearances of eyes in volute capitals, consult G. Gruben, "Das archaische Didymaion," *JdI* 78 (1963) 174 and

notes 167–168. Perhaps the technology was borrowed from the manufacture of funerary stelai where the practice was a common one.

element below the volutes. In the cases where this feature is a large leaf-decorated drum, as at Old Smyrna, Neandria, and Thasos, there is a visual (if not structural) weak point at the narrow juncture between drum and capital. The reduction of the transitional element at Klopedi may be regarded as an adjunct to the more compact nature of the capital itself.

The reduction of the element below the capital could be a local Aeolian development, but another possibility may also be considered. Fragments of painted plaster from the Persian levels at Gordion illustrate what is surely an Aeolic column (pl. 69). Painted decorations on the unfluted shaft suggest the original was of wood, but unfortunately the scene is too fragmentary for restoration. While much of the capital is missing, the lower part of the volutes and the undecorated torus beneath them are clearly visible. The date should be about the same as that of the temple at Klopedi. A member with three simple horizontal moldings had been used beneath Aeolic capitals in the Near East as early as the ninth century B.C. (see the tablet from Sippar, pl. 2), and two moldings appear at Babylon in the early sixth century B.C. (pl. 16). Simple, undecorated moldings also occur on quite a few of the East Greek vases (see app. c), some of which (notably the example from Chios) are much earlier than the temple at Klopedi. It would seem both undecorated and carved drums were used in the Near East as well as in Greece, and it is possible both notions were transmitted to the East Greek cities as separate branches of the Aeolic style. It is not the invention of a low undecorated member beneath the volutes that is novel at Klopedi, but its application to a capital with a very low profile.

Of the entablature at Klopedi, very little may be said with certainty. Like earlier Aeolic buildings, the temple used wood for this element, and only a few fragments of the terracotta revetments have been reported from the site. The ornamental quality of other parts of the building surely demands moldings (one may compare the clay model from Larisa, pls. 39–40), and

fasciae or dentils are also strong possibilities. Small bits of terracottas with human figures may have come from a raking sima or a decorative band applied to the gables or entablature, and a clay frieze with leaves and palmettes was used as well. The temple thus continued the practice visible at Larisa where ornamental friezes were applied to several parts of the wooden superstructure. It is possible this Aeolic tradition contributed to the development of the continuous Ionic frieze. The reconstruction in figure 42 is based on the evidence available at the present writing. Both fasciae and dentils are used, and a decorative molding is restored above the fasciae, a position with parallels from Ionic buildings. The restoration of the antefixes is based on small fragments of several separate examples; it is more likely some system of alternation was used, as more than one design is known, but the pieces of the other antefixes are small, and their contemporary use with the lion-attacking-deer motif used here is not completely certain. No figurative frieze is included; the fragments are simply too small for any restoration, and it is the opinion of the present writer that they were not applied to the exterior of the entablature.

There was a considerable amount of experimentation in the sixth century in several Aeolic details, but a satisfactory resolution of most problems was achieved by the time of the temples at Klopedi and Mytilene. From simple and hesitant beginnings the style had reached a design successfully balancing ornament and structural necessity. The Aeolic style had come of age.

In addition to the discussion of major stone monuments, at least a mention must be made of the illustrations of Aeolic columns in the minor arts. The largest category is on vases, both painted and decorated in relief, and it is surely no coincidence that these illustrations occur in the same area where the monumental style flourished. One cannot be sure, of course, that actual columns were used in the same cities, as one may be dealing with the dissemination of traditions in the decoration of pottery rather than with architectural styles. Only occasionally, as at Larisa, do full-sized buildings occur alongside examples in the minor arts. For convenience, vases in this group are listed in appendix c. All are most likely from the sixth century B.C.

There are two sherds from Larisa (app. c, nos. 1 and 2), both in the local gray fabric usually called *bucchero*. They are decorated in relief, with incised details. The columns are of the usual Aeolic form, with a small torus below the volute elements. Schematization and the fragmentary condition of the vases make a detailed analysis impossible.

From Assos, on the coast of Aeolis south of Neandria, comes one sherd with an incised Aeolic capital (app. c, no. 3). The volutes are placed on a handle, so it is likely they were not intended as architecture. Traces of slip show the vase was given details in white.

Aeolic columns also occur on two Klazomenian sarcophagi illustrating running chariots (app. c, nos. 4–5). Appearing as isolated columns, they support basins used as prizes for the races. There are bases to support the shafts and tori beneath the volutes. On the gable of one example (no. 5), an Aeolic capital supports the ridge beam.

A krater from Chios, found at Pitane, is decorated with the myth of Troilos and Achilles (app. c, no. 6). An interesting detail is the fountain house, a rare occurrence of the elevation of an Aeolic building from before the middle of the sixth century B.C. The vase is one piece in appendix c which can be fairly closely dated, i.e. about 570–560 B.C. The fountain is a gabled building with akroteria in the form of palmettes. Checks indicate its stone construction. The single Aeolic column has a clearly defined rectangular base and a capital with volutes separated by a design (presumably intended as a palmette) set upon a torus or leaf drum. There is no hint of a frieze.

Allowing for differences in style and schematization, the vases form a remarkably consistent group. Vertical volutes must have been standard fare for Archaic capitals in the northeast Aegean. Bases below the shafts were present, and transitions between capital and shaft were usual. The vases confirm the picture presented by the monumental stone columns, and the situation may be contrasted with the picture in Athens (app. B and chap. v) where far more variation existed both in the monuments and in the painted pottery.

By the final years of the Archaic period, the Aeolic style had progressed to a point where its development paralleled the nascent Ionic order of a generation before. The experimentation is what one might expect from a young and vigorously active artistic fashion: one can find the same mood in early Ionic buildings where there were experiments with carved drums above the bases, karyatids, neckings for the columns, and different designs for capitals and bases.

If the Ionic system of the sixth century B.C. may be called an architectural order, the same nomenclature should be extended to the Greek portion of the Aeolic style. The temple at Klopedi is easily systematized enough to call its style an order, and perhaps the term should be extended to all of the Archaic period in the north Aegean. There is a clear distinction between the Greek fashion and the usage of the (sometimes contemporary) Near Eastern styles where the volute column was simply one of several column types, to be used with whatever context the current building required. In Greece, the design was used exclusively for free-standing columns in peristyles and porticoes, along with a gradually developing set of specific architectural details. It is this change that clearly sets off the north Aegean tradition both from its predecessors and from the contemporary usage at non-Greek sites.

Chapter V

ATTICA

In the seventh and sixth centuries B.C.,[1] Athens put out many of the artistic and economic roots that would nourish its later "Golden Age." Through a series of deep-seated political and social changes, accompanied by increased urbanization and a concentration of wealth in the hands of a few powerful families, the city changed from a small state concerned mainly with its own affairs into a sophisticated and cosmopolitan polis. It was during this period of transformation that Aeolic columns were first erected in and around the city.

Most of the major Aeolic monuments in Athens seem to have been constructed within a period lasting less than a hundred years, from the second quarter of the sixth century B.C. until the time of the Persian wars. The first part of this period was dominated by the personality of the tyrant Peisistratos. His encouragement of Athenian contacts with East Greece went a long way toward determining the course Athens would take in future years, and his sons seem to have promulgated a similar policy. New political directions characterized the end of the era. The emerging democracy at the close of the sixth century and the clash with Persia in the

immediately succeeding years are difficult to assess in terms of architectural orientation, but they must certainly have pushed the city into new paths that could not fail to be reflected in the contemporary arts. By the time of the invasion of Xerxes in 480 B.C., Athenian architecture had already turned away from the Aeolic fashion with which it had flirted so briefly.

The evidence for the Aeolic style in Athens is somewhat limited in comparison with certain other regions, but the evidence that does exist suggests a tradition of considerable richness. If there were no Aeolic temples in Athens, at least there were volute designs of elegance and beauty in a variety present at few other cities. If the stone tradition was limited to isolated columns with only an occasional small building in marble, the Athenian styles showed an artistic maturity that must surely suggest a fuller tradition in perishable materials. Three different Aeolic designs[2] are known from the Attic capital: the first appears fully developed in Athens after a prior history in Aeolis; the second may have come to the city from Ionia or the Dodecanese; the third, a style known only from an isolated capital found to the north of the city and from

---

[1] Good bibliographical references for Archaic Athens can be found in V. Ehrenberg, *From Solon to Socrates* (London and New York, 1967).

[2] Variations not preserved in stone examples are excluded.

99

Athenian vase painting, has an unclear prior history, although it, too, is undoubtedly of eastern origin.

The earliest evidence for the use of vertical volutes on Athenian capitals comes not from architecture but from isolated columns used for votive or funerary purposes. Fragments of outstanding examples of this group have been found in the Agora and the Kerameikos; more schematized pieces are known from the Akropolis as well. In all cases, the capitals seem to have been used as supports for statuary.

The fragment from the Agora (pl. 52 and fig. 47) was found in a well in the northwest corner of the market, at a level assigned to the fourth century B.C. It was part of a deliberate filling. Made of poros limestone, the piece shows fine workmanship in its carving, although only a small part of the front face is preserved. The fragment was apparently part of a capital shaped very much like the one from Mytilene (pl. 50). It is the largest Aeolic capital yet known from the mainland of Greece. It had a partially drilled central eye, whorls outlined by a double molding with a channel between them (a feature occurring also at Neandria, pl. 41), and small petals at the upper corners of the cushion. Whether or not the petals were extensions of the central palmette (as at Mytilene) cannot be determined from the surviving details. The edge of a large cutting is visible in the upper surface of the block, indicating the stone held a piece of statuary, a use that is well known from Athenian vases. Since the capital from Mytilene is very late in the Aeolic series, a date at the end of the Archaic period seems likely; the monument may have been destroyed in the Persian invasions of 480 B.C., accounting for the battered condition of the block by the time it was deposited in the well in the next century.

A piece of a very similar capital comes from the Kerameikos.[3] Less than half of the poros block survives, since the stone was broken and trimmed at some point in its history for use in another structure. The back, once carved in relief like the front, was later partially smoothed (probably when the block was trimmed down). Enough details remain, however, to visualize its complete form. The delineation of the whorls with their doubled moldings and their central eye, the extension of the moldings onto the shaft (visible at the back only), and the presence of the lower part of a petal at the upper corner associate the block with the capital from Mytilene (pl. 50). Differences exist in the eye, which is not drilled in the Athenian specimen, and in the number of turns to the whorls. The fragment from the Kerameikos has only two turns in its volute, while the capital from Mytilene (as with most examples from Aeolis) has two and one half turns. Since the piece from the Agora shows a full three turns, this detail could evidently vary considerably in Athenian capitals. A cutting in the upper surface of the block from the Kerameikos shows that it, too, once supported a piece of statuary. Its date should be about the same as the block from the Agora.

From the Akropolis comes a small Parian marble capital of generally comparable design (pls. 53–55 and fig. 48).[4] Like its counterparts from elsewhere in the city, it must have capped an isolated column for statuary. Aeolic whorls are lightly incised into the front, while the back and sides are plain and undecorated. Even though all traces of paint have disappeared, one can assume other details—a central palmette and a decorative band beneath the whorls, for example—would have been added in fugitive colors. The capital from the Akropolis is greatly simplified, but the form of the whorls (with their large eyes) suggests a general relationship. The schematization makes dating difficult, but the piece must come from the late Archaic period, no earlier than the last half of the sixth century B.C.

An additional capital from the Akropolis may

[3] K. Kübler, "Ausgrabungen im Kerameikos I," *AA* (1938) col. 605 and fig. 16; *Kapitelle und Basen*, fig. 170.

[4] Akropolis Mus. no. 3794. Ht. 0.18 m.; width 0.28 m.; thickness 0.14 m. See J. Durm, *Die Baukunst der Griechen* (Leipzig, 1910) fig. 284.

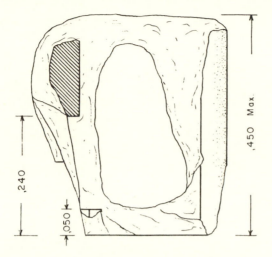

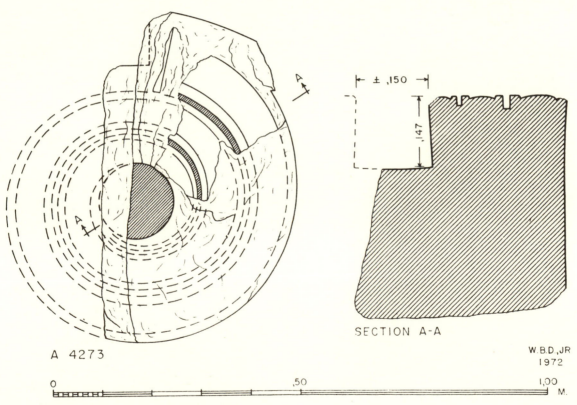

SECTION A-A

A 4273

W.B.D.,JR
1972

0   ,50   1,00   M.

Fig. 47. Fragment of an Aeolic capital found in a well
in the Agora. By courtesy of the Agora Excavations,
Athens. Drawing by William B. Dinsmoor, Jr.

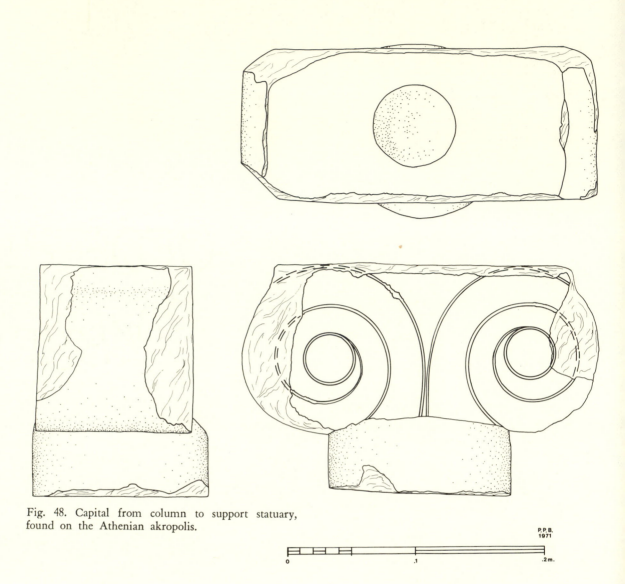

Fig. 48. Capital from column to support statuary, found on the Athenian akropolis.

P.P.B.
1971

0   .1   .2 m.

also be added to this group, although its overall form is much more schematized (fig. 49).[5] The block is very stylized, with volutes painted on the front. It is made of bluish gray Hymmettian marble. A circular cutting with a central dowel hole in the lower surface once helped fix the block to its shaft, while an ovoid recess in the top was designed to hold the plinth of a statue. Although the shape is too schematized for a

close stylistic analysis, the circular eyes and the two and one-half turns to the volutes associate the piece with the other members of the series. None can be dated closely, but the last half of the sixth century B.C. seems likely.

The second Attic style, used for stone architecture at least in one instance, had volutes of the usual vertical type, but it also included details that were seldom applied to the structural

[5] *Technik und Form*, 162ff., figs. 20–21.

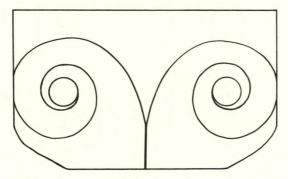

Fig. 49. Aeolic capital from the Athenian akropolis. After Raubitschek, *Technik und Form*, fig. 20.

parts of buildings. In fact, the style was more at home in stelai and the decorative arts where it was employed regularly. It was often used for antefixes, and vase paintings indicate a use in furniture as well.

A small marble capital of this type (pls. 56–59) was found on the Athenian Akropolis, northeast of the Erechtheion.[6] The front of the stone is well finished; the original appearance of the back is not known because this part was broken away in antiquity. Details were painted rather than carved, and although the paint has now completely disappeared, traces of color were still visible when the piece was discovered, and drawings were made at that time (pl. 59). They show painted volutes springing not from a triangle or from the capital's base but from a series of horizontal bands. A central palmette, small petals at the upper corners, and a flat abacus complete the design.

The fine-grained Parian marble was carefully carved. A cylindrical dowel hole appears in the center of the lower surface, which is smooth at its periphery but slightly raised at its rougher center to assure a closer fit with the stone below. The entire upper surface was leveled before it was slightly roughened with a point (pl. 58). The front is completely smooth, but the petals extend along the sides to form a molding above the slightly pinched pulvinus.

The exact stylistic position of this capital has occasioned considerable controversy. It was once regarded as an intermediary step between Aeolic and Ionic capitals,[7] but clarification of the artistic development of the Aeolic style has shown that its affinities are actually with a mature stage of the development. Its design has been called "fanciful"[8] and even "*Mischformen*,"[9] and some have suggested that it should not be included with "true" Aeolic columns.[10] Many writers have published it as a support for statuary, a view which seems to go back to an error of Trowbridge made before the turn of the century,[11] and the view has been expressed that it is not likely to have reproduced a form used in architecture.[12]

Yet a reexamination of the stone itself has shown that its original use actually was architectural, and the appearance of extremely good parallels from a building at Alâzeytin in the Halikarnassos peninsula forces a reassessment of the whole interpretation of the block. It now appears to be the only extant piece of evidence for a sixth-century B.C. building (or at least an architectural facade) on the Athenian Akropolis, in a style which was not unique in Archaic building.

[6] Athens, Akrop. Mus. 9980. R. Borrmann, "Stelen für Weihgeschenke auf der Akropolis zu Athen," *JdI* 3 (1888) 269ff.; S. B. P. Trowbridge, "Archaic Ionic Capitals Found on the Acropolis," *AJA* 4 (1888) 22ff.; R. Borrmann, "Altionische Kapitelle aus Athen," *Antike Denkmaeler* 1 (1891) 8 and pl. 18; Durm (supra n. 4) fig. 284, no. 4. More than half of the capital remains, and its original size can be computed from the arc of its circular resting surface.

[7] Trowbridge (supra n. 6).

[8] *Greek Architecture*, 132. Compare *Architecture of Ancient Greece*, 143.

[9] H. Drerup, "Architektur und Toreutik in der griechischen Frühzeit," *MdI* 5 (1952) 8.

[10] *Kapitelle und Basen*, 75.

[11] He erroneously stated that it had a cutting in its upper surface. Borrmann (supra n. 6, 1888) observed correctly that the cutting is in the lower surface. Observations and discussion about the structure of Athenian votive columns used for the support of statuary can be found in *Technik und Form, passim*.

[12] *Greek Architecture*, 132.

The argument that the capital did not crown an isolated column for statuary is based on the fact that the upper surface has no cutting to help hold a figure securely. This would have been a structural necessity for the sake of the stability of the monument, especially in a country subject to earthquakes. In Athens the cutting was omitted only if additional elements, like those in the entablature of a building, were intended to be placed on top, so that the whole construction would be held together by considerable weight. Since the capital lacks the cutting, it must have been used in an architectural context.

As for the date, the capital's find spot gives only a *terminus ante quem*. The block was found in a level assigned to the Persian destructions of 480 B.C., but there is no way to place individual objects from this stratum in a specific period in the absence of independent evidence. Some help, however, is offered by a comparison with Athenian grave stelai. Double volutes were regularly used for Attic grave monuments by the second quarter of the sixth century B.C., and although one cannot be absolutely precise about their chronology,[13] enough pieces survive to give a general idea of the relative order of the major types.

A capital in the Metropolitan Museum in New York (pl. 60) serves as a good example of the series from the second quarter of the century (although the type may have persisted a little later). It capped a tall stele and must have supported a sphinx, probably used in this context as a guardian figure for the dead.[14] The eyes of the capital's whorls have double lines as do those on the painted capital, and horizontal lines are present between the volutes, but the floral ornament above the whorls has little relation to the form of this decoration on the architectural block.

A closer correspondence exists with examples usually dated to after 550 B.C. On a lyre capital from this time, also in the Metropolitan Museum, the upper volutes are placed below an abacus in the same way as they are on the capital from the Akropolis (pls. 61–62). In both cases a small palmette is between the volutes, and small petals fill the upper corners of both capitals. A collation also exists in the shape of the volutes.

In the last quarter of the sixth century, the Athenian stelai with sphinx capitals were mostly replaced by simpler forms with palmettes above the volutes. These newer designs, evidently inspired by types used in Ionia,[15] no longer required an abacus, and they have fewer points in common with the Athenian capital.

These comparisons suggest the capital from the Akropolis is not likely to be much earlier than the middle of the sixth century B.C. The best parallels come from the period between 550 and 525 B.C., although a slightly later date would also be possible. Unfortunately, the capital cannot really be dated closely.

If the stone did not act as a pedestal for statuary, of what sort of monument is it likely to have been a part? From the capital itself, one can infer that the monument was relatively small since the column was not large—its shaft was only 25 cm. in diameter at the top. It is possible the block was used with something other than a full-sized building. Since the Akropolis had become a religious center by the second half of the sixth century, the most likely theory would

[13] A good survey is G. M. A. Richter, *The Archaic Gravestones of Attica* (London, 1961), with additional bibliography in the same author's *A Handbook of Greek Art* (London and New York, 1969) 400–401. Miss Richter drew very precise lines between her stylistic groups, but it would appear there was actually some overlapping between types. On this, see B. S. Ridgway, "Review of *The Archaic Gravestones of Attica*, by Gisela M. A. Richter," *AJA* 66 (1962) 419–422; F. Hiller, "Zur Berliner Ritzstele," *Marburger Winckelmann-Programm* (1967) 18ff.

[14] For the function and meaning of such sphinxes, see E. Buschor, "Mitteilungen aus dem Kerameikos III: Ein Kopf vom Dipylon," *AthMitt* 52 (1927) 209; Richter (supra n. 13, 1961) 6.

[15] They are also known from Aeolis. See L. D. Caskey, *Catalogue of Greek and Roman Sculpture, Museum of Fine Arts, Boston* (Cambridge, Mass., 1925) 25.

seem to be that the stone formed part of a votive monument of an architectural nature, dedicated on the Akropolis to Athena or to one of the other deities who was worshiped there.

One possibility is suggested by the painted pottery. Architecture had been occasionally included on Attic vases for many years, but the fashion became more popular at the end of the sixth century and slightly later. Columns on vases usually had Doric, Ionic, or Aeolic capitals (although an occasional stylized or poorly drawn example is hard to classify), and among the objects with Aeolic representations are two clay plaques (pls. 63–64). Both were found on the Athenian Akropolis, and both date from the end of the sixth century. They seem to illustrate small shrines or oikoi.

One of the plaques (pl. 63) shows Hermes approaching a small building from the right. Within the structure is Athena, with her owl perched on one extended arm. A small table of offerings is set before her. The shrine itself consists of an entablature with one or more Aeolic columns used as supports. Only two fragments of the plaque survive.

The second pinax also shows Athena (pl. 64), but in this case the goddess is seated within her chamber. A figure carrying a lyre, perhaps Apollo, approaches from the right. More architecture is shown in the second plaque, where the building has a gabled roof with akroteria on top, and one can see that it must have had at least four columns. Again, the entablature is supported by Aeolic columns.

The plaques are about contemporary, dating from the end of the sixth century B.C., and the capitals have eyes at the centers of the whorls, like the similarly dated fragments from the Agora and the Kerameikos. Their columns have a decorative molding beneath the volutes; there are no bases. In both cases, the entablatures consist of alternating dark and light panels, with small projections below the black rectangles.

The projections are clearly guttae, suggesting the artist was painting a Doric entablature and was showing either mutules or triglyphs. Black rectangles with guttae below them occur on many Aeolic buildings by Athenian artists, and they may have been simply an artistic convention, derived partially from Doric architecture. Their repetition by many artists, however, may indicate an echo from the entablatures of actual Aeolic buildings. One possibility is that they may be related to the use of dentils, square or rectangular blocks reflecting the ends of ceiling beams projecting through the building to support the cornice (pl. 65). Stone dentils appear in later architecture from the east Aegean,[16] and a few examples (for instance, the Lycian rock-cut tombs[17] and the stone tombs from Tamassos, Cyprus, pl. 65) seem to date from as early as the sixth century B.C. It is possible that the eastern system of using visible beam ends, or a local variation in which the projecting timbers look like mutules, was employed by the Athenians for Aeolic buildings.

The plaques, however, are too ambiguous to be used to reconstruct the superstructures of Aeolic buildings with any certainty. What they do suggest is that the application of Aeolic columns to religious buildings was not a completely foreign notion in Athens. One must remember that the two plaques were discovered on the Akropolis, in the same destruction debris that yielded the fragment of the painted Aeolic capital. Could the capital have come from a small votive shrine like those shown on the plaques? The possibility is a tempting one.

The immediate inspiration for the painted monument must also be regarded as uncertain, although a connection with East Greece seems likely. A very good comparison is offered by the pillar capitals from Alâzeytin (pls. 32–35 and fig. 19b). The form of the eastern capitals and their use in a small structure of an apparently religious nature are closely paralleled by the

[16] *Greek and Roman Architecture*, 47–48, 159; *Architecture of Ancient Greece*, 66–68; *Greek Architecture*, 137, 303; for a survey with excellent photographs see *Kunst Anatoliens*, figs. 72, 76, 79,

81, 82, 84, and 110–111. To these may be added the Carian evidence presented by P. Roos, *The Rock-Tombs of Caunus* (Göteborg, 1972).

[17] *Greek Architecture*, 137 n. 9.

Athenian specimen. Yet one must also ask if foreign inspiration is absolutely necessary in order to explain the appearance of the Aeolic monument in Athens. All of the necessary stylistic ingredients were already present in Attic votive and sepulchral monuments,[18] and if an eastern influence is to be found, it may be only in the idea of applying these forms to architecture rather than restricting their use to the decorative arts. That a local artistic vocabulary could have been applied in this way to a new idea is quite understandable because the artists who made the monument (whatever commission they may have been given) would have been more familiar with their own stylistic traditions than with the modes of some other area.

There are close parallels also in Attic vase paintings. The most distinctive trait of the painted marble capital is the series of horizontal bands aligned approximately with the eyes of the whorls. A similar capital can be seen on a calyx-krater found on the Akropolis (by the Syriskos painter, pl. 66), and the same form occurs on other vases as well.[19] The capitals on the vases are stylized and greatly simplified, but their relation to the marble block is clearly recognizable. One possible conclusion is that the paintings were copied (directly or through intermediaries) from the Aeolic monument on the Akropolis. The dating reinforces this suggestion since the vases were made in the early fifth century, and the Aeolic structure was destroyed in 480 B.C. In any case, one can be sure

that visitors to the Akropolis in the late Archaic period could see at least one small marble monument with Aeolic capitals.

A third Aeolic design may be discusesd in connection with Athens since an example in stone was found to the north of the city, and the style also occurs on Athenian vases. The stone capital, probably dating from about the middle of the sixth century B.C., was found built into the church of St. Eleussa, at Sykaminon, near Oropos, north of Athens (pl. 67).[20] A rectangular cutting with a central dowel hole in the upper surface of the block indicates a use as a base for a sphinx or some other statue. Made of fine-grained white marble, the block is well carved with details that stand out clearly in very low relief. It has slightly convex volutes without eyes, a central palmette with eleven petals, and a clearly defined abacus above whorls and palmette. At the base of the capital is a large echinus, pushed farther up under the capital than the leaf drums from Neandria and Thasos.

Especially in the shape of the whorls without eyes and in the form of the large echinus below the volutes, the votive can best be compared with a series of early Ionic and Ionic-related capitals used to support sphinxes. Examples with eyeless volutes crowned the Naxian columns from Delos[21] and Delphi,[22] a dedication at Naxos itself,[23] and a sphinx column found at Cyrene (fig. 50).[24] Other examples also are known.[25] The capital from Delphi has been

---

[18] The possibility that the use of related motifs for antefixes may have played a role in their dissemination has also been suggested. See E. B. Harrison, "Archaic Gravestones from the Athenian Agora," *Hesperia* 25 (1956) 36–37.

[19] For example, a pelike in Boston, Museum of Fine Arts no. 1971.343, and a skyphos (?) fragment in Athens, Akropolis Collection no. 641. See appendix B.

[20] Athens, Nat. Mus. no. 4797. Ht. 0.34 m.; width 0.89 m.; thickness 0.32 to 0.33 m.; rectangular cutting in upper surface 0.37 m. by 0.18 m. by 0.05 m. deep, with central dowel hole 0.09 m. by 0.06 m. by 0.07 m. deep.

[21] P. Amandry, *La Colonne des Naxiens et le Portique des Athéniens* (*Fouilles de Delphes* II, Paris, 1953) pl. 15, no. 3, pl. 16.

[22] *Ibid.*, 26–31.

[23] G. Gruben, "Die Sphinx-Säule von Aigina," *AthMitt* 80 (1965) supplementary pl. 75.

[24] D. White, "The Cyrene Sphinx, its Capital and its Column," *AJA* 75 (1971) 47ff.

[25] For a discussion of Sphinx-capitals in general, see A. Raubitschek, *Dedications from the Athenian Acropolis* (Cambridge, 1949) 3ff. The earliest known example may be a monument from the sanctuary of Athena Aphaia on Aigina, Gruben (supra n. 23) 170ff.

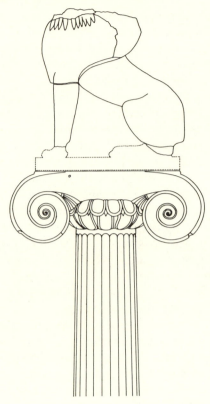

Fig. 50. Reconstruction of the sphinx and its Ionic capital from Cyrene. By courtesy of Donald White, University of Pennsylvania.

dated c. 570–560 B.C.[26] or slightly later,[27] and the date of the columns from Delos and Cyrene

should approach the middle of the century.[28] The style of the sphinxes gives a better indication of date than the capitals themselves do since neither the proportions[29] nor the presence or absence of the eyes[30] may be relied upon to fix the chronology with certainty. These details, like the concave or convex volutes,[31] can probably be ascribed to the preferences of individual schools. The narrow eggs of the Aeolic capital should make it slightly later than the votives from Delphi and Delos, but the projecting echinus and the general similarity to the other capitals from this period[32] must place it within the same generation. Since the monument thus postdates the earliest appearance of Ionic capitals, this might mean that the highly placed echinus and the long, curved triangles in the position occupied by the corner palmettes on Ionic capitals (compare the Naxian votive from Delphi, fig. 51) are a sign of Ionic influence rather than a survival from earlier practice. The same conclusion is suggested by the low profile, because East Greek architectural Aeolic capitals from the same period are always much taller; Ionic architectural capitals with a relatively low profile have a clear priority of date. That the specimen from Oropos had strong Cycladic connections is suggested by two slightly later capitals from Paros (fig. 46 and no. 33 in the catalogue).[33] The Parian volutes curve around large

[26] Amandry (supra n. 21) 26–31.

[27] J. Boardman, "Chian and Early Ionic Architecture," *AntJ* 39 (1959) 199.

[28] White (supra n. 24) 52.

[29] That the proportions vary in accordance with the dimensions of the sculpture has been noted by Amandry (supra n. 21) 18; Boardman (supra n. 27) 205; White (supra n. 24) 52.

[30] The earliest extant capitals from Samos have no eyes, O. Ziegenaus, "Die Tempelgruppe im Norden des Altarplatzes," *AthMitt* 72 (1957) 106ff., pl. 15, supplementary pls. 108–109, but seem to date from about 530 B.C., while the capitals from Ephesos, with eyes, are undoubtedly earlier. For Ephesos see W. Alzinger, "Ionische Kapitelle aus Ephesos I," *JOAI* 46 (1961–1963) 105ff., and E. Bammer, "Beobachtungen zur ephesischen Archi-

tektur," *AA* (1972) 440ff. For other examples of capitals without eyes, see G. Gruben, "Das archaische Didymaion," *JdI* 78 (1963) 174, notes 167–168.

[31] Concave volutes occur on Aigina, on Paros, in the Naxian dedications at Delphi and Delos, and at Naxos itself. The motif is discussed by W. Hahland, "Didyma im 5. Jahrhundert v. Chr.," *JdI* 79 (1964) 191ff.

[32] For architectural capitals, see especially the specimens from Ephesos, Alzinger (supra n. 30). For the projecting echinus, compare also the early capital from Aigina, Gruben (supra n. 23) 170ff.

[33] G. Gruben, "Naxos und Paros. Dritter vorläufiger Bericht über die Forschungskampagnen 1970 und 1971," *AA* (1972) 379 and fig. 35.

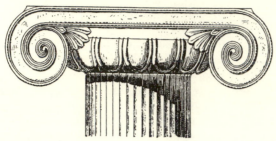

Fig. 51. Restoration of the capital from the Naxian column at Delphi. After Perrot and Chipiez, *Histoire de l'art* VII (1898) pl. 54.

eyes, but the proportions, the low profiles, and the placement of the echinus are very similar.

Since the capital from Delphi (fig. 51) has a missing center, the possibility that its volutes were not joined has occasionally been raised.[34] The present study has pointed out that the Aeolic tradition was not confined to Aeolis, and the close similarity of the capitals from Attica and Delphi could argue for vertically rising volutes on both, but the small palmettes at the inner corners of the whorls on the Naxian capital prove its volutes could not have been exactly like those of its smaller counterpart. There are no examples of true Aeolic capitals with palmettes in this position, but the Naxian dedication on Delos and a number of similar capitals that have been associated with the Cyclades (especially Paros)[35] may offer an alternative for the reconstruction. On these columns the capitals have volutes that are separated above the echinus, even though they do not rise vertically from the center of the stone. They also have tiny palmettes at the inner corners of the whorls, like the Naxian capital from Delphi. Theoretically, there could still have been room for the whorls to rise from the center of the echinus on the Naxian dedication, or the capital could have been of the usual Ionic type; there is simply not enough evidence for a full reconstruction.

Capitals like the one from Sykaminon also occur occasionally on Athenian vases. A red-

figured pelike in the Louvre (no. G 228) furnishes a good example (fig. 52) since it includes a sphinx column whose capital has most of the features characterizing this stylistic type (for the vase consult app. B). The eyeless volutes rise from a simple necking at the top of the fluted column, a design recalling a palmette fills the interstice between the whorls, and a large abacus supports the sculpture. The vase has been attributed to the Syleus painter, who was active in the first quarter of the fifth century B.C.

A more clearly architectural example can be seen on a skyphos of the Corinthian type by the Lewis Painter, now in Münster (pl. 68). Here the palmette is missing and the necking is again very small, but the eyeless volutes and the heavy abacus are unmistakable. Since the scene is a domestic one, the column is apparently intended to suggest the wooden supports of a private home. From the large number of vase painters who used Aeolic columns on their vases (see app. B), one can only conclude that capitals with vertical volutes were not an especially rare sight in the Attic capital and that they were inspired by a number of different sources.

HISTORICAL DEVELOPMENT

When taken in aggregate, the evidence from Athens indicates an Aeolic tradition of some vigor—yet its real strength and influence is difficult to judge. With three distinct Aeolic designs, all apparently in use at about the same time, the city presents a unique situation. This variety may perhaps be explained by the decorative use of the style in Athens, but it still represents an unusual amount of creativity.

The vases suggest that vertically rising volutes were far from uncommon in the Attic capital, but the paintings present some problems: they are often highly schematized or badly confused and poorly drawn; Aeolic capitals were sometimes mixed with Doric or Ionic elements (or

[34] Boardman (supra n. 27) 199; J. Boardman, J. Dörig, W. Fuchs, and M. Hirmer, *Greek Art and Architecture* (New York, 1967) 17.

[35] N. M. Kontoleon, "Πάρια ἰωνικὰ κιονόκρανα," *AAA* 1 (1968) 178–181.

Fig. 52. Capital from a sphinx column on a pelike attributed to the Syleus Painter, in the Louvre, no. G 228. After R. Vallois, *Revue Archéologique* II (1908) 382, fig. 21. For a photograph, see E. Pottier, *Vases antiques du Louvre* III, pl. 131 no. G 228.

with both); and the drawings often indicate the artists understood little about the architectural principles behind the buildings they were depicting. Still, within their own idiom, the vases can offer certain evidence not available elsewhere. The Athenian artists stylized or altered what they drew, but they made no concerted effort to create new forms. Since the Aeolic capitals on the vases almost always conform to designs known from other contexts, one must assume the painters received at least part of their inspiration from monuments they could see in Athens.

Many of these monuments must have been of wood so that no trace of them remains; others were isolated stone columns used to support sphinxes or other statues (pls. 52–55 and 67). In spite of the evidence from the vases, the small stone structure on the Akropolis (pls. 56–59) must have been an unusual sight—there was certainly never a strong tradition of stone Aeolic architecture in Athens. One must, in fact, be very careful not to reconstruct too much from the evidence of the vases. Aeolic capitals were far more decorative than Doric ones, and many vase painters may have painted Aeolic volutes because they were simply more interesting visually.

Even if the vases do reflect a tradition in

wood, it was clearly not powerful enough to achieve its own classical order in the sense that Doric and Ionic buildings came to associate a specific column type with other structural and decorative members. An Aeolic order was already nascent in the Archaic cities of Aeolis, but Athens made no further contribution to the canonization of the style. Even the capitals themselves occur in a variety of designs, and there is no common denominator among all the vases. If one element does suggest a developing architectural tradition, it is the dentillike elements at the top of the entablatures on certain vases (pls. 63–64). If this is taken as an indication of the appearance of wooden buildings, and not as a simple artistic device, it suggests Athens received the Aeolic column as a part of an architectural tradition, not as an isolated decorative feature. Unlike the Ionic system, however, the Aeolic fashion was never formalized in Athenian architecture; even Ionic buildings, however, did not conform to a regularized system in the sixth century B.C.

Chronologically, the Aeolic columns from the Greek mainland are somewhat later than those of Aeolis. There is no evidence to place any of the stone columns much before the middle of the sixth century B.C., and the paintings are almost all from the period of the red-figured vases. This suggests a relatively late development in the Archaic period, well after the style had developed in East Greece.

Unlike their eastern cousins, however, the Athenians did not apply the Aeolic style to their temples; during the sixth century, these buildings were invariably in the Doric order at Athens, perhaps because elegant Baroque-like curves did not conform to the simple dignity demanded of Attic religious architecture. In consequence, temples remained somewhat austere, even when other architectural traditions had begun to change.

This may partially explain why there was no Aeolic order in Attica. The Aeolic fashion entered the city at a time when local tastes restricted its use to decorative columns and perhaps an occasional minor building in wood or stone. By the fifth century, when Athens was more receptive to floral motifs as an architectural embellishment for major religious structures, Aeolic influences were no longer coming into the city. Only Ionic architecture had an impact in Classical times.

The sources of the Athenian motifs are not difficult to discover, at least in their broad outlines. In the case of the first of the three forms discussed in this section, the antecedents clearly come from Aeolis. In the second, the predecessors are not so well defined, but they must certainly come from East Greece, probably from Ionia or even more southern Greek areas. In the third case, too little is known of this particular eastern style to trace the antecedents with certainty. The vertically rising volutes without eyes recall a few Aeolic capitals from East Greece, as at Larisa and Old Smyrna, but the many similar Ionic votive columns from other regions may also have played a role.

These architectural styles can only be understood against the background of Athenian relations with the east. The exact position of Athens in the general pattern of Archaic Greek foreign contacts is a problem that has posed some difficulties,[36] but there can be little doubt where the Aeolic capital is concerned. Etruscan, Carthaginian, and other western variations cannot be assigned a clear priority of date, and the historical situation of their originating areas cannot be related directly enough to the situation of the Athenians to suggest a movement from west to east.[37] It is eastward, then, that one must look to explain the genesis of the Attic style.

From the morphological comparisons one can exclude all areas except the eastern Aegean and the nearby Anatolian coast, and the history of the period seems to confirm this conclusion. Significant quantities of Attic black-figured pottery began to travel eastward in the mid-sixth century B.C., appearing first in southern Ionia and the Dodecanese and then in northern East Greece.[38] While there is considerable evidence for commercial exchange, the evidence rapidly decreases when the areas beyond the Anatolian coastline are considered. Finds of Athenian pottery from as far inland as Gordion and as far south as Egypt show there was at least some relation with the Near East,[39] but contacts (direct or indirect) are never likely to have been close. Athens enjoyed a closer relationship only with the east Aegean.

For these areas, and especially for Ionia, factors that do not involve trade must be added to the mercantile picture. Historic and ethnic ties bound the Athenians to the Ionian colonies, and the unsettled conditions that existed in Asia Minor as a result of the Persian conquests of the sixth century B.C. encouraged many of the

[36] The general configurations of such contacts are well known. Good surveys include A. R. Burn, *The Lyric Age of Greece* (London and New York, 1960); C. G. Starr, *The Origins of Greek Civilization, 1100–650 B.C.* (New York, 1961); J. Boardman, *The Greeks Overseas* (London and Baltimore, 1964); M. I. Finley, *Early Greece: The Bronze and Archaic Ages* (London, 1970). For the east, see T. J. Dunbabin, *The Greeks and their Eastern Neighbors* (London, 1957); M. B. Sakellariou, *La Migration grecque en Ionie* (Athens, 1958); C. Roebuck, *Ionian Trade and Colonization* (New York, 1959); J. M. Cook, *The Greeks in Ionia and the East* (New York, 1963); G. L. Huxley, *The Early Ionians* (London, 1966). For the West, see T. J. Dunbabin, *The Western Greeks* (Oxford, 1948); R. van Compernolle, *Etude de chronologie et d'historiographie siciliotes* (Brussels, 1960); A. G. Woodhead, *The Greeks in the West* (New York, 1962); M. I. Finley, *Ancient Sicily to the Arab Conquest* (London and New York, 1968); M. Miller, *The Sicilian Colony Dates* (New York, 1970).

[37] The evidence is discusesd by Antonia Ciasca, *Capitello Eolico,* 27ff.

[38] Roebuck (supra n. 36) 81.

[39] R. M. Cook, "Die Bedeutung der bemalten Keramik für den griechischen Handel," *JdI* 74 (1959) 114ff. See also C. Clairmont, "Greek Pottery from the Near East," *Berytus* 11 (1955) 109ff.; Roebuck (supra n. 36) 79ff.; D. Auscher, "Les Relations entre la Grèce et la Palestine avant la conquête d'Alexandre," *Vetus Testamentum* 17 (1967) 8ff.

East Greeks to seek new homes. Athens was usually receptive to foreign residents, especially artisans, and the new feeling for grace and elegance in the painted pottery and the other Attic crafts of this century can be partially ascribed to these new residents. Ionian influence in Athens can be traced in many areas, and the economic and cultural bond between the two regions gradually increased as wheels were set in motion that would not cease until the city had made herself mistress of the Aegean, the head of a fifth-century maritime empire.

A somewhat different situation existed with respect to Aeolis, where relations were often competitive and hence not so amicable. Here it was undoubtedly trade that most influenced Attic contacts since Athenians and Aeolians were both interested in the sea route to the Black Sea. By the middle of the sixth century B.C., the Athenian need for grain was increasing rapidly.[40] The Black Sea ports offered one possible source, but way stations were essential if this supply was to be exploited. Both the literary[41] and the archaeological[42] evidence show that Athens made a concerted effort to secure colonies on both sides of the Hellespont early in the reign of Peisistratos (i.e. at Sigeion and Elaious), and this colonization must have had economic causes behind it.[43] The Aeolic cities in the northeast were far from friendly toward the Athenian newcomers. There was constant friction between the two groups, and the Athenian strength gradually decreased. With additional pressures from the Scythians at the end of the sixth century and from the Persian empire at

the beginning of the fifth, Athens retreated to return only after the Persian wars.[44]

One result of these relations with East Greece —friendly contacts with the southern cities, more hostile contacts with Aeolis—was a gradual infiltration of East Greek influence into Athenian art. Combining with the city's own traditions and with a pastiche of influences from other cities, the eastern fashion helped fuse the style that would finally emerge as Athenian. An important aspect of East Greek influence was a taste for graceful ornament, especially tendrils, volutes, whorls, and other curvilinear floral motifs. The encroachment of these forms into Attic art can perhaps be traced most easily in a decorative tradition like that of the grave stelai,[45] but it also appears in many other contexts. It is surely no accident that Aeolic capitals first appeared in Athens during this same era.

The background of eastern contacts goes a long way toward explaining the architectural development of the Aeolic column in Athens. Aeolic influences seem to have begun in Athens at about the same time that quantities of Attic pottery started appearing in East Greece, a time which also coincides with the city's foundations at Elaious and Sigeion in the Hellespont. The style was a vigorous tradition in Athens only until the beginning of the fifth century B.C. After that, a change occurred, and the Athenians began using the Ionic style and their native Doric tradition almost exclusively. Perhaps the magnificent Ionic temples, as at Samos and Ephesos, proved more influential than their more modest Aeolic counterparts. Perhaps the

[40] Solon, for example, had banned the export of all agricultural produce except olive oil (Plut., *Sol.*, 24).

[41] The version in Herodotos (4. 38; 5. 94; 6. 34ff.) is well known. For additional references, see *PW*, vol. v, cols. 2227–2228, ser. 2, vol. ii, cols. 2275–2276.

[42] Good summaries are in S. Casson, *Macedonia, Thrace and Illyria* (Oxford, 1926) 201ff.; J. Boardman (supra n. 36) 236ff.

[43] While most writers would agree with the eco-

nomic reasons for this colonization, the role of Peisistratos is disputed. For review of the evidence, with previous bibliography, see A. J. Graham, *Colony and Mother City in Ancient Greece* (New York, 1964) 32ff.

[44] An increased percentage of Athenian currency from Egyptian coin hoards during this period suggests that Athens may have turned to a new source for its grain. C. Roebuck, "The Grain Trade between Greece and Egypt," *CP* 45 (1950) 236ff.

[45] See above, note 13.

Athenian retreat from the northeast influenced the change in style, or maybe the architecture simply reflected the tastes of the more viable economic regions. Whatever the underlying reasons, by the fifth century B.C. the Aeolic motif was virtually excluded as an architectural decoration for stone monuments in Athens. Unlike the Ionic tradition, it would not become a Classical order, and later Athenian evidence of it is limited to an occasional form in the minor arts.

PART III

Chapter VI

A SUMMARY OF THE STYLISTIC DEVELOPMENT
IN THE EASTERN MEDITERRANEAN

As can be seen from even the briefest survey of the relevant floral decorations of the Late Bronze Age (see chap. 1), the artistic antecedents of the Aeolic style were widely disseminated in the late second millennium B.C. Columnar forms with paired volutes were used with both flowers and palms, and they were incorporated into the artistic repertories of many different peoples. It is possible that no single area developed the Aeolic column as a complete stylistic entity.[1] Columns with floral capitals of wood or stucco can be traced to the eighteenth dynasty in Egypt (figs. 1–3) because they were depicted in tomb paintings, but somewhat later evidence in other regions (pl. 2) suggests the practice may have been a common one. The gradual stylization of these patterns and their eventual application to stone architecture resulted in the Aeolic style of the Iron Age and later. Since the designs from the Iron Age show a great diversity of form, it is surely better to regard them as representing a series of related traditions instead of a single artistic progression.

We do not know exactly where the double volute motif was first applied to stone architecture, but several pieces of evidence point to a spot somewhere in the Syro-Palestinian area as the most likely possibility. This region's art had absorbed the Egyptian and Asian mannerisms that seem to have come together to form the style as it appears in the succeeding periods, and its decorative tradition made much use of elegant floral embellishment. It is also in this area that the earliest known stone capitals appear, at Shechem (pl. 17)[2] and Megiddo (pl. 8).

With the end of the Bronze Age, Egypt ceased to play a role in the style's development. There are no true Aeolic buildings from the Nile valley, and the Egyptian floral capitals must have exerted their influence on the style

---

[1] An alternative is that the style goes back to a single source dated well back in the Bronze Age, no later than the mid second millennium B.C. and perhaps considerably earlier. Certainly the style was well dispersed by the beginning of the Iron Age.

[2] Dated to the Bronze Age by E. Sellin, "Die Ausgrabung von Sichem," *Zeitschrift des Deutschen Palästina-Vereins* 49 (1926) 311, pl. 39 b, and to the Iron Age by G. Welter, "Stand der Ausgrabungen in Sichem," *AA* (1932) col. 313. The lack of symmetry could make the piece quite early, if it is, indeed, architectural.

at a very early stage. After the nineteenth dynasty, Egypt seems to have pursued a path that allowed no further contact with Aeolic architectural fashions until the Greek Archaic period.[3]

The earliest clearly datable stone volute capitals are the tenth- to ninth-century B.C. specimens from Megiddo (pl. 8). Their origin is most likely to be sought in the Phoenician cities to the north of Palestine since Phoenician influence can be traced in other aspects of Palestinian architecture from the same period, but archaeological proof is lacking. The similar volute designs from Cyprus and the Phoenician colonies in the western Mediterranean surely represent aspects of the same artistic tradition.

In spite of the fact that only scanty remains survive from a Phoenician style, the tradition must have been extremely influential. From the tombs at Tamassos[4] and other fragments, one may reconstruct a system making liberal use of carved wooden members, particularly Aeolic pilasters that had no carved leaf drums when used as major architectural supports.[5] The dissemination of several elements, like the use of dentils, the application of volute members to doorjambs or antae, the employment of small petals and a molding to delineate the whorls around a tiny dot, the use of a central triangle for volute capitals, and even the concept of decorating the main facade of a building with structural members in the form of floral ornaments may be partly due to Phoenician influence. If the Aeolic balustrades were originally Phoenician as well, one may add other influences also.

Since the finest Phoenician architectural decorations were evidently executed in perishable materials, as is suggested by several types of evidence, one can understand the scarcity of the remains. Few actual examples could be expected except when they were copied secondhand in stone. This is what one finds in Phoenicia and its colonies and in Cyprus, where volute designs survive because of occasional symbolic facades for tombs, grave stelai, and other monuments of a derivative nature. The originals, executed in stucco, in carved wood, or in wood sheathed with bronze,[6] are no longer extant.

The Palestinian capitals form the most complete Iron Age sequence to survive. They were used to enhance some of the most impressive monuments of the Palestinian cities, where they were given a variety of architectural functions. With the exception of the broken block from Shechem, they crowned only pillars; some were engaged, while others were used as free-standing supports. Related designs decorated balustrades (pl. 26), and there were undoubtedly other uses as well. A distinct stylistic break can be detected at the schism between north and south that resulted in the dissolution of the Israelite united monarchy. After the tenth century B.C., the southern capitals included horizontal abaci, triple lines to outline the triangles, and circles in the backgrounds, giving the blocks an entirely different appearance from that of their counterparts from the north.

While there is far more evidence from Palestine than from other Iron Age localities, scattered bits of information suggest the Israelite situation was not unique. Probably the stone tradition of Palestine was paralleled by a wooden carpentry tradition in a great many Near Eastern communities where volute designs were only occasionally applied to media that would effect their preservation.

No single movement of people or artistic influence can explain the appearance of volute capitals in Assyria, Mesopotamia, Greece, Anatolia,

---

[3] It has occasionally been suggested that Egypt played a role in Archaic Greek architecture parallelling its role in Greek monumental stone sculpture because concepts like the employment of stone columns in series on the exterior of buildings could have been inspired from this region.

[4] See the discussion in chapter II, with references

in note 85.

[5] The Aeolic balustrades, of course, employ leaf drums at an early date and may be Phoenician as well.

[6] For the use of bronze decorations, see H. Drerup, "Architektur und Toreutik in der griechische Frühzeit," *MdI* 5 (1952) 10–11.

Etruria, and elsewhere. Rather, one must suppose the architectural traditions inherited from the Bronze Age crossed many national and ethnic boundaries. Among these loosely related styles one can distinguish a number of separate Near Eastern traditions, including the series of pillar capitals from Palestine and elsewhere (chap. II), a group with animal protomes above vertical volutes best known from Persian specimens (fig. 53),[7] a division made up of double-tiered capitals with the volutes rising from triangles (as at Tell Tainat, pl. 24, and Babylon, pl. 16), and a type with elaborate floral ornament above the whorls (pls. 18 and 20). While our evidence can only give us the slightest hints about these largely nonsurviving wooden forms, we must suppose a number of related traditions that could be applied (as was the case in Palestine) to both columns and pillars, engaged or free-standing. Volute capitals were simply one crowning member for architectural supports, and they seldom formed a part of a concerted architectural scheme. It is in this respect that the Greek orders stand somewhat apart.

The antecedents of the Greek style must be sought in Near Eastern designs of the seventh century B.C. While the exact source cannot be pinpointed at our present level of knowledge, several indications can narrow the area this influence must have come from. The pilaster

tradition from Palestine and elsewhere can be ruled out[8] because of its structural usage and because its morphology is very different.[9] Egypt can also be excluded from the picture.[10] A movement from the west or a Mycenaean survival seems very unlikely,[11] and Mesopotamia and Iran appear to have had no close historical connections with Greece at this period. Very few Anatolian volute designs are known from the seventh or eighth century B.C., although the appearance of the style at Gordion in later times (pl. 69)[12] could conceivably imply an earlier tradition we know nothing about. It is most likely that the Greeks borrowed the volute capital from some nearby region in Anatolia or North Syria, although an Assyrian origin cannot be completely ruled out. Because of the form, architectural usage, and artistic style of the earliest Greek columns, the most plausible theory is that they were derived from oriental traditions visible to us only in the minor arts, in the Assyrian palace reliefs, and in ornamental window balustrades like those of the plaques illustrating the "Woman at the Window." Of these the window balustrades show the closest stylistic affinities with the later Greek style.

We have an excellent series of actual balustrades from Ramat Raḥel (pl. 26). Carved in stone, they preserve the shape of the wooden examples known from illustrations in the minor

[7] For the separate nature of the Persian development, perhaps with some influence from the minor arts, see H. H. von der Osten, *Die Welt der Perser* (Stuttgart, 1956) 75. For the wide geographic distribution of this form note the evidence presented by B. Rowland, "Notes on Ionic Architecture in the East," *AJA* 39 (1935) 489ff. Additonal discussion and bibliography is presented in *Figuralkapitelle*, 27ff.

[8] An opposite view has been expressed by R. Martin, *Problème des ordres*, 130.

[9] There is no central palmette and no pendant girdle of leaves, and the volutes often rise from triangles. The use with pilasters is extremely different from the articulated Greek column composed of base, shaft, and capital.

[10] It has been suggested, however, that the idea of regularly associating several specific architectural

details to form an "order" could have been inspired by Egyptian practice. See J. Boardman, "Chian and Early Ionic Architecture," *AntJ* 39 (1959) 215 n. 1.

[11] Mycenaean designs belong in the "International Style" (see chap. 1). Intermediary steps between this style and the Archaic period can be clearly traced in the Near East but are completely absent from Greece. In addition, the Aegean Bronze Age columns are completely different in form and conception. Most recently on this, see *Kapitelle und Basen*, chapter 1.

[12] R. S. Young, "The Campaign of 1955 at Gordion," *AJA* 60 (1956) 256, pl. 85 fig. 18. The human figures in the fragments are either East Greek or represent heavy Greek influence; lines of influence are most likely from west to east.

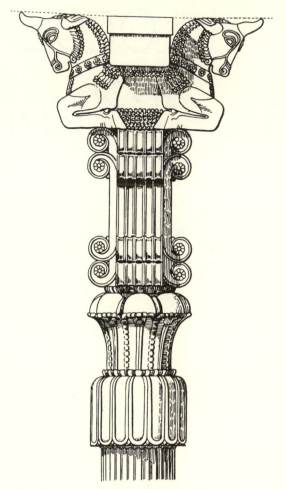

Fig. 53. Persian composite capital from Susa, from the time of Darius I. After O. Puchstein, *Die ionische Säule* (1907) fig. 48.

arts from several sites (see app. A). The longest series of objects illustrating this motif is the group of ivory plaques showing the "Woman at the Window" (pl. 23), usually attributed to North Syria/Phoenicia.[13]

The stone balusters have several traits in common with the Greek tradition. They consist of true columns, used in series to support a horizontal beam. The capitals' whorls, with only

one turn (as in the earliest Greek examples), do not rise from triangles. Pendant girdles of leaves lie between shaft and capital. One important difference in the balustrade capitals is the absence of the central palmette; it is obvious we do not have the exact prototypes. Since many of the plaques illustrating balustrades have been assigned to the North Syrian/Phoenician artistic sphere, one could suppose a similar origin for the Greek columns, but this is not completely assured. The style of the plaques need not imply a restricted distribution for the subjects portrayed on them, and the appearance of similar motifs from Cyprus and Palestine as well as Assyria may imply a relatively widespread artistic fashion. Even if the Greek style could be surely traced to North Syria, one would prefer to see it borrowed from the more monumental designs known to exist in this area (as in the porticoes used with the *bit hilani*), even though the columns themselves have not survived.

The emergence of North Syria and Phoenicia as good candidates for the origin of the Greek columns points up several other analogies between the architectural styles of these regions and Greece. In the Neo-Hittite cities of North Syria, decorative motifs were applied to architecture in a tectonic arrangement in which base, shaft, and capital were clearly articulated.[14] Each element in a column was set off from the others both by its structure and by its own surface decoration (see pls. 24 and 70). The result conveys a feeling of strength and solidity because of the clear structural relationships, while the ornament of the individual parts enhances the work's decorative quality as a whole. A similar combination of tectonic arrangement with precise and elegant detail would be used by the Hellenic architects.

A correspondence between the two regions' architecture may also exist in several details. Barnett has suggested that fasciae may have been derived from Near Eastern carpentry practices

[13] *Nimrud Ivories*, 145ff. For possible Egyptian parallels, see A. Hermann, "Die Katze im Fenster über der Tür," *Zeitschrift für ägyptische Sprache und Altertumskunde* 73 (1937) 68ff., fig. 1.

[14] On this tectonic arrangement, see especially E. Akurgal, *The Art of Greece; Its Origins in the Mediterranean and Near East* (New York, 1968) 79–94.

visible in "recessed niches" like those of the plaques showing the "Woman at the Window" (pl. 23).[15] He has proposed a similar origin for the stone moldings around the doors of Greek temples. One can also note the North Syrian practice of placing plinths below bases (which also occurs at Ephesos)[16] and the use of moldings at the top of the shafts, below the capitals.[17] Singly, these isolated elements mean little, but taken in aggregate they represent the largest group of Near Eastern affinities with the earliest East Greek architecture that have so far come to light. If their pattern is corroborated by future discoveries, they could suggest that the volute capitals represent more than a simple borrowing of an isolated Near Eastern detail. They could imply a much deeper relationship in which several aspects of Near Eastern architecture were transmitted to the Greek cities.

One must be very cautious in assessing the collation of these details. It must be remembered that the comparable details are isolated traits taken from a broad geographic region, not from a specific city. In many cases (as with the "recessed niches"), we may be dealing with characteristics familiar to much larger areas of the eastern Mediterranean. The artistic parallels may suggest where one should look for additional comparanda, but the problem of the origins of the Greek volute capitals is still far from solved.

The East Greek styles in building construction were preceded by a considerable development of similar motifs in the minor arts. Ceramics,

metalwork, and several other media had used paired volutes on a regular basis in Greece from the beginning of the eighth century B.C., so the monumental uses did not represent an influx of any new artistic designs. The application to architecture was a fresh aesthetic direction, but the climate for the style was already set. Our best indication of the uses of Aeolic-like forms in the minor arts comes from furniture making, a craft offering considerable extant evidence. It has, in fact, been occasionally suggested that the Aeolic style was simply an expansion and an enlargement of a furniture-making tradition.

Ivory panels with Aeolic-like designs were set into woodwork as early as the Late Bronze and Early Iron Ages (pl. 19), and continuity with later times is suggested by examples like the relief from Tell Tainat illustrating a throne decorated with Aeolic columns (pl. 24). The piece from Tell Tainat, however, is unusual for its time and place; most North Syrian thrones were not so decorated.[18] The style reached the heights of its popularity somewhat later and is best known from the Assyrian reliefs from Khorsabad and from Greek examples of the sixth and fifth centuries B.C.[19]

Ornaments shaped like Aeolic capitals must have decorated the furniture of a number of areas. The furniture from Khorsabad is certainly Near Eastern rather than Greek, though Greek examples are more numerous. Many illustrations survive on Athenian vases.[20] Etruscan examples[21] and pieces from the Greek areas

---

[15] *Nimrud Ivories*, 99.

[16] For Carchemish see C. L. Woolley, *Carchemish* II (London, 1921) 55, fig. 61; for Khorsabad, see G. Loud and C. B. Altman, *Khorsabad* II (Chicago, 1938) 30, fig. 2, pls. 38, 41 b and c, considered a North Syrian import by Akurgal (supra n. 14) 83; for Zincirli, see *Ausgrabungen in Sendschirli* (*Mitteilungen aus den orientalischen Sammlungen der Berliner Museen*, Berlin, 1893–1911) 320, figs. 226 no. 361 and 260; for Arslan-Tash, see F. Thureau-Dangin *et al., Arslan-Tash* (Paris, 1931) pl. 5 no. 2.

[17] *Histoire de l'art*, II, 726 fig. 386.

[18] H. Kyrieleis, *Throne und Klinen* (Berlin, 1969) 54ff.

[19] The best discussion of the style in general is that of Kyrieleis (supra n. 18). For the table with legs decorated with Aeolic-like designs from Khorsabad, see H. Baker, *Furniture in the Ancient World* (New York, 1966) 184–187, fig. 294 and color pl. 13.

[20] A partial list is in P. Oliver-Smith, "Representations of Aeolic Capitals on Greek Vases before 400 B.C.," *Essays in Memory of Karl Lehmann* (Locust Valley, N.Y., 1964).

[21] G. M. A. Richter, *The Furniture of the Greeks, Etruscans and Romans* (London, 1966) pls. 451 and 454–455.

of southern Italy[22] show the westward dispersion of the style, and Roman furniture[23] illustrates its long popularity.

As one might expect from such a varied and long-lived tradition, there was much differentiation in style. The usual practice was to place the volutes near the top of the legs, as in plate 71. The motifs were rendered as shallow reliefs carved from wood, or as inlay. Metal additions are known as well, and ivory insets survive from Athens and from Kul Oba on the Black Sea.[24] The ornaments might or might not have leaf drums, eyes, or a central palmette; furniture used all variations found in the architectural capitals plus many others. An important departure from the architectural style is the absence of the separation into base, shaft, and capital; usually it is the capital alone that adorns the furniture. Thus a structural role plays no part in the tradition, and the designs are simply used as surface ornamentation. This function sometimes affects the style, so that the motifs may lack the abacus or may not lie immediately below any horizontal element, completely denying their roles as supporting members.

In considering the role of the minor arts in Aeolic architecture, a very strong case may be made for influence from some of the woodworking crafts, like the carving of balusters. Much less evidence survives for any influence from furniture. The most comparable examples are relatively late chronologically, and the nonsupporting role of the paired volute seems quite distinct from its first application as a structural member. It is more likely the two styles were simply part of the same milieu; a common heritage and constant contact between disciplines resulted in a close relationship of architectural decoration not only with woodcarving, but with metalworking, the carving of grave markers, and the other arts as well. The decorative aspects of paired vertical helices were exploited much longer in furniture and other craftwork than they were in stone buildings, and it is their derivative nature that has resulted in the survival of so many related forms.

The exclusion of furniture from the nascence of the Greek architectural style, however, need not rule out occasional instances of later influence. One possibility is the design visible in the painted capital from Athens (pl. 59) and the similar pillars from Alâzeytin (pls. 32–35). This design cannot be traced to earlier monumental predecessors, and it is similar to decorations used in furniture. A connection is possible, but influence from ornamental stonework (like stelai) cannot be ruled out either. One may also note the unusual form of some of the votive capitals (as in pls. 53–55 and fig. 49), which could suggest a relation with the decorative arts. For most of the monumental examples in stone, however, more evidence exists for an architectural genesis than for a derivation from furniture.

Greek volute capitals in architectural contexts can be traced from the end of the seventh century B.C. There is a possibility that earlier and more widely distributed Hellenic forms existed, but so far no actual examples have come to light.[25] The earliest Greek capitals have vertical volutes without eyes applied to rather tall architectural blocks. Palmettes between the whorls were present from the beginning, and an element was regularly included as a transition between capital and shaft. By the end of the sixth century B.C., the capitals were lowered considerably in profile, and the weight-bearing surface was increased in size. Well-formed eyes for the

[22] *Ibid.*, pl. 487.

[23] Kyrieleis (supra n. 18) pl. 21 no. 2; Richter (supra n. 21) pls. 486 and 562.

[24] Kyrieleis (supra n. 18) pl. 21 nos. 1 and 2.

[25] A fragment of a volute was found at the temple at Prinias, Crete. It has been considered an akroterion by L. Pernier, "Templi arcaici sulla patela di Prinias," *ASAA* 1 (1914) 64; "New Ele-

ments for the Study of the Archaic Temple of Prinias," *AJA* 38 (1934) 176, but a suggestion that it could be a piece of a volute capital has been raised by C. Weickert, *Typen der archaischen Architektur in Griechenland und Kleinasien* (Augsburg, 1929) 58–59. The depth of the piece seems too shallow to regard it as a capital.

whorls had appeared by the second quarter of the same century. The substitution of a smooth torus flanked by smaller moldings for the leaf-decorated element marks the end of the Archaic development; it complemented the more compact nature of the rest of the capital.

Once they were incorporated into the Greek architectural traditions, the Aeolic designs underwent a subtle transformation. For the first time, free-standing columns were monumentalized in stone on a regular basis. Employed in series on the exterior of buildings, they offered the viewer an architectural facade of an entirely new type. Their combination with a specific set of structural and decorative elements created an on-going and viable architectural tradition.

Where evidence exists for the complete arrangement, the Greek Aeolic order used columns with base, shaft, and capital, but—unlike the Ionic column which also had a tripartite division—there was no emphasis on the carved surface decoration of individual elements. In the Old Palace at Larisa, for example, the bases were very much like the slightly earlier ones from Samos except that they had no horizontal fluting. A similar idea can be detected in the shafts, which were regularly fluted in Ionic buildings but (except at Old Smyrna, a building which is very early in the series) were always left smooth in the Aeolic system. As a result, the Aeolic buildings must have presented the viewer with an entirely different visual impression than the more decorative Ionic structures, where the play of light and shadow over flutes and moldings would have created a much more ornate effect. Without suggesting the extreme strength and solidity of the massive Doric

buildings of this time, the Aeolic facades must have seemed elegant and reserved, with their graceful capitals and tall proportions tempered by a quiet simplicity and a clear relationship between the component parts. The capitals always supported an entablature of wood to which were applied terracotta revetments of various types. Roofs were tiled, with akroteria and antefixes adding a final decorative touch.

Although the strongest Archaic Greek development was in Aeolis, and adjacent parts of Ionia and the Cyclades, suggestions of other regional Hellenic styles also survive. From Attica come votive columns of the type found in Aeolis, as well as capitals whose stylistic origins in East Greece cannot be so easily traced (chap. v). The long series of columns on Attic vases (app. B) implies a large number of Athenian houses with wooden Aeolic columns, and decorated vases also survive from Ionian and Aeolian regions in the northeast Aegean (app. c). Alâ-zeytin in the Halikarnassos peninsula used Aeolic buildings with a probable Greek connection (chap. III), which may suggest an as yet unknown Aeolic style in the adjacent Hellenic areas. Fragments of evidence from other regions include the stone votive columns from the Cyclades (chap. IV), some related architectural decorations from Samos,[26] and painted pottery from Boeotia,[27] and elsewhere. These bits of evidence seem far too numerous and too disparate to be based on anything except a rather widely spread style. The gradually mounting body of evidence seems to point toward an important tradition in the northeast Aegean with occasional monuments in other parts of Greece as well.

[26] Compare a volute-decorated anta capital, E. Buschor, "Altsamischer Bauschmuck," *AthMitt* 72 (1957) 4.

[27] *CVA, Schloss Fasanerie (Adolphseck)* fasc. 2 (Deutschland, fasc. 16) pl. 63.

Chapter VII

THE RELATION BETWEEN THE AEOLIC AND IONIC ORDERS

The relation between the Aeolic and Ionic systems has been a vexing problem since the first discovery of Aeolic capitals. Scholarship has been sharply divided between the theory that holds the Aeolic columns to be the ancestors of the Ionic ones[1] and that which holds them to be a completely separate development, based on common or related antecedents.[2] Since the chronology of the major Aeolic monuments can now be more firmly fixed than was once the case, the entire problem can be clarified considerably. The emerging picture suggests that both artistic fashions were rooted in the orientalizing styles of the seventh century B.C. Impulses derived from the east merged with the native Greek traditions to create the architectural orders so typical of later East Greek architecture.

The earliest known Aeolic building in Greece is the temple of Athena at Old Smyrna, built at (or slightly after) the end of the seventh century B.C. The Ionic style can be first studied in two slightly later temples, at Ephesos and Samos, both apparently begun around or shortly before the middle of the next century. Less is known of contemporary Ionic buildings from other cities, but the temple at Naukratis is from the same period, the one at Didyma may be this early, and there are also fragments from Miletos. The *oikos* of the Naxians on Delos also seems to date from near the middle of the century, and scattered remains survive from Phokaia, Myus, Naxos, Paros, and elsewhere.[3] To these structures may be added a series of votive columns in both the Ionic and the Aeolic styles

[1] *Architecture of Ancient Greece*, 58ff.; H. Drerup, "Architektur und Toreutik in der griechischen Frühzeit," *MdI* 5 (1952) 7ff.; E. Akurgal, *Kunst Anatoliens*, 288ff.; "Vom äolischen zum ionischen Kapitell," *Anatolia* 5 (1960) 1–7; J. Boardman, J. Dörig, W. Fuchs, and M. Hirmer, *Greek Art and Architecture* (New York, 1967) 16–17.

[2] J. Braun-Vogelstein, "Die ionische Säule," *JdI* 35 (1920) 27ff.; *Die ionische Säule* (Berlin and Leipzig, 1921); *Äolische Kapitell*, 42ff.; *Greek Architecture*, 131–132; *Problème des ordres*.

[3] Good surveys of the remains include J. Boardman, "Chian and Early Ionic Architecture," *AntJ* 39 (1959) 199ff.; E. Akurgal, *Kunst Anatoliens; Ancient Civilizations and Ruins of Turkey* (Istanbul, 1973). For Naxos, add G. Gruben, "Naxos und Paros. Dritter Vorläufiger Bericht über die Forschungskampagnen 1970 und 1971," *AA* (1972) 358ff. For Delos, add R. Martin, "Chapiteaux ioniques de Thasos," *BCH* 96 (1972) 313–314 and fig. 7.

—a few of the Ionic votives may be even earlier than the earliest known Ionic buildings.[4] Stelai, altars, and other related monuments add evidence as well, suggesting that by the second quarter of the sixth century B.C., the two styles were already widespread regional manifestations.

The history of the Ionic capital cannot be traced before its first appearance in Greek monuments. Near Eastern sources have been occasionally suggested, but they do not offer truly convincing parallels. The rare occurrence of Ionic-like volutes in the Near Eastern minor arts[5] cannot be clearly related to the Archaic architectural usage, and some proposed antecedents, like the rock-cut tomb at Dar-u-Dukhtar,[6] have been discounted in recent years. Even the Assyrian palace reliefs offer no good synchronisms.[7] From the available evidence, we can conclude only that the Ionic capital was invented in Greece during the sixth century B.C., or was developed from the Aeolic tradition which goes back in Hellenic areas at least to the end of the previous century.

On a superficial level, the Aeolic and Ionic columns seem closely related. Both were applied as decorative or symbolic elements to the structural parts of architecture. Both were two-sided, in strict contrast with the circular concept of the Doric and most Near Eastern floral capitals, as well as with the columns used by the Minoans

and Mycenaeans. Both capital types used whorls set above carved drums, with subsidiary palmettes in a secondary position. They were accorded a similar usage, and the change from vertically rising to horizontally placed whorls could easily be regarded as a stylistic change to better accommodate the supported architectural members. Any study of a possible relationship, however, must also examine the contexts in which the columns were used.

The gigantic temples at Samos and Ephesos must have gone a long way toward establishing the patterns architects would follow in subsequent years. Because the earliest architectural usage of the Ionic order can be studied in detail from these buildings only, any consideration of the origins of the style must begin here. The buildings themselves as well as the morphology of the capitals must be taken into account, for it is important to determine whether the Aeolic and Ionic styles were related to each other by more than the outward form of the architectural supports. Any really close relationship should produce more than a general correspondence of isolated details taken out of context. In order to isolate the exact nature of the stylistic relationship, the constructions as a whole must be considered.

Not a single capital has survived from the Heraion at Samos which was built a little before the middle of the sixth century B.C.[8] The colos-

---

[4] G. Gruben, "Die Sphinx-Säule von Aigina," *AthMitt* 80 (1965) 207.

[5] *MRMC*, 40, fig. 12; Ch. Kardara, "Ὑπαίθριοι στῦλοι καὶ δένδρα ὡς μέσα ἐπιφανείας τοῦ θεοῦ τοῦ κεραυνοῦ," *ArchEph* (1966) 175, fig. 24; H. Berve and G. Gruben, *Greek Temples, Theatres, and Shrines* (New York, 1962) fig. 104.

[6] H. von Gall, "Zu den 'Medischen' Felsgräbern in Nordwestiran und Iraqi Kurdistan," *AA* 81 (1966) 19ff. and fig. 22. Its affinities are with fifth-century rather than sixth-century capitals.

[7] Some of the early drawings made from the Assyrian reliefs (for example, *Histoire de l'art*, II, fig. 41) are extremely misleading, resulting in theories about the early stages of the Ionic capital which may not be correct, as, for example, that in L. W. King, "Sennacherib and the Ionians," *JHS*

30 (1910) 327ff. The present writer has examined the reliefs in London and Chicago. The most likely possibility for an Ionic parallel seems to be a relief from Khorsabad in the Oriental Institute, Chicago, no. A 11255, but the carving is extremely ambiguous, and it is possible that no volutes of any type were intended. For photographs, see G. Loud, *Khorsabad* 1 (Chicago, 1936) 72, fig. 83 and 77, fig. 89.

[8] E. Buschor, "Heraion von Samos: Frühe Bauten," *AthMitt* 55 (1930) 1–99; O. Reuther, *Der Heratempel von Samos* (Berlin, 1957). For a reconstruction without Ionic capitals see H. Walter, *Der griechische Heiligtum: Heraion von Samos* (Munich, 1965) 57, fig. 58. Berve and Gruben (supra n. 5) 453 have suggested the capitals were carved from wood.

sal limestone structure (on a stylobate c. 52.5 x 105 m.) was so badly destroyed that its restoration is very uncertain, but it was evidently dipteral, with two rows of columns at least on the sides. Built of fine masonry upon a platform with two steps, it had an east front with eight columns spaced to give a greater intercolumniation at the center; both nine and ten supports have been proposed for the rear, while the flanks had about twenty-one.[9] All bases were set back from the edge of the platform to produce an ambulatory around the building. The massing of columns at the front was emphasized by a pronaos with two rows of ten columns, and there were additional supports within the cella, but there was no opisthodomos. Some shafts had forty shallow flutes (with sharp arrises), while others were unfluted—apparently the temple was still unfinished when it was destroyed by fire about half a century after work was begun. Each base consisted of a convex torus above a cylindrical spira, both fluted horizontally (fig. 54).[10] The roof was tiled using the Corinthian system, and the entablature was apparently of wood. According to the ancient tradition, the architects were Rhoikos and Theodoros.[11]

A date in the second quarter of the sixth century B.C. seems indicated: Buschor once considered c. 560–550 B.C.,[12] although he has pointed out more recently that a slightly earlier date is possible if Samos is to be regarded as the fore-runner of other Ionic buildings;[13] Dinsmoor preferred c. 575 B.C.;[14] Walter has suggested about 570 B.C.;[15] Berve and Gruben have proposed c. 570–550 B.C.[16] The dating is based on stylistic analogies of a very general nature since really precise stratigraphic evidence is wanting, and the last view is about as close as is possible.

The second major architectural undertaking of the East Greeks in this generation, the temple of Artemis at Ephesos,[17] was also a dipteral building. It was built by Chersiphron and Metagenes of Knossos, while the same Theodoros who worked at Samos assisted with the foundations.[18] Very little remains of the original structure, but a fourth-century B.C. rebuilding used the same (or at least a similar) ground plan, and this furnishes additional information.

The temple has several traits in common with the Samian one it was apparently designed to rival. There were two steps to the platform, which was built as a solid podium, a stylobate 55.10 x 115.14 m. in size. The columns were perhaps set back from the edge as in the Samian structure; they were of marble, while the walls were of limestone, faced with marble. The front (on the west, following earlier practice at the site) used eight columns with the widest intercolumniation at the center. From twenty to twenty-four columns have been proposed for the flanks, and both eight and nine have been suggested for the rear.[19] The plan has been recon-

---

[9] For computations, see *Architecture of Ancient Greece*, 125.

[10] The bases varied slightly in their diameters, perhaps in accordance with variations in the intercolumniation, or perhaps simply because of individual differences in the workmanship. See H. Johannes, "Die Säulenbasen vom Heratempel des Rhoikos," *AthMitt* 62 (1937) 13–37.

[11] Hdt., 3. 60; Paus., 7. 5. 4; Plin., *HN*, 34. 83; 36. 90; Vitr., 7, *praef.* 12.

[12] Buschor (supra n. 8) 50ff.

[13] E. Buschor, "Altsamischer Bauschmuck," *AthMitt* 72 (1957) 4.

[14] *Architecture of Ancient Greece*, 124.

[15] Walter (supra n. 8) 57.

[16] Berve and Gruben (supra n. 5) 451. See also G. Gruben, *Die Tempel der Griechen* (Munich, 1966) 321ff.

[17] The British excavations of the Archaic temple were published by D. G. Hogarth, *Excavations at Ephesus: the Archaic Artemisia* (London, 1908). Additional bibliography is listed by Dinsmoor, *Greek Architecture*, 311. For more recent bibliography, including the Austrian excavations, see E. Akurgal, *Ancient Civilizations and Ruins of Turkey* (Istanbul, 1970) 362. See also E. Bammer, "Beobachtungen zur ephesischen Architektur," *AA* (1972) 440ff.

[18] Vitr., 3. 2. 7; 7. *praef.* 12; 10. 2. 11–12; Plin., *HN*, 36. 95–97.

[19] The scholarship is reviewed by Dinsmoor, *Architecture of Ancient Greece*, 128, who concludes that twenty-one and nine are the most likely estimates. More recently see Gruben (supra n. 16) 329ff.

structed both with and without an opisthodomos, as dipteral with an extra row of columns at the front, as dipteral on the front and flanks with only a single row of columns at the rear, and as dipteral on the flanks and tripteral on the front and rear.[20] We do not know whether or not supports were required in the cella, which may have been open to the sky. One of the few points about the plan that is agreed upon is the presence of a pronaos, which suggests a strong emphasis on frontality, with columns massed at the front of the building. The practice (which also occurs at Samos) has occasionally been compared with the Egyptian treatment of hypostyle halls where a use of monumental entrances had a long history.

The bases at Ephesos (fig. 55) consisted of large horizontally fluted tori set upon discs with two wide flutes (scotiae) separated by double moldings. A similar design occurs on an Assyrian sphinx base from the reign of Esarhaddon,[21] and a Near Eastern connection for this detail has occasionally been suggested.[22] A relation with Samos seems more likely since the Assyrian base is rectangular rather than cylindrical. At Ephesos the bases were set upon square plinths (a practice which also has Near Eastern predecessors),[23] and in a few instances sculpted drums were placed above them. The carving of the bases varied considerably from piece to piece, and in a few cases the tori were carved with leaves.

Like the bases, the shafts and capitals admitted more than a single variety (fig. 56). Shafts could follow schemes with either forty or forty-four flutes or a design with forty-eight alternating narrow and wide flutes (all with sharp arrises). Capitals were of two types, one using Ionic volutes with convex whorls and small eyes, the second substituting rosettes for the whorls. Both used a single molding to delineate the details. The echinus had an egg-and-dart, while below it was a bead decoration carved on the upper drum of the shaft. An additional molding with egg-and-dart (or sometimes a heart-and-dart) decorated the edges of the very long abaci. At the sides of the capitals were deep scotiae divided by double moldings. Neckings with lotus-and-palmette decorations also survive, most likely from the columns on the front (used along with the sculpted bases and rosette capitals?).

Little survives of the entablature. Most writers have supposed it was of marble,[24] which agrees with the tradition preserved in Vitruvius[25] and Pliny,[26] probably based on a monograph about the temple written by its architects. There are no fragments from the architrave. Pieces of a large egg-and-dart survive, and there was also a marble sima carved in low relief, executed many years after work had begun. Other details must be conjectured.

The date of the temple is usually given as 560–550 B.C. As both the literary tradition[27] and inscriptions on the sculpted column drums indicate, part of the cost was underwritten by Croesus of Lydia, who reigned from about 560–546 B.C. This should provide a good date for portions of the building, but work must have progressed rather slowly. The fifth-century B.C. style of figures on the marble sima and on some of the sculpted column drums[28] must be regarded as a note of severe caution.

The Archaic temple at Didyma may be as-

[20] For a résumé of the scholarship, see Akurgal (supra n. 17) 149.

[21] R. D. Barnett, and M. Falkner, *The Sculptures of Assur-Nasir-apali II (883–859 B.C.), Tiglath-Pileser III, Esarhaddon (681–669 B.C.)* (London, 1962) 23, pls. 110–111.

[22] E. Akurgal, *The Art of Greece: Its Origins in the Mediterranean and Near East* (New York, 1968) 222, trans. from *Orient und Okzident: Die Geburt der griechischen Kunst* (Baden-Baden,

1966).

[23] See above, chapter VI, note 16.

[24] *Architecture of Ancient Greece*, 131.

[25] 10. 2. 11.

[26] *HN*, 36. 96.

[27] Hdt., 1. 92.

[28] G. Lippold, "Die griechische Plastik," in *Handbuch der Archäologie* (5. Lieferung, Munich, 1950) 60.

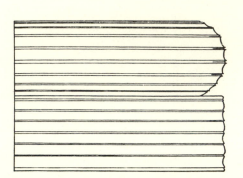

Fig. 54. Column base from the temple of Hera at Samos, dating from just before the middle of the sixth century B.C., composed of a horizontally fluted torus above a spira. After C. Nylander, *Ionians in Pasargadae* (1970) fig. 37a.

Fig. 55. Column base from the temple of Artemis at Ephesos, begun during the reign of Croesus of Lydia. After C. Nylander, *Ionians in Pasargadae* (1970) fig. 37c.

signed to the same generation as its cousins from Samos and Ephesos,[29] though most writers have dated it slightly after the middle of the century.[30] It was evidently a dipteral building left open to the sky in the interior, as perhaps was the case at Ephesos. Nothing survives of the eastern doorway, but there was surely a pronaos with no back room. Details of the individual elements betray a strong debt to Ephesos; the bases were closely copied from the Ephesian design, and reliefs were added to the lower parts of the shafts.

Additional evidence for the Ionic style is furnished by the temple of Apollo at the Greek colony of Naukratis in Egypt,[31] although the building itself does not survive. As reconstructed

by its excavator Sir Flinders Petrie, the limestone columns had several individualistic traits (fig. 57). Their bases consisted of horizontally fluted tori above cylinders with flutes and moldings somewhat like the ones from Samos. Above each base Petrie restored two smooth truncated cones, giving considerable diminution (in two steps) below the shaft. These are without parallel, and their correctness has occasionally been questioned.[32] Arrises were sharp, as was usual in the period,[33] and there were twenty-five shallow flutes. At the top, some shafts ended in a large astragal carved with a bead-and-reel, while others placed a necking band carved with lotus patterns (fig. 58) between the top of the fluting and a plain molding.

[29] H. Knackfuss, in T. Wiegand, *Didyma I: Die Baubeschreibung* (Berlin, 1941) 121ff.

[30] See Berve and Gruben (supra n. 6) 463ff., and Gruben (supra n. 16) 340, each with an excellent summary of the remains, and with additional bibliography.

[31] W. M. F. Petrie, *Naukratis* (London, 1886–1888); E. Gjerstad, "Studies in Archaic Greek

Chronology I, Naucratis," *Annals of Archaeology and Anthropology* 21 (1934) 67ff.

[32] Boardman (supra n. 3) 203.

[33] For the fluting of contemporary Ionic votive columns, see P. Amandry, *La Colonne des Naxiens et le Portique des Athéniens* (*Fouilles de Delphes* II, Paris, 1953) 8; D. White, "The Cyrene Sphinx, its Capital and its Column," *AJA* 75 (1971) 53.

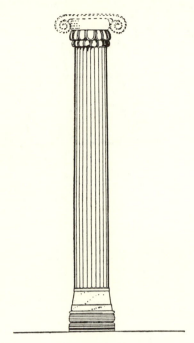

Fig. 56. Reconstructed columns from the temple of Artemis at Ephesos, begun during the reign of Croesus (c. 560–546 B.C.). After D. Hogarth, *Excavations at Ephesus* (1908) pl. 15.

Fig. 57. Column from the temple of Apollo at Naukratis, in Egypt, as reconstructed by W. M. Flinders Petrie. The blocks placed above the base and below the volute element are surely not correct. After W. M. F. Petrie, *Naukratis* I (1886) pl. 3.

Although one fragment of a capital was found, it was smashed by the local villagers before it could be photographed. The published sketch (presumably from memory) indicates a design without eyes reminiscent of several Ionic votive capitals from about this time.[34] The echinus was carved from a separate block,[35] so that the volutes were not joined to its sides. This is a char-

acteristic of Aeolic rather than Ionic columns, and Boardman has pointed out we are "at liberty to speculate whether it was not from an Aeolic capital."[36] A theoretical member, supposed by Petrie to have lain between the echinus and the volutes, has been discounted.[37]

The date at Naukratis is not completely certain. The early 560s B.C. have been proposed,[38]

[34] For a discussion of the problem of eyes in capitals see G. Gruben, "Das archaische Didymaion," *JdI* 78 (1963) 174.

[35] A similar situation exists in the capitals from the temple at Samos usually assigned to the time of Polykrates.

[36] Boardman (supra n. 3) 203 n. 3.

[37] *Problème des ordres*, 127.

[38] *Architecture of Ancient Greece*, 125; the stratigraphy allows some latitude either way. See Gjerstad (supra n. 31).

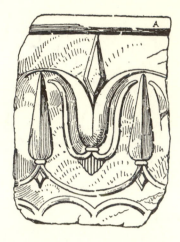

Fig. 58. Necking from the upper part of the shaft of one of the columns of the temple of Apollo at Naukratis. After W. M. F. Petrie, *Naukratis* 1 (1886) pl. 3.

coinciding with the reign of Amasis II,[39] but the building need not have been erected at the very beginning of the reign. Since the bases cannot be very far removed in date from those of Samos, and since the moldings seem very Archaic, a date before the middle of the century is surely indicated.

From about the same time or even slightly earlier is the oikos of the Naxians at Delos,[40] a closed room with a central "spine" of columns supported on simple cylindrical bases. The exact purpose of the oikos is unknown. Small fragments of volutes show its roof was supported by Ionic columns, but since it was not a temple, its style may not have conformed to the tradition used for more monumental buildings.

The fragmentary evidence from other quarters does not seriously contradict our picture of early Ionic architecture derived from these sources, and we thus have a fairly coherent if fragmentary picture of the early stages of the

[39] *Hdt.*, 2. 178.
[40] H. Gallet de Santerre, *Délos primitive et archaique* (Paris, 1958) *passim*, dated the structure

Ionic order. It would seem that influential buildings like those at Ephesos and Samos were already setting norms for the style. A pronaos was used before the cella at both Samos and Ephesos, and the latter may have used an opisthodomos or an adyton as well. Ionic moldings with egg-and-dart and other Greek designs were becoming firmly established. More than a single column type was used occasionally, but a consensus was emerging in regard to capitals, bases, and other details. Volute capitals were appearing on a regular basis, with fluted as opposed to smooth shafts. There was an emphasis on elegant surface decoration, especially with moldings and carved floral designs. The design and placement of the fictile revetments was also becoming regularized. Peristyles were usual, with columns often massed at the front of the building to create an impressive entrance way. A few important later characteristics, like the Classical system of fluting the Ionic columns, had not yet appeared; others, like dentils and fasciae, must be conjectured by analogies with other structures. The construction techniques made use of finely joined blocks (where evidence is extant), on much better foundations than at the early Neandrian or Larisan temples.

Many details set the style at Neandria and the other Aeolic sites apart from the temples at Ephesos, Samos, Didyma, and elsewhere. Except at Old Smyrna, the northern columns were not fluted. Aeolic bases never conformed to the usual Ionic designs, although the bases in the Old Palace at Larisa are probably derived from the Ionic pattern, and the final form of the Aeolic base (from Klopedi, fig. 59) is completely independent of Ionic influence. The moldings, the sima, and the other Aeolic architectural details were made exclusively in terracotta, and costly materials were seldom used. Fewer carved moldings and floral motifs were employed, and surfaces were often left smooth where an Ionic architect would employ rich surface elaboration. The massing of columns at the front was never

to c. 600 B.C. (p. 293). Berve and Gruben (supra n. 5) 364, prefer c. 570 B.C., while Martin (supra n. 3) has suggested the middle of the century.

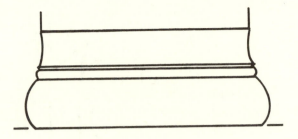

Fig. 59. Base from the Aeolic temple at Klopedi.

attempted at the northern sites, and in the examples where evidence survives, the altar was placed behind the building (*i.e.* a denial of emphasis on frontality in favor of an overall view). Yet perhaps the greatest difference between the Aeolic and the Ionic temples lies in their ground plans. As can be seen from the early temple at Larisa (fig. 37), one of the traditional temple plans in Aeolis was that of the single rectangular room without porch or peristyle, a very simple design which must have been invented independently at many points in history. In Ionia, by the time of the temples at Samos and Ephesos, this plan had been modified and made more complex by the addition of a pronaos, a peristyle, and perhaps other features as well. While the peristyle was added in Aeolis, the pronaos and adyton or opisthodomos were not. Complex plans (as in the early temple at Klopedi, fig. 39) were not to become the rule in Archaic Aeolis, and the later temple at Klopedi (fig. 40), like its predecessors from Neandria (fig. 31) and Larisa (figs. 37–38), was a simple, rectangular room without front or back porch.

There is a difference, too, in the degree of informality. While still conforming to the broad tenets of the style, each Aeolic structure was a highly individualistic monument. Freedom from the restraints of a tight canon was even extended to the design of specific elements, and Aeolic details (such as capitals or bases) admitted far more variation within a single building than was usual in Ionic architecture. Construction techniques were so informal that buildings like the one at Neandria have occasionally been considered to be rather poorly built.

These differences must have produced entirely different moods in Aeolic and Ionic temples. The magnificent grandeur of the huge buildings at Ephesos and Samos would surely have awed the casual visitor. Their giant columns, massed at the front in an impressive echo of the Egyptian hypostyle halls that might have amazed the earliest East Greek colonists of Naukratis, were surely a wonder to behold. Finely carved floral and figural decorations, fluted columns and bases, and elegant moldings and revetments would have created a dazzling display of light and shadow, subtly changing the visual impact of heavy marble and transforming it into a rich tapestry of surface decoration that was both elegant and grandiose. Aeolic temples, on the other hand, placed little emphasis on monumental dimensions. Their more modest size and their smooth moldings and unfluted columns advocated a greater dignity and simplicity. Architectural members were carefully set off from each other, producing a clear differentiation between each component part. Floral ornament was used selectively to emphasize particular portions and complement the remaining surfaces. The slender columns and organic capitals must have created the same lightness associated with the Ionic style, but the Aeolic tradition was more modest, with a clarity of parts that was uniquely its own.

Still, there are also many points of similarity between the two styles. The use of the peristyle, the stonecarving techniques, and the design of some of the elements are often closely related. Common traditions existed for moldings, terracotta revetments, and other decorative ornaments. While some similarities (like the exterior altar or the need for a cella) may be ascribed to similar cult practices, most of the parallels can be explained only on the basis of a close relationship between the styles and techniques of the architecture itself. The similarities between Ionic and Aeolic buildings seem especially close when the two East Greek styles are compared with the Doric style where baseless circular columns support a complex stone entablature quite unrelated to East Greek traditions. Since the Near Eastern connections for the Ionic style (as for the Aeolic) exist only in an occasional detail taken out of its oriental context, the similarities in the East Greek architectural styles cannot be explained by proposing a common eastern origin. The relationship can have developed only in Greece itself. The two orders must have inherited many of their characteristics from the immediately preceding orientalizing period, when the Greeks first began using two-sided volute capitals with articulated columns to create exterior colonnades for their buildings. Other features, like the terracotta revetments, were joined to the style at a later stage, according to some authors perhaps well into the sixth century B.C.[41]

The two styles had evidently already taken different directions by the second quarter of the sixth century. The best known examples of the Aeolic style seem to represent an independent Archaic development, mostly distinct from the Ionic order. The votives from the Athenian Akropolis, once thought to be "intermediate steps" in a stylistic progression from vertical to horizontal volutes, are now known to be relatively late in the Aeolic series. Even the temple at Neandria cannot be regarded as the inspiration for Ionic buildings, though it may offer some information about those sources because of its conservatism which preserved earlier practice.

The style that preceded the sixth-century Aeolic and Ionic orders must be examined chiefly in the unfinished temple at Old Smyrna. Here was an impressive stone building set upon a massive podium. Fluted columns with sharp arrises supported capitals with vertical volutes whose whorls had no eyes. The ornate capitals, elaborated with additional floral decoration, were arranged in an exterior peristyle. Many of the Greek techniques and practices were already established along the lines they would later follow, but some sixth-century features, like bases and moldings, had not yet appeared.

The best theory to explain the available facts would seem to be that the Aeolic and Ionic styles of the sixth century B.C. represent contemporary artistic developments. They must have developed from the building styles of the previous century, and the long Near Eastern tradition of capitals with paired volutes was surely the antecedent of both systems. Combining this earlier inspiration with a measure of native Greek influence, the Hellenic architects created the Archaic East Greek orders.

Apparently the Ionic and Aeolic floral decorations—palmettes, volutes, rosettes, and foliate ornaments of various types—were first applied to Greek buildings in the orientalizing period which reached its climax in the seventh century B.C. The designs first appeared in the same organic way they were used in the Near East where they had been developed for carpentry, metalwork, and other decorative arts.

The Aeolic temple of Athena at Old Smyrna makes almost no modification in the designs to suit the structural requirements of the building itself. It was only later, over a period of many years, that adjustments were made to conform to the needs of monumental architecture. These adjustments were present in both orders, but the Aeolic system retained much more of the organic plasticity that had characterized its antecedents.

The theory that earlier capitals with vertical volutes led to both Archaic East Greek orders seems to be supported by some details of the columns themselves. At Naukratis, as in the Samian temple from the time of Polykrates, the echinus was distinct from the overhanging volutes; the conception of the echinus as a separate member also occurs in Ionic votive columns, as in the early sphinx capital from Aigina. The idea may go back to Aeolic practice where it can be traced in stone examples from as early as the mid-seventh century B.C.[42] An inward curve to the top of the echinus, present

---

[41] On this, see Å. Åkerström, *Die architektonischen Terrakotten Kleinasiens* (Lund, 1966) *passim.*

[42] I.e. the balusters from Ramat Raḥel.

at Samos and Ephesos but abandoned in later Ionic capitals, also seems to recall the Aeolic leaf drum. A change from vertical to horizontal volutes may be partially explained by a simple stylistic development which compressed the capital, but structural considerations must also be examined. One of the problems of the volute capitals was the small size of their upper surfaces. Moabite and southern Palestinian stonemasons had experimented with a rectangular abacus at an early date (see chap. II), but the feature does not appear in the architectural capitals of the Aeolians. The size of the upper surface is undoubtedly related to the weight of the superstructure, presenting an acute problem only in the north Aegean when the builders had to contend with the increased weight of stone construction—in fact, this may be one reason why the superstructures of Aeolic buildings were built of wood throughout their history. The horizontal volutes of Ionic capitals may represent one way of dealing with the problem since the earliest known Ionic buildings are heavy stone structures. If one accepts the reconstructions with girdles of leaves beneath the Aeolic capitals, the leaf drum can easily be regarded as the ancestor of the Ionic echinus. The increased weight of stone entablatures and tile roofs (or of heavy sculpture with a wide base if one regards the Ionic votive columns as the originators of the style)[43] could have suggested the spreading of the volutes, with a concomitant flattening of the capital that brought the lower block up under the whorls. This produces a much larger supporting area for the upper elements.

The horizontal form of simple wooden block capitals may also have influenced the stylistic development. Rectangular blocks (fig. 60) have surely been used in all periods as a useful transition between upright posts and their horizontal supported members. Besides transferring the weight satisfactorily, they allow minor irregularities to be adjusted in small, easily managed

boards instead of in the larger architectural elements. The retention of such a scheme of construction could have suggested the horizontal format of the Ionic capital; its practicality would certainly have contributed to the triumph of horizontal over vertical formats. By the end of the Archaic period, even the Aeolic capital had become horizontal, and the two styles had converged considerably in their schemes of construction.

A few of the architectural relations must imply a knowledge of contemporary building styles by both Aeolic and Ionic architects. Thus the bases in the Old Palace at Larisa may be simplifications of Ionic bases like those at Samos, and common artistic traditions can be traced in ornaments like the egg-and-dart or the bead-and-reel. The temple at Klopedi, the last major monument of Aeolic architecture, shows such a thorough knowledge of late Archaic trends in sizes, proportions, and the design of its individual parts, that it can only reflect a familiarity with Ionic architecture. On the other hand, the continuous frieze occurs only sporadically in architecture before its emergence as a dominant element in Aeolic buildings in the third quarter of the sixth century B.C.[44] Its incorporation into the Ionic system comes later, and an Aeolic use could be partly responsible for the tradition.

Aeolic influence could also be present in two groups of Ionic votive capitals from the mid-sixth century B.C. The two series have been discussed by Roland Martin, who has noted that the first group (known from Delos, Paros, Naxos, and Thasos) employs a large projecting echinus that is not completely integrated with the capital's design.[45] The second series, noted from the central and northeast Aegean but with ties in the west as well, is characterized by, among other things, proportions so short they allow only two or three eggs in the echinus. Both series lack the abacus, already well formed at both Ephesos and Didyma. It is possible that the Aeolic capital with its separate leaf drum,

43 See above, note 4.

44 For the Ionic frieze, see R. Demangel, *La Frise ionique* (Paris, 1932). A good recent discussion is

by B. S. Ridgway, "Notes on the Development of the Greek Frieze," *Hesperia* 35 (1966) 188ff.

45 Martin (supra, n. 3) 303–325.

Fig. 60. A block capital, a simple rectangle used between shaft and architrave in wooden construction.

high proportions, and simple upper surface, exerted a measure of influence on these votives from the Aegean. It is surely noteworthy that Delos, Paros, and Thasos, as well as the nearby coast of Asia Minor, have all yielded traces of Aeolic monuments.

Many details confirm the depth of the interchange of architectural knowledge throughout East Greece. Both the Aeolic and the Ionic styles were known outside their own areas, and by the time of the Persian wars, the Ionic order had emerged as the dominant East Greek fashion.

The decline of the Aeolic tradition at the end of the Archaic period raises several questions. That it did not end completely in Greek areas is shown by several pieces of evidence, including the Athenian vases (app. B) and an occasional relief from as late as the Roman period.[46] In temple building, however, the Aeolic order ceased to play any role of importance. The later representations in the minor arts are most likely derived from the wooden supports for houses.

As with any complex stylistic problem, several factors must have contributed to the eventual dominance of the Ionic style. Structurally, there

is no reason to suppose that the final Archaic stages of the Aeolic usage were not as well suited to the resolution of the problems presented by Classical buildings as were their Ionic counterparts. Yet the broad weight-bearing surface was slow to develop in Aeolic capitals, and the priority of the Ionic solution was bound to make it influential. Political dominance must also have played a role, and even Herodotos noted that the Aeolians seemed to follow the political lead of their southern neighbors.[47] Economically, the Ionian cities could afford to erect far larger and more costly structures. They could employ the best architects of their day, men capable of producing work that would command the attention of all Greece. The small, conservative Aeolic buildings must have seemed pale in contrast with the magnificent monuments at Ephesos and Samos. In the light of all these considerations, it comes as little surprise that even Aeolic cities were using the Ionic order by the beginning of the fifth century B.C.[48]

But did the Aeolic style in fact decline, or did it simply evolve into something else? Antonia Ciasca has raised some interesting questions about the origins of the Corinthian order.[49] Noting that it first appears at Bassai as an isolated column occupying the position usually held by the cult image, she has compared its symbolism with that of the many isolated Aeolic columns that graced the sacred precincts at Athens and elsewhere.[50] The columns with vertical volutes may have never completely lost the symbolic character relating them to palms, which they had had from their earliest days, and palms were often associated with the god Apollo. Even if there were three Corinthian capitals at Bassai, as is now thought, the symbolism remains germane.

In many ways, the Corinthian capitals seem like Aeolic members that have been embellished

[46] For example the funerary stele of Ioulios Plocamos, Archaeological Museum, Istanbul, no. 237, from the first century B.C./A.D.

[47] Hdt., 1. 151.

[48] For the redating of the earliest Ionic buildings at Larisa to the fifth century B.C., consult Board-

man (supra n. 3) 209.

[49] Capitello Eolico, 22.

[50] On the symbolism, see A. Wotschitzky, "Um die Entstehung des korinthischen Baustils," JOAI 38 (1950) 122 and 131.

with additional decorations and given a circular form. Their context remained the Ionic system throughout their history, suggesting an East Greek tie that is easily explained if the Aeolic style served as their inspiration. We cannot know for certain if the small tendrils at the corners of the Corinthian capitals are attenuated Aeolic volutes, if their rows of acanthus leaves are related to the earlier leaf drums, or if the central palmette of the earliest capital (at Bassai) was influenced by the Aeolic palmette in this position, but the development is plausible, at least on a morphological level. If true, it suggests the Aeolic style did not end abruptly with the close of the Archaic era. After a generation of only limited usage, it may have reappeared to take a different direction as the inspiration for an entirely new style of Greek architecture.

Catalogue

This listing is not intended as a complete *catalogue raisonné* but as a compendium of the Palestinian, Carian, and Greek monuments discussed in this study, presented in tabular form for easy reference, with brief descriptions and selected bibliography. For the Palestinian capitals the reader is also referred to the forthcoming corpus being prepared by Yigal Shiloh which will include additional information on these pieces. The order of the catalogue follows the chapters in this work. Votive monuments and small pottery objects are included, but forms from furniture, small bronzes, and other objects which are not suggestive of an architectural context are not included. For window balustrades and the "Woman at the Window" motif, see appendix A. For Athenian vases, see appendix B. For vases from the northeast Aegean, see appendix C. Sizes are given height by width by thickness unless noted otherwise.

PALESTINE

Hazor

Pls. 4–6

1. Two capitals for pillars, of limestone, one bifacial and the other carved on the front only. Volutes have single turn, with small eyes; petals at upper and lower corners; marginal borders delineate details; small design (not palmette) between volutes; no triangle. In Israel Department of Antiquities, Jerusalem, on display in Israel Museum. Dimensions: bifacial capital: 0.58 x 1.60 x 0.52 m.; other capital: 0.62 x 1.60 x 0.69 m.

Y. Yadin, "Excavations at Hazor, 1958," *IEJ* 9 (1959) 79; "The Fourth Season of Excavations at Hazor," *BA* 22 (1959) 10ff.; *Hazor* III–IV, pls. 48 nos. 1 and 3–4, 49 nos. 1–3, 362, and 363; *Hazor* (London, 1972) pl. 28b; *Capitello Eolico*, 16, pl. 2 no. 1; *Kapitelle und Basen*, figs. 127–128.

Megiddo

Pl. 8 and Figs. 5–6

2. Two capitals for pillars, of limestone, one carved on the front only, the other smooth on both faces; both carved on sides. Volutes flanking triangle have one turn and terminate in eyes; petals at upper and lower corners; marginal borders delineate details. Israel Department of Antiquities, Jerusalem, nos. M 5339 (smooth capital) and M 5340 (carved capital). Dimensions: carved capital (M 5340) 0.57 x 2.44 x 0.57 m.; smooth capital (M 5339) 0.57 x 2.39 x 0.56 m.

Megiddo I, 14–15 and fig. 17; *MRMC*, pl. 11; H. Th. Bossert, *Altsyrien* (Tübingen, 1951) fig.

1013; D. Ussishkin, "On the Original Position of Two Proto-Ionic Capitals at Megiddo," *IEJ* 20 (1970) 213ff.; *Kapitelle und Basen*, figs. 118–120; D. Ussishkin, "King Solomon's Palaces," *BA* 36 (1973) 94ff.

Pls. 9–12

3. Series of ten capitals for pillars and pilasters, of limestone, three carved on both faces, the others carved on the front only. Volutes with single turn and small eyes rise from triangle; petals at upper and lower corners; marginal borders delineate details. Bifacial capitals: Israel Department of Antiquities, Jerusalem, no. 36.2189 and another; the Megiddo Museum. Capitals carved on one face: Israel Department of Antiquities, no. 36.2187 and others; G. Schumacher, *Tell el-Mutesellim*, fig. 178; Oriental Institute, Chicago, no. 3657; the Megiddo Museum. Dimensions: bifacial capitals: 0.44 x 1.03 x 0.43 m. (Israel Department of Antiquities, no. 36.2189); 0.60 x 1.10 x 0.28 m. (Megiddo Museum). Capitals carved on one face: 0.40 x 0.95 x 0.30 m. (*Tell el-Mutesellim*, fig. 178); 0.435 x 1.025 x 0.46 m. (Oriental Institute, Chicago, no. 3657); 0.44 x 1.14 x 0.48 m. (Israel Department of Antiquities, no. 36.2187); 0.50 x 1.50 x 0.50 m. (reconstructed) (Megiddo Museum).

G. Schumacher, *Tell el-Mutesellim* (Leipzig, 1908) fig. 178; *Megiddo* I, 55–56, fig. 67; *MRMC*, pl. 10; H. Th. Bossert, *Altsyrien* (Tübingen, 1951) fig. 1012; D. Ussishkin, "On the Original Position of Two Proto-Ionic Capitals at Megiddo," *IEJ* 20 (1970) 213ff.; *Capitello Eolico*, 16, pl. 1 no. 2; *Kapitelle und Basen*, figs. 116–117. Shiloh, *BASOR* 222 (1976) 67ff.

Pl. 13

4. Fragments of a pottery shrine. Clay, gray to yellowish, covered with a red wash. Vertical volutes occur at the corners, above vertically standing sphinxes; male figure stands at center of side wall; walls rise above molding at roof level; windows and small circular openings pierce walls; probably used as incense altar. Israel Department of Antiquities, Jerusalem, no. 1.4447 (Megiddo, no. 2986).

MRMC, 13ff. and pls. 13–14, with additional bibliography; H. Th. Bossert, *Altsyrien* (Tübingen, 1951) fig. 1015; R. Amiran, *Ancient Pottery of the Holy Land* (New Brunswick, 1970) photo 347.

5. Fragments of a pottery shrine, style similar to above. Columns or pilasters occur at corners; windows pierce sides; walls rise above roof level; moldings above and below roof level, on outside of walls; probably used as incense altar. Israel Department of Antiquities, Jerusalem, Megiddo, no. 2985.

MRMC, 17 and pl. 15.

Pl. 14 and Fig. 8

6. Fragment of a miniature limestone capital, carved on front and sides only. Volute has single turn and small eye, within a border. Painting on front: red petals and borders; blue background of volute. Solid red on top and bottom. Painting on the side includes small red, white and gray (originally black or blue?) squares between red and red-brown borders. Oriental Institute, Chicago. Preserved length 0.17 m.

Megiddo I, 55 n. 37; *Megiddo* II, pl. 270 no. 1; *Kapitelle und Basen*, fig. 115.

Samaria

Pl. 15

7. Series of capitals for pilasters, of limestone, carved on front and sides. Volutes with single turn and small eyes rise from triangle; petals at upper and lower corners; marginal borders delineate details. Israel Department of Antiquities, Jerusalem. Dimensions: 0.50 x 1.16 x 0.47 m.; 0.495 x 1.15 x 0.40 m.; 0.49 x 1.10 x 0.48 m. (*Samaria-Sebaste* I, 14–15); 0.53 x 1.08 x 0.44 m. (Israel Department of Antiquities, no. 36.2186); others fragmentary.

Samaria-Sebaste I, 14–15, figs. 6–7 and pl. 29; *Capitello Eolico*, 16, pl. 1 no. 1; *Kapitelle und Basen*, figs. 121–122.

8. Two capitals for pillars, of limestone, carved on sides only. Design as above, but larger. Israel

Department of Antiquities, Jerusalem. Dimensions: 0.65 x 2.50 x 0.45 m.; 0.65 x 1.40 x 0.67 m. (both reconstructed).

Samaria-Sebaste I, 14–15; Shiloh, *BASOR* 122 (1976) 67ff.

Shechem

Pl. 17

9. Fragment of a capital. Bottom of volutes and element between them extant; has no central triangle; volutes spring vertically, without marginal borders; appears to be from a free-standing column. Not fully published. Present whereabouts unknown.

E. Sellin, "Die Ausgrabung von Sichem," *Zeitschrift des Deutschen Palästina-Vereins* 49 (1926) 311, pl. 39B; G. Welter, "Stand der Ausgrabungen in Sichem," *AA* (1932) col. 313.

Unknown Site, said to be "in Transjordan"

Pl. 18

10. Pottery shrine, of coarse clay, brownish with a blue-gray core, with reddish-brown slip. Back rounded like a jug; front in the form of a portico with two columns with volute capitals arranged prostyle but partially engaged; roof flat, raised above level of ceiling; bird with spread wings below lintel. Israel Department of Antiquities, Jerusalem, no. 40.286. Ht. 0.235 m.

J. H. Iliffe, "A Model Shrine of Phoenician Style," *QDAP* 11 (1944) 99–100 and pl. 21; S. Yeivin, "Jachin and Boaz," *PEQ* 91 (1959) 9ff.

Jerusalem

Pl. 21

11. Capital for a pilaster, of limestone. Volutes with single turn and small eyes rise from triangle outlined by three moldings; marginal borders delineate details elsewhere; circles decorate flat areas between triangle and volutes; horizontal weight-bearing member is above whorls; petals occur at upper and lower corners. Israel Department of Antiquities, Jerusalem, on

display in Israel Museum. Dimensions: 0.61 x 1.24 x 0.43 m.

K. M. Kenyon, "Excavation at Jerusalem, 1962," *PEQ* 95 (1963) 16 and pl. VIII B; *Jerusalem; Excavating 3000 Years of History* (London, 1967) 59 and pl. 20; *Kapitelle und Basen*, 64 no. 5. J. Gray, *Near Eastern Mythology* (London, New York, Sydney, and Toronto, 1969) pl. on p. 135.

Ramat Raḥel

Pl. 22

12. Series of pilaster capitals, of limestone. Volutes with single turn and small eyes rise from triangle outlined by three moldings; single marginal borders delineate details elsewhere. Circles decorate flat areas between triangle and volutes; horizontal weight-bearing member is above whorls; petals occur at upper and lower corners. Israel Department of Antiquities, Jerusalem. Dimensions of best preserved example: 0.50 x 1.05 x 0.43 m. (Israel Department of Antiquities, no. 55.27).

Ramath Rahel 1954, 141ff., pls. 22B, 27B; "Excavations at Ramat Raḥel," *BA* 24 (1961) 103–104, fig. 6; *Ramat Raḥel 1959–60*, 14, 39, fig. 13, 2, pls. 11, 1 and 15, 2; *Capitello Eolico*, 16, pl. 1 no. 3; *Kapitelle und Basen*, figs. 123–125.

13. Single fragment of a capital for a pillar, of limestone. Bifacial; fragment too small to determine complete design, but appears to be like above series, but smaller. Israel Department of Antiquities, Jerusalem. Dimensions: 0.35 x c. 0.78 to 0.79 x 0.29 m.

Ramat Raḥel 1959–60, 14–15, fig. 13, 1 and pl. 11, 1.

14. Fragmentary frieze depicting Aeolic columns or balusters supporting an architrave. Each column has short shaft, large transitional element between shaft and capital, and large volute element; whorls rise from oval area (i.e. a volute in frontal view?) and support an abacus, with horizontal lintel extending above all columns. Israel Department of Antiquities, Jeru-

salem, no. 31. 345. Dimensions: 0.50 x 0.77 x 0.35 m.

B. Maisler, "Ramat Raḥel ve-Hirbet Tselaḥ (Giv'at Eliahu)," *Kovets* (Jerusalem, 1934) 14; M. Stekelis, "Me'arat Kevarim Yehudim be-Ramat-Raḥel," *Kovets* (Jerusalem, 1934) 27–29, fig. 3; M. Kon, "The Stone Capitals from Ramat Rahel," *Bulletin of the Jewish Palestine Exploration Society* 13 (1947) 83–86, fig. 3; Y. Aharoni, *Ramath Rahel 1954*, 104 n. 5; *Ramat Raḥel 1959–60*, 15 n. 45, 39.

Medeibîyeh

Pl. 25 and Fig. 12

15. Square citadel, c. 82 x 80 m. Square towers at the corners and rectangular towers in the center of the north and south sides; gates in the east and west sides. One limestone pilaster capital survives, probably from a doorjamb of the east gate; triangle outlined by double lines covers base of capital, with volutes rising from the sides of the triangle; circles occur in the background field, between the whorls and the triangle; volutes delineated by marginal borders have small eyes and single turn. Dimensions: 0.87 x 1.90 x 0.50 m.

C. M. Doughty, *Travels in Arabia Deserta* (Cambridge, 1888) 20, and drawing on p. 49; N. Glueck, "Further Explorations in Eastern Palestine," *BASOR* 51 (1933) 13 and fig. 2; "Explorations in Eastern Palestine I," *AASOR* 14 (1933–1934) 66ff. and pl. 11; "The Civilization of the Moabites," *AJA* 38 (1934) 216, fig. 5; H. Th. Bossert, *Altsyrien* (Tübingen, 1951) fig. 1014; *Kapitelle und Basen*, fig. 126.

THE HALIKARNASSOS PENINSULA

Alâzeytin

Pls. 29–31 and Figs. 15–17

16. Rectangular building (Building 30) consisting of two floors, not bonded together. Lower level has two vaulted rooms, interconnected. Upper floor is 11.9 x 6.4 m., with door in south end; built as single room, with Aeolic pilasters as doorjambs. Capitals have volutes rising from horizontal lines; palmette between eyed volutes on one capital; elaborate heart-shaped figure between volutes without eyes on other example; material is gray limestone. Capitals in Bodrum Museum, no. 2251 (capital with palmette) and no. 2252 (capital with heart-shaped figure). Dimensions: no. 2251: ht. 0.53 m.; width of resting surface 0.625 m.; thickness 0.25 m.; reconstructed width 1.365 m.; reconstructed width of upper surface 0.975 m.; no. 2252: ht. 0.53 m.; width of resting surface 0.625 m.; thickness 0.25 m.; reconstructed width 1.51 m.; reconstructed width of upper surface 1.055 m.

W. Radt, *Siedlungen und Bauten auf der Halbinsel von Halikarnassos* (*IstMitt*, Beiheft 3, Tübingen, 1970) 39ff., 237ff., figs. 1–5, 22–24, pls. 13–16, 39–41.

Pls. 32–35 and Figs. 18–19

17. Rectangular building (Building 31) consisting of two floors, not bonded together. Lower floor with two vaulted rooms, interconnected. Upper floor is rectangular room 9.45 x 4.25 m. with one open side; series of five steps within building, with third step forming one meter wide platform; roof probably supported on two Aeolic pillars between antae; lintel and ceiling beams of stone. Capitals have eyed volutes rising from bands placed level with the eyes, with three-petaled palmettes between them; capitals and shafts carved from one piece; material is gray limestone. Capitals in Bodrum Museum, nos. 3582 (complete example) and 3583 (fragment). Dimensions of best preserved capital (no. 3582): 0.53 x 0.98 x 0.195 to 0.200 m.; width of resting surface 0.503 m.; width of upper surface about 0.61 m.

W. R. Paton and J. L. Myres, "Karian Sites and Inscriptions," *JHS* 16 (1896) 199–200; W. Radt, *Siedlungen und Bauten auf der Halbinsel von Halikarnassos* (*IstMitt*, Beiheft 3, Tübingen, 1970) 55ff., 255ff., figs. 3–4, 6, 24 nos. 3–4, pls. 17, 41 nos. 3–5, and 42 nos. 1–2.

AEOLIS, NORTHERN IONIA, AND THE NORTH AEGEAN

Old Smyrna

Pl. 36 and Fig. 20

18. Temple of Athena, peripteral, perhaps 6 x 11 columns. Columns of tufa, with fluted shafts (32 flutes, sharp arrises); Aeolic capitals, with leaf drums between capitals and shafts; capitals have vertical volutes with floral ornament as eyes, five-petaled palmettes between volutes, and abacus at top of capital. Elements in Izmir Museum.

J. M. Cook, "Archaeology in Greece, 1951," *JHS* 72 (1952) 104–106; E. Akurgal, *Kunst Anatoliens*, 285, pl. 251; "The Early Period and the Golden Age of Ionia," *AJA* 66 (1962) pl. 101 fig. 22; *Ancient Civilizations and Ruins of Turkey* (Istanbul, 1970) 119–121; (1973) 119–121.

Neandria

Pl. 41 and Figs. 24–32

19. Temple, peripteral(?), perhaps 7 x 11 or 7 x 12 columns, 12.87 x 25.71 m. Columns of gray tufa. Seven columns as a central "spine" within the cella. Volute capitals have two and one-half turns to whorls, central eyes, and seven-petaled palmettes, with five petals forming the weight-bearing surface; channels are slightly convex; single leaf-decorated torus should probably be placed below each volute element. Architectural elements in Archaeological Museum, Istanbul. Dimensions of best preserved capital (no. 704, Mendel no. 275): ht. (volute element only) 0.60 m.; dia. of lower surface 0.40 m.; width (restored) c. 1.20 m. One smaller capital 0.95 m. wide.

J. T. Clarke, "A Proto-Ionic Capital from the Site of Neandreia," *AJA* 2 (1886) 1–20, 136–148; *Neandria*, 23ff.; *Catalogue*, 33ff., no. 275; J. Durm, *Die Baukunst der Griechen* (Leipzig, 1910) figs. 284, 7, and 285, A–B; L. Curtius, *Die antike Kunst* II (Potsdam, 1938) 127, fig. 167; *Äolische Kapitell*, 42ff.; *Architecture of Ancient Greece*, 61–62 and figs. 21–22; *Kunst Anatoliens*, 288; *Capitello Eolico*, pl. 6 no. 1; *Kapitelle und Basen*, figs. 158–164.

Larisa on the Hermos

Pls. 42, 44, and Fig. 34

20. Capital from a building or isolated column, of gray tufa. Whorls have two and one-half turns, without eyes; five-petaled palmette is between volutes; small additional volutes stemming from a heart-shaped nucleus with double-whorl design occur below volutes; upper surface roughly worked. Archaeological Museum, Istanbul, no. 1924 (Mendel no. 277). Dimensions: 0.68 x 1.30 x 0.393 m.; dia. of base 0.40 x 0.425 m.

Catalogue, 37ff., no. 277; L. Kjellberg, "Das äolische Kapitell von Larisa," *Corolla Archaeologica Principi Hereditario Regni Sueciae Gustavo Adolpho dedicata* (Lund, 1932) 238ff.; *Larisa* I, 142–143, pls. 19a, 29, and 40; *Äolische Kapitell*, 42ff., fig. 17; *Architecture of Ancient Greece*, pl. 18, below; *Capitello Eolico*, pl. 4 no. 1; *Kapitelle und Basen*, figs. 153–154.

Pls. 45–47 and Fig. 35

21. "Old Palace." Building includes portico with four (or three?) tufa columns with Aeolic capitals; portico flanked by square towers; two chambers behind portico. Reconstructed width, c. 23 m. Architectural elements in Archaeological Museum, Istanbul. Dimensions of best preserved capital (no. 1925, Mendel no. 278): ht. 0.56 m.; width 0.95 m. (as preserved); reconstructed width 1.22 m.; thickness 0.31 m.; dimensions at the base 0.385 m. (length) x 0.335 m. (thickness). Second capital (fragment, no. 1926, Mendel no. 279): ht. 0.45 m.; preserved length 0.425 m.; thickness 0.21 m.

Catalogue, 39–40, nos. 278–279; *Larisa* I, 84ff. and *passim*, pls. 19b, 22a, 30, 41 nos. 5 and 7. For capitals, see p. 123, nos. 2–3 and perhaps also no. 6, pl. 22c; *Äolische Kapitell*, 51; *Capitello Eolico*, 21, pl. 4 no. 2; *Kapitelle und Basen*, figs. 152, 155.

22. Small fragment of an unfinished Aeolic capital, of gray tufa. Not fully published. Archaeological Museum, Istanbul.

Larisa I, 123 no. 5; *Kapitelle und Basen*, 76 no. 5.

Pl. 48

23. Fragment of a small Aeolic capital, probably from a votive column, of yellowish tufa. Volute has slightly convex channels, outlined by marginal borders and a deep incision; eye is round. Archaeological Museum, Istanbul, no. 1926. Reconstructed width c. 0.65 m.; thickness 0.182 m.; dia. of eye 0.055 m.
Larisa I, 123 no. 4, pls. 22b, 41a, 4; *Kapitelle und Basen*, fig. 156.

24. Fragment of an Aeolic capital, known only from a photograph (excavated in 1902). Dimensions unknown.
Larisa I, 123 no. 6, pl. 22c; *Kapitelle und Basen*, fig. 157.

Pls. 39–40

25. Building model, fragmentary, of terracotta. Building is peripteral or prostyle, with one Aeolic-like capital extant; visible are upper part of doorway, architrave, gabled roof, and upper part of one column. Archaeological Museum, Istanbul, no. 72.4. Reconstructed width of model 0.23 m.; length not extant.
Äolische Kapitell, 43ff., figs. 19–20; *Kapitelle und Basen*, figs. 171–172.

26. Two miniature votive capitals, of brown clay. Incised details are somewhat schematized, with two and one-half turns to the whorls and horizontal lines below the volutes; traces of white slip remain. Archaeological Museum, Istanbul. Ht. 0.057 m. (*Larisa* III, pl. 10 no. 42); 0.047 m. (*Larisa* III, pl. 10 no. 43).
Larisa III, 48, pl. 10 nos. 42–43; *Capitello Eolico*, 21, pl. 5 no. 2; *Kapitelle und Basen*, fig. 173.

Klopedi

Pl. 49 and Figs. 40–42 and 59

27. Temple, peripteral, 8 x 17 columns, 16.25 x 37.50 m. Within cella was interior colonnade.

Aeolic capitals from peristyle have slightly convex whorls with two and one-half turns, large eyes (sunken), and palmette between volutes (which also forms weight-bearing surface); below volute element was element composed of two small moldings with a larger molding between them. Elements in Archaeological Museum, Mytilene, and at the site. Dimensions: 0.61 x 1.36 x 0.48 m. (capital found by Koldewey).
R. Koldewey, *Die antiken Baureste der Insel Lesbos* (Berlin, 1890) pls. 16–17; D. Evangelides, "12η Ἀρχαιολογικὴ Περιφέρεια 1) Ἀνασκαφαὶ ἐν Λέσβῳ," *Deltion, Parartema* (1924–1925) 41–44; "Ἀνασκαφαὶ ἐν Λέσβῳ," *Praktika* (1927) 57–59; "Ἀνασκαφὴ Κλοπεδῆς Λέσβου," *Praktika* (1928) 126–137; *Kapitelle und Basen*, figs. 166–169; D. Hatzi, "Εἰδήσεις ἐκ Λέσβου," *AAA* 5 (1972) 43ff.

Mytilene

Pl. 50

28. Capital, architectural, of limestone. Design as at Klopedi but with doubled marginal borders separated by groove and with eyes bored through the stone. Archaeological Museum, Istanbul, no. 985 (Mendel cat. no. 276). Dimensions: ht. 0.58 m.; length 1.26 m.; broken at back (restored thickness c. 0.40 m.); dia. of eye 0.105 m.; dia. of base 0.36 to 0.39 m.
Catalogue, 36–37 no. 276; *Äolische Kapitell*, 46, fig. 18; J. D. Condis, "Capitello eolico di Eresso," *ASAA*, new series, 8–10 (1946–1948) 29–30; *Kunst Anatoliens*, 290–291, fig. 255; *Capitello Eolico*, 21, pl. 6 no. 2; *Kapitelle und Basen*, fig. 165.

Eressos

Pl. 51 and Fig. 43

29. Capital, apparently architectural, of granite. Carved on the front and smooth on the back. Doubled slightly convex volutes with two and one-half turns and large eyes begin below level of whorls; area between volutes plain, for painted decoration(?). Archaeological Museum, Mytilene. Upper surface smooth; dowel hole in lower

surface. 0.33 x 0.555 x 0.26 m. Dia. of dowel hole 0.047 m., depth 0.025 m.

O. Walter, "Archäologische Funde in Griechenland von Frühjahr 1939 bis Frühjahr 1940. Inseln des Aigaion," *AA* (1940) col. 288; J. D. Condis, "Capitello eolico di Eresso," *ASAA* new series, 8–10 (1946–1948) 25ff.

Thasos

Pl. 37

30. Leaf drum from an Aeolic capital, of marble. Decorated in relief with leaf-and-dart. Archaeological Museum, Thasos, no. 1385. Ht. 0.215 m.; upper dia. 0.316 m.; lower dia. 0.22 m.; dowel hole in upper surface: dia. 0.065 m.; depth 0.045 m.

F. Salviat, "Chronique des fouilles en 1955, Thasos VI, Architecture," *BCH* 80 (1956) 421; Martin, *Problème des ordres*, 125, pl. 26 no. 3; *Kapitelle und Basen*, 135.

Delos

Fig. 45

31. Capital from a votive column, of marble. Vertical volutes with two and one-half turns and large eyes, with palmette between them; cylinder below decorated portion of capital, forming a neck. Archaeological Museum, Delos. 0.90 m. wide by 0.39 m. deep.

Histoire de l'art, VII, pl. 53 no. 1; J. Durm, *Die Baukunst der Griechen* (Leipzig, 1910) 302, fig. 279 no. 3; *Problème des ordres*, pl. 27 no. 5.

Paros

Fig. 46

32. Column used for statuary, of Parian marble. Cylindrical section acts as base; shaft diminishes with concave profile, supporting capital with two and one-quarter turns to the volutes and large eyes; echinus is between volutes; large abacus is at top of capital; back of capital is rough. Shallow dowel hole is in upper surface, with pour channel leading from back to cutting. Archaeological Museum, Paros, no. 737. Ht. 0.905 m.; width at base 0.495 m.; width across eyes 0.45 m.; abacus is 0.095 x 0.655 x 0.46 m.

A. Orlandos, "Πάρος," Τὸ Ἔργον τῆς Ἀρχαιολογικῆς Ἑταιρείας (1960) 178–179 and fig. 194; (1961) 192–193 and figs. 198–199; G. Daux, "Chronique des fouilles, 1960; Paros," *BCH* 85 (1961) 844 and fig. 14; "Chronique des fouilles, 1961; Paros," *BCH* 86 (1962) 858 and figs. 6–7; G. Gruben, "Naxos und Paros. Dritter vorläufiger Bericht über die Forschungskampagnen 1970 und 1971," *AA* (1972) 379 and fig. 37.

33. Capital from a votive column, of Parian marble. Volutes have two and one-half turns, with large eyes. Central palmette has five petals. Large echinus is between volutes. (Published only in a preliminary report as of this writing.)

G. Gruben, "Naxos und Paros. Dritter vorläufiger Bericht über die Forschungskampagnen 1970 und 1971," *AA* (1972) 379 and fig. 35.

ATTICA

Athens

Pl. 42 and Fig. 47

34. Fragment of a capital, from an isolated column for statuary, of poros. Found July 23, 1971, in well J 5:1 at the northwest corner of the Agora (level 10.80–11.20 m. in depth), in a context of the second half of the fourth century B.C. Volutes, delineated by doubled marginal borders with a groove between them, have three turns and a large eye, partially drilled. Traces of stucco remain. Cutting for statuary is in upper surface. Agora Museum, Athens, no. A 4273. Max. length of fragment 0.68 m. Restored dia. of eye c. 0.150 m.

35. Fragment of a capital from an isolated column for statuary, of poros. Found in the Kerameikos. Whorls, delineated by doubled marginal borders with groove between them, have two and one-half turns and terminate in large eyes; block is bifacial. Kerameikos Museum, Athens, no cat. number. Dimensions: ht. 0.29 m.; width (as preserved) 0.40 m.; thickness (as preserved) 0.35 m. at top to 0.33 m. at bottom.

K. Kübler, "Ausgrabungen im Kerameikos I,"

AA (1938) col. 605 and fig. 16; *Kapitelle und Basen*, fig. 170.

Pls. 53–55 and Fig. 48

36. Capital from an isolated column for statuary, of Parian marble. Found on the Akropolis. Incised volutes have two and one-half turns, with large flat eyes; no design extant between helices. Akropolis Museum, Athens, no. 3794. 0.18 x 0.28 x 0.14 m.

M. Meurer, *Vergleichende Formenlehre des Ornaments und der Pflanze* (Dresden, 1909) 502, pl. 8 no. 7; J. Durn, *Die Baukunst der Griechen* (Leipzig, 1910) fig. 284 no. 6; Raubitschek, *Technik und Form*, 164–165, fig. 23; M. Jacob-Felsch, *Die Entwicklung griechischer Statuenbasen und die Aufstellung der Statuen* (Waldsassen/Bayern, 1969) 34 n. 105.

Fig. 49

37. Capital from an isolated column for statuary, of bluish gray Hymettian marble. Found on the Akropolis. Painted Aeolic volutes on the front only; ovoid recess for plinth of statue in upper surface; circular cutting with central dowel hole in lower surface. Akropolis Museum, Athens, no. 10261. Dimensions: 0.20 x 0.33 x 0.24 m.

Raubitschek, *Technik und Form*, figs. 20–21.

Pls. 56–59

38. Capital from a small building or shrine, of Parian marble. Found on the Akropolis in the stratum from the Persian destructions. Front smoothed and painted; whorls rise from horizontal bands and have two and one-half turns, terminating in eyes; palmette has three petals; horizontal weight-bearing surface is above whorls, and small petals occur at upper corners only; back is not extant. Akropolis Museum, Athens, no. 9980. Dimensions: ht. 0.30 m.; width 0.50 m.; thickness (as preserved) 0.21 m.; dia. of shaft 0.25 m.

R. Borrmann, "Stelen für Weihgeschenke auf der Akropolis zu Athen," *JdI* 3 (1888) 275–276, fig. 16; S. B. P. Trowbridge, "Archaic Ionic Capitals Found on the Acropolis," *AJA* 4 (1888) 22ff.; R. Borrmann, "Altionische Kapitelle aus Athen," *Antike Denkmaeler* 1 (1888) 8 and pl. 18 no. 3; G. Kawerau, "Ionische Säule von der Akropolis zu Athen," *JdI* 22 (1907) 197ff., fig. 5; M. Meurer, *Vergleichende Formenlehre des Ornaments und der Pflanze* (Dresden, 1909) 492, pl. 2 no. 4; J. Durm, *Die Baukunst der Griechen* (Leipzig, 1910) fig. 284 no. 4; L. Curtius, *Die antike Kunst* II (Potsdam, 1938) fig. 155.

Sykaminon-Oropos

Pl. 67

39. Capital, from an isolated column for statuary. Found north of Athens at Sykaminon, near Oropos. Made of white marble; carved in low relief, with volutes that have two and one-quarter turns, without eyes; central palmette has eleven petals; large echinus with egg-and-dart is at center, below volutes; thin abacus is at top of block. National Museum, Athens, no. 4797. 0.34 x 0.89 x 0.32 to 0.33 m.

E. Bammer, "Beobachtungen zur ephesischen Architektur," *AA* (1972) 453.

Appendix A

SITES YIELDING AEOLIC BALUSTERS AND ILLUSTRATIONS OF BALUSTRADES WITH VOLUTE CAPITALS

Windows in which small columns support a railing across the lower part of the fenestration are illustrated by a number of ancient objects. The largest category consists of plaques of stone or ivory in which the window itself forms the main part of the design; often, but not always, a facing female head shows above the railing (pl. 23). While the precise origin of this motif is not known, several authors (see especially Barnett in *Nimrud Ivories*) have made a strong case for Phoenician connections on both literary and artistic evidence. The motif seems to have been most popular in the late eighth and seventh centuries B.C.

That the illustrations of the "Woman at the Window" (pl. 23) are religious symbols portraying temple prostitutes is a view held by most writers who have examined the motif in detail; some scholars have extended the symbolism to plaques where the woman's head does not appear, but this need not be true in all cases. It is possible that some of the Cypriot reliefs (see P. Dikaios, "The Excavations at Vounous-Bellapais in Cyprus, 1931–1932," *Archaeologia* 88 [1940] 122 n. 5) were used as windows in house tombs where an entirely different significance is likely. A few illustrations, such as those on the Assyrian reliefs, provide clear evidence for the architectural placement of the balustrades, leaving no doubt that they were actually used with windows.

The motif was evidently applied to both religious and secular buildings. One of the best examples of the context is shown in figure 11, a relief from the palace of Sennacherib at Nineveh (ancient Kuyunjik). Other variations are seen in the plaques of the "Woman at the Window," which seem to show a temple, while the carved and painted members from Ramat Raḥel evidently decorated a palace. In all cases the balusters were used similarly, forming a barrier across the lower parts of windows; the area above the railing was completely open. The details of the carving can be seen most clearly in the full-sized limestone balusters from Ramat Raḥel (pl. 26) where Aeolic capitals were set upon leaf drums, with small shafts below. On the art objects the number of balusters ranges from two to four. At Ramat Raḥel three balusters seemed to form the norm, though there was not enough evidence to be certain in all cases. Obviously the usual material was wood or wood with added metal or stucco; the style of the relief work, with its deep undercutting, is unlikely to have been developed for stone. In addition, the absence of weight on the railings made stone unnecessary structurally. Because of this situation, the stone pieces from Ramat Raḥel must have been a rare exception to the usual construction practices; one may not expect the future appearance of many new pieces in stone.

A relation between the Aeolic balusters and the East Greek architectural orders must at least be examined, though it is far from definite. The dating would be consistent since the balustrades were especially popular in the seventh century B.C. when the Aeolic order first appeared in East Greece. The artistic style also seems related, especially now that the earliest known Greek Aeolic columns (from Old Smyrna) have confirmed the presence of a leaf drum below the volute element at this period. Yet one must be cautious in matters of this nature, and there is clearly not enough evidence yet to permit a conclusion. Since the same areas that used the balustrades also had a tradition of monumental columned porticoes where the design of the columns is not known, perhaps the best conclusion to be drawn from the balusters is only a hope: they suggest where one might look for further evidence.

The balusters on the art objects in the following list are often rather ambiguous, and one cannot always be certain what design was intended. The examples from Ramat Raḥel clearly belong to the Aeolic style, and they have been used as a guide, but other designs must also have been employed occasionally. It is at least conceivable that some of the following representations were intended as palm capitals or leaf capitals.

PALESTINE

Ramat Raḥel:
Series of limestone columns with volute capitals for window balustrades. Y. Aharoni, *Ramat Raḥel 1961–62*, 56ff., fig. 38, and pl. 48.

Samaria:
Ivory plaques of the "Woman at the Window." J. W. Crowfoot *et al., Early Ivories from Samaria* (London, 1938) pl. 13 no. 2.

PHOENICIA

Umm el'Amad, Jordan:
Stone plaque. Perrot and Chipiez, *Histoire de l'art* III, fig. 80.

NORTH SYRIA

Arslan-Tash:
Ivory plaques of the "Woman at the Window." F. Thureau-Dangin *et al., Arslan-Tash* (Paris, 1931) 112ff. and *Atlas*, pls. 34–36 nos. 45–58.

ASSYRIA

Khorsabad:
Ivory plaques of the "Woman at the Window." G. Loud and C. B. Altman, *Khorsabad* II (Chicago, 1938) 96–97, nos. 29–37, pls. 51–52.

Nimrud:
Ivory plaques of the "Woman at the Window." M. E. L. Mallowan, *Nimrud and its Remains* (London, 1966) 522, 584, color plate V, pls. 429 and 555; Barnett, *Nimrud Ivories*, pl. 4.

Nineveh (Kuyunjik), Palace of Sennacherib:
Stone relief. Barnett, *Nimrud Ivories*, fig. 53.

———, Palace of Assurbanipal:
Stone relief. R. D. Barnett, *Assyrian Palace Reliefs* (London, n.d.) pl. 105; A. Parrot, *Nineveh and Babylon* (Paris, 1961) 52, fig. 60.

CYPRUS

Ialysos:
Ivory plaque. Barnett, *Nimrud Ivories*, fig. 55.

Kouklia (Old Paphos) and vicinity:
Stone plaques. H. Gesche, H. Beckedorf, and

F. G. Maier, "Ausgrabungen in Alt-Paphos," *AA* (1969) 388, fig. 1; F. G. Maier, "Excavations at Kouklia (Palaepaphos): Third Preliminary Report: Season 1968," *Report of the Department of Antiquities, Cyprus* (1969) pl. 2 no. 1; V. Karageorghis, "Chronique des fouilles et découvertes archéologiques à Chypre en 1969," *BCH* 94 (1970) 216 and fig. 55.

Kourion and vicinity:
Stone plaques. V. Karageorghis, "Chronique des fouilles et découvertes archéologiques à Chypre en 1969, 7. Episkopi, 'Curium House,'" *BCH* 94 (1970) 226ff., fig. 80a–b; P. Dikaios, "The Excavations at Vounous-Bellapais in Cyprus, 1931–32," *Archaeologia* 88 (1940) 122 n. 5 and pl. 43c.

Appendix B

ATHENIAN VASES ILLUSTRATING AEOLIC COLUMNS

The most complete study of Aeolic capitals on Greek vases is that of Philip Oliver-Smith ("Representations of Aeolic Capitals on Greek Vases before 400 B.C.," in *Essays in Memory of Karl Lehmann*, Locust Valley, 1964). Oliver-Smith discussed more than three dozen examples of Aeolic columns in architectural contexts, and although it has been possible to add several vases to his list, most of his conclusions still stand. Noting that similar Aeolic designs appear in the work of several different artists, and that these same vase painters often faithfully reproduced other details of life around them, he concluded that the painted columns were probably derived from contemporary architecture, particularly architecture in wood. Schematization, differences in the scale, and a general summarizing of the architectural motifs caused problems in the interpretation of the Aeolic designs, but he concluded that the presence of the style in Athens over several generations seems almost incontrovertible.

Architecture on vases was usually used to illumine the action of the main figures, or to set the scene where the action occurred. Most of the Aeolic structures do not appear to have been intended as monumental stone buildings but as houses or other minor constructions in perishable materials. This circumstance may explain the lack of a uniform style for proportions or details, since minor buildings surely did not use the more rigid canons set up for their monumental counterparts, but one must still be very cautious in deriving architectural conclusions from motifs in the minor arts. The present writer has a few reservations about the derivation of some of the painted representations since they may copy other paintings rather than actual buildings. One can never be certain where a reflection of actual building practices stops and artistic license begins, and it is possible that at least some of the vase painters used the elegant and highly decorative Aeolic column in preference to the more reserved Doric one for purely artistic reasons. That there were at least some Aeolic buildings in Athens, however, is surely correct, a fact which is now confirmed by the identification of an architectural Aeolic capital from the Athenian Akropolis (see discussion in chap. v).

Oliver-Smith found that the style was popular on the vases from the second half of the sixth century B.C. until the time of Perikles. New examples may now push the style back to the middle of the century in Athens (see the vase by the Heidelberg Painter, Taranto, Museo Nazionale, I. G. 4342), and it appears even earlier in East Greece (app. c, no. 6). Vases from other areas suggest a parallel development in other Greek cities (chap. vi, n. 27, and app. c). While an occasional vase has appeared which may imply a rare survival of the motif into much later times (Athens, Agora Museum, white-ground Panathenaic Amphora no. P 8522), the conclusion that Aeolic buildings were mostly superseded by Ionic ones during the second half of the fifth century B.C. still seems correct. During their main period, Aeolic capitals were used on the vases with many types of buildings: temples, shrines, palaces, houses, fountain houses, a palaestra, a portico, a stable or hippodrome, and the labyrinth of the Minotaur. They also supported statuary or stood alone, and they formed a part of couches and other articles of wood and metal. Some artists apparently had a special liking for the style, and a few painters—especially the Painter of Half-Palmettes and the Nikoxenos Painter—employed it on a regular basis. It is interesting to note that these two artists used the columns on some vase shapes but not on others, even though most of their contemporaries probably recognized no correlation between the vase shape and the presence or absence of architectural elements (with the exception, of course, of the panathenaic amphoras).

By far the most common context of the columns (when they are used with architecture) is the private dwelling. Even a single Aeolic column with a small fragment of entablature could suggest a domestic setting, and a pair of columns provided a good frame for a figural scene. It is likely that this follows the actual use of the style in Athens where volute capitals were surely used more for private homes than for public buildings.

In the minor arts, Aeolic capitals were given a variety of uses. Basins were often supported by columnlike stands, and it is worth noting that the same artists who used Aeolic capitals in their architectural scenes sometimes used the same design to support a laver (for example, the fragmentary pelike in Oxford by the Syriskos Painter, *ARV²*, p. 262 no. 31).

If we may believe the vases, the most common use of the Aeolic motif in the minor arts was as a decoration for furniture, especially the legs of couches (see pl. 71). These ornaments show the same artistic variations as their more monumen-

tal cousins, and they begin as early (shortly before the middle of the sixth century B.C.). A number of examples are discussed by Oliver-Smith, who concluded that the Aeolic motif was regarded as an especially suitable decoration for wooden construction; it was thus applied to both furniture and architecture. The fashion in furniture has been discussed previously, in chapter VI. Since the examples on furniture are peripheral to the main thrust of this study, they are omitted from this appendix.

The following list is arranged by vase painters, following the chronological order established by J. D. Beazley in *ABV* and *ARV²*. Isolated columns and columns supporting statuary or other objects and beings (like Athena's owl or the Sphinx) are included, but ornamental designs and examples of Aeolic or Aeolic-like capitals on grave stelai, couches, the supports of basins, decorative chariot fittings, and other works from the minor arts are excluded. Only Attic vases are listed, and the reader is referred to the text for examples from elsewhere. If the identification of the column as Aeolic is doubtful or uncertain, this fact is noted.

BLACK-FIGURED VASES

The Heidelberg Painter

1. Kylix, in Taranto, Museo Nazionale, I. G. 4342. I, Herakles and the lion. A, man stealing up to two women at a fountain; B, Herakles and the lion. *CVA, Taranto, Museo Nazionale*, fasc. 2 (Italia, fasc. 35) pl. 27 no. 2; *ABV*, 66 no. 55.

The Leagros Group

1. Hydria, in Munich, Antikensammlungen, 1715. Women at a fountain. On the shoulder, youth mounting chariot. *ABV*, 366 no. 74.

2. Hydria, in Paris, Louvre, F 302. Women at the fountain. On the shoulder, chariot. *CVA, France, Musée du Louvre*, fasc. 6 (France, fasc. 9) pl. 72 nos. 4 and 7; *Paralipomena*, 165 no. 174 *bis*.

The Theseus Painter

1. Lekythos, in Paris, Louvre, CA 1837. Bull led to sacrifice. C. H. E. Haspels, *Attic Black-figured Lekythoi* (Paris, 1936) pl. 43 no. 2.

The Painter of Vatican G 49

1. Oinochoe, in Paris, Bibliothèque Nationale, Cabinet des Médailles, 269. Hermes (?) and Kerberos. *ABV*, 535 no. 20.

The Pholos Group

1. Lekythos, in Paris, Louvre, CA 1705. The Sphinx with visitors. C. H. E. Haspels, *Attic Black-figured Lekythoi* (Paris, 1936) pl. 42 no. 2a, with incorrect museum number.

The Painter of Half-Palmettes

1. Hydria (kalpis), in London, British Museum, 64.10–7.182. Altar before temple. C. H. E. Haspels, *Attic Black-figured Lekythoi* (Paris, 1936) 248 no. 6.

2. Hydria (kalpis), in London, British Museum, 64.10–7.184. Altar before temple. C. H. E. Haspels, *Attic Black-figured Lekythoi* (Paris, 1936) 248 no. 7.

3. Oinochoe, in Tübingen, Universität Tübingen, D 62. Two owls with a column between them. *ABV*, 573 no. 1.

4. Oinochoe, in London, British Museum, B 506. Komast. *ABV*, 573 no. 5.

5. Oinochoe, in Paris, Louvre, N 3374. Komast. *ABV*, 573 no. 7 (listed as F 350?, an incorrect museum number).

6. Oinochoe, in Gotha, Schlossmuseum, 43. Woman seated, in a sanctuary. *CVA, Gotha, Schlossmuseum*, fasc. 1 (Deutschland, fasc. 24) pl. 41 no. 6; *Paralipomena*, 288.

7. Oinochoe, in Gotha, Schlossmuseum, 42. Head of goddess, in a sanctuary. *CVA, Gotha, Schlossmuseum*, fasc. 1 (Deutschland, fasc. 24) pl. 41 no. 7; *Paralipomena*, 288.

8. Oinochoe, in Paris, Louvre, G 15. P. Oliver-Smith, in *Essays in Memory of Karl Lehmann*, 237 n. 28.

9. Oinochoe fragment, in Bologna, Museo Civico, Ar. 9. Athena standing beside an altar, before a temple. *CVA, Bologna, Museo Civico*, fasc. 2 (Italia, fasc. 7) pl. 36 no. 3.

10. Oinochoe, in Ferrara, Museo Nazionale di Spina, 16269. Maenad before an altar. *CVA, Ferrara, Museo Nazionale*, fasc. 2 (Italia, fasc. 48) pl. 24 nos. 1–2.

11. Oinochoe, in Ferrara, Museo Nazionale di Spina, 186. Dancing Maenad. *CVA, Ferrara, Museo Nazionale*, fasc. 2 (Italia, fasc. 48) pl. 24 nos. 3–4.

The Emporion Painter

1. Lekythos, in Athens, National Archaeological Museum, 608. The Sphinx with visitors. *ABV*, 585 no. 17.

Unattributed Vases

1. Amphora, in London, British Museum, B 49. A, sanctuary of a goddess (Cybele?), with her image in the shrine; B, warrior, and horseman leading the warrior's horse. Third quarter of the sixth century B.C. *CVA, London, British Museum*, fasc. 3 (Great Britain, fasc. 4) pl. 35 no. 2a; *ABV*, 326.

2. Panathenaic amphora, in Princeton, Art Museum, Princeton University, 50.10. A, Athena; B, Charioteer. Last quarter of the sixth century B.C. F. F. Jones, *Ancient Art in the Art Museum, Princeton University* (Princeton, 1960) 34–35.

3. Plaque, in Athens, National Archaeological Museum, Akropolis Collection, 2547. Athena within her shrine, with Hermes at right. End of the sixth century B.C. Graef, *Akropolis* I, pl. 105 no. 2547.

4. Plaque, in Athens, National Archaeological Museum, Akropolis Collection, 2549. Athena seated within a building, with lyre player ap-

proaching from right. End of the sixth century B.C. Graef, *Akropolis* I, pl. 105 no. 2549.

5. Calyx krater fragment, in Amsterdam, Allard Pierson Museum, 2113. Man reclining on a *kline*, with a silen approaching from the right. End of the sixth century B.C. *CVA, Pays-Bas, Musée-Scheurleer (La Haye)* fasc. 2 (Pays-Bas, fasc. 2) III He, pl. 6 no. 2.

6. Panathenaic amphora fragments, in Athens, Agora Museum, P 3631. Fourth century B.C.

RED-FIGURED VASES

The Nikosthenes Painter

1. Skyphos, in Paris, Louvre, G 66. Gigantomachy? A, Athena in battle; B, Herakles in battle. *ARV²*, 126 no. 25.

The Nikoxenos Painter

1. Amphora, in Paestum, Museo di Paestum. A, Herakles and Kerberos; B, Amazons arming. *ARV²*, 220 no. 2. (No design at center of capital.)

2. Panathenaic amphora, in Boston, Museum of Fine Arts, 95.19. A, Athena; B, Athena. *ARV²*, 220 no. 5.

3. Panathenaic amphora, in Oxford, Mississippi, University of Mississippi. A, Athena; B, Athena. *ARV²*, 221 no. 6.

4. Panathenaic amphora, in Berlin, Staatliche Museen, 2161. A, Athena with kithara; B, kitharode. *ARV²*, 221 no. 7.

5. Panathenaic amphora, in Munich, Antikensammlungen, 8728. A, Athena; B, jumper and flute player. *ARV²*, 221 no. 8. (No design at center of capital.)

6. Panathenaic amphora, Basel market, 1961. A, Hermes; B, Hermes. *ARV²*, 221 no. 8 *bis* and 1636.

7. Panathenaic amphora, in New York, private collection. A, Athena; B, trainer between jumper

and discus thrower. Attributed by D. von Bothmer.

The Eucharides Painter

1. Stamnos, in Leningrad, Museum of the Hermitage, 642. A, Danae and Perseus; B, Amazons. *ARV²*, 228 no. 30; A. A. Peredolskaya, *Krasnofigurnye attischeskie vazy* (Leningrad, 1967) pl. 25; *Paralipomena*, 347, 510.

2. Kylix, in Ferrara, Museo Nazionale di Spina, from Tomb no. 503 at Spina. I, Danae, Perseus, and Akrisios. S. Aurigemma, *La Necropoli di Spina in Valle Trebba* (Rome, 1960) pl. 167; *ARV²*, 231 no. 79. (Column perhaps Ionic.)

The Syleus Painter

1. Amphora, in Würzburg, Martin von Wagner-Museum der Universität Würzburg, 509. A, kitharode and man; B, jumper and trainer. *ARV²*, 249 no. 5.

2. Pelike, in Paris, Louvre, G 228. A, Gigantomachy (Athena, Herakles, and Giant); B, the Sphinx. *ARV²*, 250 no. 14 and 254.

3. Pelike, in Boston, Museum of Fine Arts, 71.343. The Sphinx between seated youths. C. Vermeule, "Department of Classical Art Purchases," *The Ninety-Sixth Annual Report of the Museum of Fine Arts, Boston* (Boston, 1971–1972) 44 and pl. on p. 43.

4. Pelike, in a Swiss private collection. A, kitharist and listeners; B, men and youth. Attributed by D. von Bothmer.

5. Hydria, in Paris, Bibliothèque Nationale, Cabinet des Médailles, 440. Zeus entrusting the infant Dionysos to the Nymphs. *ARV²*, 252 no. 51.

The Copenhagen Painter

1. Stamnos, in a Swiss private collection. A, Theseus and the Minotaur (on the left, Ariadne; on the right, Minos); B, unexplained: three women and three young boys; two of the wom-

en show concern: mothers at Athens, in fear of the tribute? *ARV²*, 257 no. 11.

The Syriskos Painter

1. Calyx krater, in Athens, National Archaeological Museum, Akropolis Collection, 735. A, Theseus and the Minotaur. B, Orneus, Pallas, Nisos, and Lykos. Langlotz, *Akropolis* II, pl. 61 no. 735; *ARV²*, 259 no. 1.

The Harrow Painter

1. Hydria, in Maplewood, New Jersey, Joseph V. Noble collection. Boy and seated woman within a building, with man and youth standing outside. On the shoulder, fight. *ARV²*, 276 no. 70.

The Brygos Painter

1. Kylix, in Paris, Louvre, G 154. 1, warrior and old man. A–B, Achilles pursuing Troilos. *ARV²*, 369 no. 3.

2. Skyphos (?) fragment, in Athens, National Archaeological Museum, Akropolis Collection, 546. Youth seated, singing and playing the kithara. Langlotz, *Akropolis* II, pl. 41 no. 546; *ARV²*, 383 no. 197 (listed under kyathoi).

The Foundry Painter

1. Kylix, in Rome, Museo Nazionale di Villa Giulia, 50407. 1, horseman. A, hoplite and cavalry; B, cavalryman with horses. *ARV²*, 402 no. 24.

The Dokimasia Painter

1. Calyx krater, in Boston, Museum of Fine Arts, 63.1246. A, death of Agamemnon; B, death of Aigisthos. *ARV²*, 1652; *Paralipomena* 373 no. 34.

Douris

1. Kylix, in New York, private collection, with fragments in Paris, Louvre, S 1351, C 222, C 11394, C 11398, C 11404–11406 and one fragment listed under C 201. 1, maeander. Group of male figures. *ARV²*, 434 no. 81, 436 nos. 99, 102, 103, 107, and 441 nos. 194–196.

Vaguely Akin to Douris

1. Kylix, in Florence, Museo Archeologico Etrusco, 3910 (part *ex* Villa Giulia) and Boston, Museum of Fine Arts, Res. 08.31a. 1, athlete (*hoplitodromos*) and boy. A–B, *hoplitodromoi*. *CVA, Firenze, Museo Archeologico*, fasc. 3 (Italia, fasc. 30) pl. 89 no. 1; *ARV²*, 1565 no. 3; E. Vermeule, "Some Erotica in Boston," *Antike Kunst* 12 (1969) 13–14 no. 13 and pl. 11 no. 1.

Hermonax

1. Pelike, in Vienna, Kunsthistorisches Museum, 3728. The Sphinx. Signed by Hermonax as painter. *CVA, Wien*, fasc. 2 (Österreich, fasc. 2) pl. 74 nos. 1 and 4; *ARV²*, 485 no. 24.

The Group of Naples 3169

1. Column krater, in Rome, Museo Nazionale di Villa Giulia, 3579. A, Tereus; B, youths and boys. *ARV²*, 514 no. 3.

Near the Mykonos Painter

1. Column krater, in Perugia, Museo Civico, 73. A, infant Herakles and the snakes. *ARV²*, 516.

The Orchard Painter

1. Column krater, in Rome, Museo Nazionale di Villa Giulia, 50391. A, men and women; B, men and woman. *ARV²*, 523 no. 12.

The Altamura Painter

1. Stamnos, in Munich, Antikensammlungen, SL. 471. A, Theseus and the Minotaur; B, rescued youths and maidens. *CVA, München, Museum antiker Kleinkunst*, fasc. 5 (Deutschland, fasc. 20) pls. 246 and 248 no. 3; *ARV²*, 593 no. 44.

2. Oinochoe, in Boston, Museum of Fine Arts, 97.370. Apollo and Artemis. *ARV²*, 594 no. 62.

The Niobid Painter

1. Calyx krater, in Paris, Louvre, G 165. A, Athena mounting chariot; B, horseman leaving home. *ARV*², 601 no. 21.

The Group of Berlin 2415

1. Oinochoe, in New York, Metropolitan Museum, 08.258.25. Man at a statue of Athena. *ARV*², 776 no. 3. (Perhaps intended as Ionic.)

The Painter of Philadelphia 2449

1. Pyxis, in New York, Metropolitan Museum, 06.1117. Women at work with wool. *ARV*², 815 no. 3.

The Painter of London E 80

1. Kylix, in London, British Museum, E 80, with fragment in the Villa Giulia. I, Apollo seated at an altar. A–B, men ("kings") and women. *ARV*², 815 no. 1.

2. Kylix, in Orvieto, Museo Claudio Faina, from Tomb 2 at the Necropolis of Crocifisso del Tufo. I, nude woman. A, nude woman, man, and youth; B, woman and two men. Attributed by D. von Bothmer. M. Bizzarri, "La necropoli di Crocifisso del Tufo in Orvieto," *Studi Etruschi* 30 (1962) pl. 1.

The Pistoxenos Painter

1. Kylix, in Stockholm, National Museum, G 2335. I, Dionysos. A–B, youths with horses. *ARV*², 860 no. 8 *bis* and 1672.

The Telephos Painter

1. Kylix, in Boston, Museum of Fine Arts, 98.931. I, Telephos and Teuthras (?). A–B, Telephos in the house of Agamemnon. Signed by Hieron (*epoiesen*). *ARV*², 482 no. 33 and 817 no. 2; *Paralipomena*, 420 no. 2.

2. Kylix fragment, in Paris, Louvre, G 246. I, youth with lyre. *ARV*², 819 no. 45.

The Penthesilea Painter

1. Kylix, in Paris, Louvre, G 448. I, satyr and maenad. A, youths with horse; B, man and youths. *ARV*², 880 no. 5.

The Comacchio Painter

1. Column krater, in Vienna, Kunsthistorisches Museum, 825. A, uncertain subject (travelers); B, youths. *ARV*², 958 no. 62.

The Lewis Painter (Polygnotos II)

1. Skyphos of Corinthian type, in Basel, Antikenmuseum, BS 426. A, woman (mistress) with mirror; B, woman bringing chair. *Paralipomena*, 436 no. 38.

2. Skyphos of Corinthian type, in Münster, Westfälische Wilhelms-Universität, Archäologisches Museum, 45. Domestic scene. Attributed by D. von Bothmer.

The Agathon Painter

1. Pyxis, in Berlin, Staatliche Museen, 3308. Zeus, with Hera, Iris, and Nike. Signed by Agathon (*epoiesen*). *ARV*², 977 no. 1.

The Kadmos Painter

1. Neck amphora, in Boston, Museum of Fine Arts, 03.821. A, Hippodame, Asteria, Iaso, and Eurynoe; B, youth with spears (Theseus?) pursuing a woman. *ARV*², 1186 no. 29.

The Painter of Berlin 2536

1. Kylix, in Berlin, Staatliche Museen, 2536. I, warrior leaving home (youth and old man). In the exergue, two cocks. A, judgment of Paris; B, meeting of Paris and Helen. *CVA, Berlin, Antiquarium*, fasc. 3 (Deutschland, fasc. 22) pl. 117 no. 3, 118 no. 1; *ARV*², 1287 no. 1.

In the Manner of the Meidias Painter

1. Pyxis, in New York, Metropolitan Museum, 09.221.40. Aphrodite with Peitho and Hygieia;

Aponia and Eukleia; Eudaimonia and Paidia. *ARV²*, 1328 no. 99; *Paralipomena*, 479.

Unattributed Vases

1. Fragments of a head kantharos, in Carlsruhe, Badisches Landesmuseum, joining with fragment in New York, Metropolitan Museum, 1973.175.3. Several figures before a colonnade. About 500 B.C.

2. Fragmentary kylix, in Greenwich, Connecticut, Walter Bareiss collection. Decorated on the inside only, fountain house with girl washing her hair under stream of water. About 500 B.C.

3. Hydria fragment, probably a kalpis, in Bryn Mawr, Ella Riegel Memorial Museum, Bryn Mawr College, P–215. Fountain house scene, with a woman stooping to fill her vase. About 500–475 B.C. *CVA, Bryn Mawr College, Bryn Mawr, Pennsylvania*, fasc. 1 (United States of America, fasc. 13) pl. 35 no. 7.

4. Loutrophoros fragment, in Athens, National Archaeological Museum, Akropolis Collection, 641. A, women, some with torches; B, quadriga. About 480 B.C. Langlotz, *Akropolis* II, pl. 51 no. 641.

5. Column krater, in Brunswick, Maine, Bowdoin College Museum of Art, 1913.8. A, Oidipous and the Sphinx; B, woman offering a phiale to an old man. Compared with the school of Polygnotos by Herbert. K. Herbert, *Ancient Art in Bowdoin College* (Cambridge, Mass., 1964) 72 no. 196.

6. Kylix, in Athens, National Archaeological Museum, 17302. I, maenad. A–B, youths in the palaistra. Mid-fifth century B.C. *CVA, Athènes, Musée National*, fasc. 2 (Greece, fasc. 2) pl. 13 no. 4.

7. Pyxis, in Boston, Museum of Fine Arts, 93.108. A, domestic scene; B, youth crowned by Nike. About 450 B.C. to 425 B.C. L. D. Caskey, *Geometry of Greek Vases* (Boston, 1922) 226 and 181.

8. Calyx krater, in Athens, National Archaeological Museum, 14902. A, Herakles in a temple; B, Nike flanked by attendants. Fourth century B.C.

WHITE-GROUND VASES

The Painter of London D 14

1. Pyxis, in New York, Metropolitan Museum, 40.11.2. Nereids. *ARV²*, 1213 no. 1.

Unattributed Vases

1. Lekythos, in Bologna, Museo Civico, PU 354. Youth leaning on his stick. Compared with the group of Athens 2025. *ARV²*, 723 no. 2.

2. Lekythos, in London, British Museum, D 47. Two women. About 475 B.C. C. H. Smith, *Catalogue of the Greek and Etruscan Vases in the British Museum* III (London, 1896) pl. 25.

3. Panathenaic amphora, in Athens, Agora Museum, P 8522. A, Athena; B, kitharist or kitharode. First half of the second century B.C. G. R. Edwards, "Panathenaics of Hellenistic and Roman Times," *Hesperia* 26 (1957) pl. 84c. (Capital perhaps Corinthian.)

Appendix C

VASES FROM THE NORTHEAST AEGEAN WITH ILLUSTRATIONS OF AEOLIC COLUMNS

For a discussion of these vases see chapter IV. Examples with tendrils or volutelike designs which do not seem to be architectural are not included.

LARISA

1. Vase fragment from a krater, with Aeolic capital in relief. Gray fabric (*bucchero*); details are schematized, with approximately two turns to the whorls; transitional member is visible between shaft and volute element. In Archaeological Museum, Istanbul. Max. width 0.088 m.

J. F. Crome, "Ausgrabungen in Larisa am Hermos im Frühjahr 1934," *AA* (1934) cols. 404–405, fig. 40; *Capitello Eolico*, 21, pl. 5 no. 3.

2. Vase fragment, from a basin, with Aeolic capital in relief. Gray fabric (*bucchero*); incised details; a torus is below the whorls, which have approximately two turns. Archaeological Museum, Istanbul. Max. length 0.152 m.

Larisa III, pl. 45, 9, p. 106; *Capitello Eolico*, 21, pl. 5 no. 1.

ASSOS

3. Fragment of handle of large jar. Red clay, with red slip; traces of added white slip; vertical volutes incised into surface of clay. In Mu-

seum of Fine Arts, Boston, no. P 4121. Length of sherd 0.078 m. Volutes are 0.052 m. high and 0.06 m. across the whorls.

J. T. Clarke, *Report on the Investigations at Assos, 1882, 1883* (New York, 1898) 176, fig. 42.

KLAZOMENAI

4. Sarcophagus illustrated with scene of running chariots. Aeolic column supports basin. Column has base, shaft, torus or leaf drum, and volute member. In Archaeological Museum, Istanbul, no. 1426. 2.24 m. long x 0.99 m. wide x 0.685 m. high; opening 1.825 m. x 0.615 m.

Å. Åkerström, *Architektonische Terrakottaplatten in Stockholm* (Lund, 1951), 86ff. and figs. 38 no. 1 and 46; *Kapitelle und Basen*, 77 no. 15 and fig. 176.

5. Sarcophagus illustrated with scene of running chariots. One Aeolic column supports a basin, another is in the gable. Each column has base, shaft, torus or leaf drum, and volute member. In British Museum, London, no. 1896.6–15.1. 2.328 m. long x 1.158 m. wide x 0.832 m. high.

A. S. Murray, *Terracotta Sarcophagi, Greek and Etruscan, in the British Museum* (London, 1898) 88ff., fig. 1 no. 12 and figs. 4–5, pls. 1–7; Å. Åkerström, *Architektonische Terrakottaplatten in Stockholm* (Lund, 1951), fig. 47; *Die architektonischen Terrakotten Kleinasiens* (Lund, 1966) fig. 57; *Kapitelle und Basen*, 77 no. 16 and figs. 177–178.

CHIOS

6. Painted krater illustrating the ambush of Troilos, with a fountain house with one Aeolic column. Column has base, unfluted shaft, and capital with volutes having one and one-half turns, with element between them. Small molding or leaf drum is between shaft and capital. In Archaeological Museum, Istanbul.

K. Schauenburg, "Zu griechischen Mythen in der etruskischen Kunst," *JdI* 85 (1970) 48–50, figs. 14–15.

Glossary

Abacus—The uppermost element of a capital, used to transfer the weight of the entablature to the column.

Adyton—An inner room in a Greek temple, entered through a door at the back of the cella.

Aeolic capital—A capital with paired, vertically rising volutes.

Aeolic order—The Greek tradition of architecture using the Aeolic column, evolved during the sixth century B.C.

Aeolic style—A generic term used to describe the tradition of capitals with paired, vertically rising volutes.

Akroterion—A sculpture or some other ornament placed upon a roof, above the lower angles or the apex of the pediment.

Anta—A pilaster which projects slightly from the end of a lateral wall.

Antefix—An ornament placed at the end of a roof's covering tiles.

Architrave—A lintel, placed immediately above the columns.

Arris—The sharp ridge at the angular contact of two curved or plane surfaces, as in the ridge separating the flutes on Doric and on some early Ionic and Aeolic columns.

Astragal—A half-round molding carved with a bead-and-reel.

Balteus—A carved band encircling the pulvinus of a capital as if it were compressing it.

Base—The lowest or supporting portion of anything.

Bead-and-reel—An ornament applied to narrow half-round moldings, consisting of an alternation of elongated shapes (beads) with two shorter shapes (reels).

Bît hilani—A Near Eastern palace usually consisting of a portico approached by steps and flanked by one or two towers, with the major rooms beyond the portico.

Capital—The uppermost member of a column or pillar.

Cella—The Latin term for the *naos*, the principal room of a Greek temple.

Channel—The canalis, the space between the marginal borders on the face of an Aeolic or Ionic capital.

Colonnade—A row of columns used to support an entablature.

Column—An architectural support which is circular or elliptical in section.

Corinthian capital—A capital with a circular aspect decorated with volutes and acanthus leaves.

Cornice—The uppermost member of the entablature.

Covering tile—A tile used to cover the joints between pan tiles.

Dentils—Rectangular projections apparently reflecting the ends of wooden beams used to support the cornice.

Dipteral—Having a double row of columns.

Distyle—Having two columns.

Doric capital—A capital consisting of a large circular molding (echinus) supporting an abacus.

Doric order—The system of architecture using the Doric capital and entablature.

Drum—A cylindrical or semicylindrical stone, such as the section of a column.

Echinus—The convex molding between the volutes of an Ionic capital. Also the convex molding below the abacus of a Doric capital.

Egg-and-dart—An ornament applied to convex moldings, consisting of an alternation of pendant ovals (eggs) with more narrow, pointed shapes (darts).

Entablature—The superstructure of a building, usually supported by columns or pillars.

Epistyle—The Greek term for the architrave.

Euthynteria—A leveling course for a building, at the top of the foundation.

Eye—The circular center of a volute.

Fasciae—Horizontal bands on the architrave of some Ionic buildings. Each band projects slightly beyond the one below it.

Flat tile—See pan tile.

Flutes—The vertical channels in the shafts of columns. Also used for the horizontal channels of the tori of early Ionic bases.

Frieze—Any horizontal band enriched with ornament, especially sculpted or molded figures. Applied to the member on the entablature of Greek buildings between the architrave and the cornice.

Geison—The Greek term for the cornice, the uppermost member of the entablature.

Guttae—Small pegs placed beneath a mutule or a regula on a Doric building.

Heart-and-dart—The leaf-and-dart, an ornament applied to convex-concave moldings consisting of alternating leaf shapes (hearts) and pointed shapes (darts).

Helix—The spiral of a volute.

Heroon—A shrine dedicated to a deceased hero.

In antis—A column arrangement for a portico in which the columns are placed between antae.

Ionic capital—A capital decorated with paired volutes connected across the top of an echinus.

Ionic order—The system of architecture using the Ionic column, evolved in Ionia by the sixth century B.C.

Jamb—The vertical member at the side of a door or window.

Karyatid—A female figure used to support an entablature.

Krepidoma—The stepped platform of a temple.

Leaf-and-dart—See heart-and-dart.

Leaf drum—A block carved with foliate ornament, usually cylindrical or semicylindrical.

Lintel—A horizontal beam supported by two or more uprights.

Lotus-and-palmette—An ornamental band consisting of alternating palmettes and lotus-blossoms.

Megaron—A building consisting of a square or rectangular main room preceded by a porch or a porch and an antechamber, with an axially arranged doorway.

Metope—The panel between the triglyphs on a Doric frieze.

Molding—A narrow decorative band with a continuous outline or contour, used on the edge or surface of an architectural element.

Monolithic—Composed of a single piece of stone.

Mutule—A projecting slab on the exposed lower surface of the Doric cornice.

Naos—The Greek term for the principal room of a Greek temple, also called the cella.

Necking, or necking band—A narrow, transitional element between a column's shaft and its capital.

Oikos—A small Greek building composed of a single room.

Opisthodomos—The porch at the rear of a Greek temple.

Order—An architectural system in which a specific column type, an entablature, and other architectural elements are employed on a regular basis.

Palmette—A bilaterally symmetrical floral ornament composed of a series of petals in a fan-like arrangement or radiating from a central stem.

Pan tile—A flat tile used in series with covering tiles over the joints.

Pediment—The triangular area at the front or rear of a gabled roof.

Peristyle—A covered colonnade surrounding a building or lining an inner court. Also applied to the inner court itself.

Pilaster—An engaged pillar.

Pillar—An architectural support which is square or rectangular in section.

Plinth—A bricklike rectangular block, such as the blocks occasionally placed below the bases in some Near Eastern and Greek buildings.

Poros—A brownish, sometimes fossiliferous limestone.

Portico—A colonnaded porch at the front or back of a building.

Pronaos—The front porch in a Greek temple.

Propylon—A roofed entrance gate.

Prostyle—A temple with a portico whose columns are in front of the walls rather than *in antis*.

Proto-Aeolic capital—A term occasionally used to describe the Aeolic capital, not employed in this work (see Introduction).

Proto-Ionic capital—A term occasionally used to describe the Aeolic capital, not employed in this work (see Introduction).

Pteroma—The walkway between the walls of a temple and its colonnade.

Pulvinus—The side of an Aeolic or Ionic capital.

Regula—A narrow strip beneath the taenia of the Doric entablature, under each triglyph of the frieze.

Rosette—A round floral ornament.

Scene building—A building used as the architectural background in a Greek theater.

Scotia—A wide flute.

Sima—The roof gutter of a building.

Spira—The lower, cylindrical part of an Asian Ionic or an Aeolic column base.

Stele—An upright slab, such as those used for grave markers.

Stoa—A building with a long open side, usually supported by one or more colonnades placed parallel to the long axis of the building.

Stylobate—The step or platform upon which the columns are placed in a Greek building.

Stucco—A plasterlike coating applied to sculpture, architecture, etc.

Taenia—A band at the top of the architrave on a Doric entablature.

Temenos—A sacred precinct.

Torus—A large convex molding.

Triglyph—The member between the metopes on the Doric frieze.

Tripteral—Having a triple row of columns.

Tufa—A rock formed from volcanic ash.

Volute—An ornament in the shape of a spiral.

Selected Bibliography

FOR THE REGIONS DISCUSSED IN THIS STUDY, ARRANGED GEOGRAPHICALLY

GENERAL WORKS

Åkerström, Å., *Die architektonischen Terrakotten Kleinasiens* (Lund, 1966).

Akurgal, E., "Vom äolischen zum ionischen Kapitell," *Anatolia* 5 (1960) 1ff.

——, *Die Kunst Anatoliens* (Berlin, 1961).

——, *Orient und Okzident: Die Geburt der griechischen Kunst* (Baden-Baden, 1966) published in English as *The Art of Greece: Its Origins in the Mediterranean and Near East* (New York, 1968).

——, "The Early Period and the Golden Age of Ionia," *AJA* 66 (1962) 369ff.

Alsopp, B., *A History of Classical Architecture* (New York, London, and Toronto, 1965).

Andrae, W., *Die ionische Säule: Bauform oder Symbol?* (Berlin, 1933).

——, "Die griechischen Säulenordnungen," in *Kleinasien und Byzanz* (Berlin, 1950) 1ff.

Auscher, D., "Le Problème des chapiteaux dits 'Proto-Ioniques,'" in "Les Relations entre la Grèce et la Palestine avant la conquête d'Alexandre," *Vetus Testamentum* 17 (1967) 27ff.

Bergquist, B., *The Archaic Greek Temenos* (Lund, 1967) 38–39.

Berve, H., and G. Gruben, *Griechische Tempel und Heiligtümer* (Munich, 1961), published in English as *Greek Temples, Theaters, and Shrines* (New York, 1962).

Boardman, J., "Chian and Early Ionic Architecture," *The Antiquaries Journal* 39 (1959) 170ff.

Bossert, H. Th., *Altsyrien* (Tübingen, 1951).

Braun-Vogelstein, J., "Die ionische Säule," *JdI* 35 (1920) 1ff.

——, *Die ionische Säule* (Berlin and Leipzig, 1921).

Buren, E. D. van, *Greek Fictile Revetments in the Archaic Period* (London, 1926).

Ciasca, A., "I capitelli a volute in Palestina," *Rivista degli studi orientali* 36 (1961) 189–197.

——, *Il capitello detto eolico in Etruria* (Florence, 1962).

Curtius, L., *Die antike Kunst* II (Potsdam, 1938).

Demangel, R., *La Frise ionique* (Paris, 1932).

Dinsmoor, W. B., *The Architecture of Ancient Greece* (London, New York, Toronto, and Sydney, 1950).

Drerup, H., "Architektur und Toreutik in der griechischen Frühzeit," *MdI* 5 (1952) 7ff.

Durm, J., *Die Baukunst der Griechen* (Leipzig, 1910).

Groote, M. von, *Die Enstehung des jonischen Kapitells und Seine Bedeutung für die griechische Baukunst* (Strassburg, 1905).

Koch, H., *Von ionischer Baukunst* (Köln, 1956).

Krischen, F., "Werden und Wesen der jonischen

Formensprache," *Antike und Abendland* 2 (1946) 77ff.

———, *Weltwunder der Baukunst in Babylonien und Jonien* (Tübingen, 1956).

Lawrence, A. W., *Greek Architecture* (Baltimore, 1962).

Marquand, A., *Greek Architecture* (New York, 1909).

Martin, R., "Problème des origines des ordres à volutes," *Etudes d'archéologie classique* 1 (1955–1956) 117–131.

———, *Manuel d'architecture grecque* (Paris, 1965).

Mendel, G., *Catalogue des sculptures grecques, romaines, et byzantines* (Constantinople, 1912) vol. II.

Mercklin, E. von, *Antike Figuralkapitelle* (Berlin, 1962).

Meurer, M., *Vergleichende Formenlehre des Ornaments und der Pflanze* (Dresden, 1909).

Naumann, R., "Das Hausmodell vom Tell Halaf und die nach Unten verjüngten Säulen Nordsyriens," *Jahrbuch für kleinasiatische Forschung* 2 (1951–1953) 246ff.

———, *Architektur Kleinasiens* (Tübingen, 1971).

Perrot, G., and C. Chipiez, *Histoire de l'art dans l'antiquité* (Paris, 1882–1914).

Persson, A., *New Tombs at Dendra near Midea* (Lund, 1942).

Przyluski, J., "La Colonne ionique et le symbolisme oriental," *Revue archéologique*, ser. 6 no. 7 (1936) 3ff.

Puchstein, O., *Das ionische Capitell* (47. Programm zum Winckelmannsfeste, Berlin, 1887).

———, *Die ionische Säule als klassisches Bauglied orientalischer Herkunft* (Leipzig, 1907).

Richter, G. M. A., *A Handbook of Greek Art* (London and New York, 1969).

Ridgeway, B. S., "Notes on the Development of the Greek Frieze," *Hesperia* 35 (1966) 188ff.

Riemann, H., *Zum griechischen Peripteraltempel* (Frankfurt, 1935).

Robertson, D. S., *A Handbook of Greek and Roman Architecture* (London, 1945), reprinted under the title *Greek and Roman Architecture* (1969).

Schefold, K., "Das äolische Kapitell," *JOAI* 31 (1939) 42ff.

———, *Die Griechen und ihre Nachbarn* (Berlin, 1967).

Scranton, R. L., *Greek Architecture* (New York, 1962).

Shiloh, Y., "New Proto-Aeolic Capitals Found in Israel," *BASOR* 222 (1976) 67–77.

Shoe, L. T., *Profiles of Greek Mouldings* (Cambridge, Mass., 1936).

Warren, H. L., *The Foundations of Classical Architecture* (New York, 1919).

Weickert, C., *Das lesbische Kymation* (Leipzig, 1913).

———, *Typen der archaischen Architektur in Griechenland und Kleinasien* (Augsburg, 1929).

———, *Antike Architektur* (Berlin, 1949).

Wesenberg, B., *Kapitelle und Basen: Beobachtungen zur Entstehung der griechischen Säulenformen* (Düsseldorf, 1971).

Wurz, E. and R., *Die Entstehung der Säulenbasen des Altertums unter Berücksichtigung verwandter Kapitelle* (Heidelberg, 1925).

Yavis, C. G., *Greek Altars: Origins and Typology* (St. Louis, 1949).

PALESTINE

Hazor

Aharoni, Y., and R. Amiran, "A New Scheme for the Sub-Division of the Iron Age in Palestine," *IEJ* 8 (1958) 171ff.

Kenyon, K. M., "Megiddo, Hazor, Samaria and Chronology," *BIA* 4 (1964) 143ff.

Yadin, Y., "Excavations at Hazor, 1958," *IEJ* 9 (1959) 74ff.

———, "The Fourth Season of Excavations at Hazor," *BA* 22 (1959) 10ff.

———, *Hazor* (London, 1972).

Yadin, Y., Y. Aharoni, R. Amiran, T. Dohan, I. Dunayevsky, and J. Perrot, *The James A. de Rothschild Expedition at Hazor* (Jerusalem, 1958–1961).

Megiddo

Aharoni, Y., "The Stratigraphy of Israelite Megiddo," *Journal of Near Eastern Studies* 31 (1972) 302ff.

Aharoni, Y., and R. Amiran, "A New Scheme for the Sub-Division of the Iron Age in Palestine," *IEJ* 8 (1958) 171ff.

Fisher, C. S., *The Excavations of Armageddon* (Chicago, 1929).

Kenyon, K. M., "Megiddo, Hazor, Samaria and Chronology," *BIA* 4 (1964) 143ff.

Lamon, R. S., *The Megiddo Water System* (Chicago, 1935).

Lamon, R. S., and G. M. Shipton, *Megiddo* I (Chicago, 1939).

Loud, G., *The Megiddo Ivories* (Chicago, 1939).

———, *Megiddo* II (Chicago, 1948).

May, H. G., *Material Remains of the Megiddo Cult* (Chicago, 1935).

Pritchard, J. B., "The Megiddo Stables: A Reassessment," in *Near Eastern Archaeology in the Twentieth Century* (Essays in Honor of Nelson Glueck, J. A. Sanders, ed., Garden City, 1970) 268ff.

Schumacher, G., *Tell el-Mutesellim* (Leipzig, 1908).

Ussishkin, D., "King Solomon's Palace and Building 1723 in Megiddo," *IEJ* 16 (1966) 174ff.

———, "On the Original Position of Two Proto-Ionic Capitals at Megiddo," *IEJ* 20 (1970) 213ff.

———, "King Solomon's Palaces," *BA* 36 (1973) 94ff.

Watzinger, C., *Tell el-Mutesellim* II (Leipzig, 1929).

Yadin, Y., "New Light on Solomon's Megiddo," *BA* 23 (1960) 62ff.

———, "Notes and News; Megiddo," *IEJ* 16 (1966) 178ff.

———, "Notes and News; Megiddo," *IEJ* 17 (1967) 119ff.

———, "Megiddo of the Kings of Israel," *BA* 33 (1970) 66ff.

———, *Hazor* (London, 1972) 150ff.

———, "A Note on the Stratigraphy of Israel-ite Megiddo," *Journal of Near Eastern Studies* 32 (1973) 330.

Yadin, Y., Y. Shiloh, and A. Eitan, "Notes and News; Megiddo," *IEJ* 22 (1972) 161ff.

Samaria

Aharoni, Y., and R. Amiran, "A New Scheme for the Sub-Division of the Iron Age in Palestine," *IEJ* 8 (1958) 171ff.

Crowfoot, J. W., K. M. Kenyon, and E. L. Sukenik, *Samaria-Sebaste I; The Buildings* (London, 1942).

Jack, J. W., *Samaria in Ahab's Time* (Edinburgh, 1929).

Kenyon, K. M., "Megiddo, Hazor, Samaria and Chronology," *BIA* 4 (1964) 143ff.

Parrot, A., *Samarie, capitale du royaume d'Israel* (Paris, 1955).

Reisner, G. A., C. S. Fisher, and D. G. Lyon, *Harvard Excavations at Samaria* (Cambridge, Mass., 1924).

Sukenik, E. L., "Die neuen Ausgrabungen in Samaria," *AA* (1933) cols. 85ff.

Wright, G. E., "Israelite Samaria and Iron Age Chronology," *BASOR* 155 (1959) 13–29.

Shechem

Bull, R. J., "A Re-examination of the Shechem Temple," *BA* 23 (1960) 110ff.

Sellin, E., "Die Ausgrabung von Sichem," *Zeitschrift des Deutschen Palästina-Vereins* 49 (1926) 229ff.

Welter, G., "Stand der Ausgrabungen in Sichem," *AA* (1932) col. 313.

Wright, G. E., *Shechem; The Biography of a Biblical City* (New York, 1964), with much additional bibliography.

Unknown Site, said to be "in Transjordan"

Iliffe, J. H., "A Model Shrine of Phoenician Style," *QDAP* 11 (1944) 99–100 and pl. 21.

Yeivin, S., "Jachin and Boaz," *PEQ* 91 (1959) 9ff.

Jerusalem

Bliss, F. J., and A. C. Dickie, *Excavations at Jerusalem 1894–1897* (London, 1898).

Busink, Th. A., *Der Tempel von Jerusalem* (Leiden, 1970), with much additional bibliography.

Crowfoot, J. W., and G. M. Fitzgerald, *Excavations in the Tyropoeon Valley, Jerusalem, 1927, Annual of the Palestine Exploration Fund V* (London, 1929).

Kenyon, K. M., "Excavations in Jerusalem," *PEQ* (1962) 72ff.; (1963) 7ff.; (1964) 7ff.; (1965) 9ff.; (1966) 73ff.; (1967) 63ff.

——, *Jerusalem: Excavating 3000 Years of History* (London, 1967).

——, "Israelite Jerusalem," in *Near Eastern Archaeology in the Twentieth Century* (Essays in Honor of Nelson Glueck, J. A. Sanders, ed., Garden City, 1970) 232ff.

——, *Archaeology in the Holy Land* (New York and London, 1970) 240ff., 316–318, 343ff.

——, *Royal Cities of the Old Testament* (New York, 1971).

Macalister, R. A. S., and J. G. Duncan, *Excavations on the Hill of Ophel, Jerusalem, 1923–1925, Annual of the Palestine Exploration Fund IV* (London, 1926).

Simmons, J., *Jerusalem in the Old Testament* (Leiden, 1952).

Vincent, H., *Jérusalem sous terre. Les récentes fouilles d'Ophel* (London, 1911).

——, *Jérusalem: recherches de topographie, d'archéologie et d'histoire* (Paris, 1912–1926).

Vincent, L. H. *et al., Jérusalem de l'Ancien Testament* (Paris, 1954 and 1956).

Warren, Captain Charles, *Excavations at Jerusalem 1867–70* (London, 1884).

Weill, R., *La Cité de David* I-II (Paris, 1920 and 1947).

Yeivin, S., "Jachin and Boaz," *PEQ* 91 (1959) 6ff.

Ramat Raḥel

Aharoni, Y., "Excavations at Ramath Raḥel 1954," *IEJ* 6 (1956) 102–111, 137–157.

——, "The Citadel of Ramat Rahel," *Archaeology* 18 (1965) 15ff.

——, *Excavations at Ramat Raḥel 1959–1960* (Rome, 1962).

——, *Excavations at Ramat Raḥel 1961–1962* (Rome, 1964).

Garbini, G., "Sul nome antico di Ramat Rahel," *Rivista degli studi orientali* 36 (1961) 199–205.

Kon, M., "The Stone Capitals from Ramat Rahel," *Bulletin of the Jewish Palestine Exploration Society* 13 (1947) 83–86.

Maisler, B., "Ramat Raḥel ve-Ḥirbet Tselaḥ (Giv'at Eliahu)" *Kovets* (Jerusalem, 1934) 4–18.

Stekelis, M., "Me'arat Kevarim Yehudim be-Ramat-Raḥel," *Kovets* (Jerusalem, 1934) 19–40.

Medeibîyeh

Glueck, N., "Further Explorations in Eastern Palestine," *BASOR* 51 (1933) 13, and fig. 2.

——, "Explorations in Eastern Palestine I," *AASOR* 14 (1933–1934) 66ff., and pl. 11.

——, "The Civilization of the Moabites," *AJA* 38 (1934) 216, fig. 5.

THE HALIKARNASSOS PENINSULA

Alâzeytin

Bean, G. E., and J. M. Cook, "The Halicarnassus Peninsula," *BSA* 50 (1955) 125–127.

Maiuri, A., "Viaggio di esplorazione in Caria, Parte II–B, Monumenti Lelego-Carii," *ASAA* 4–5 (1921–1922) 432ff.

Paton, W. R., and J. L. Myres, "Karian Sites and Inscriptions," *JHS* 16 (1896) 199–200.

Radt, W., *Siedlungen und Bauten auf der Halbinsel von Halikarnassos* (*IstMitt*, Beiheft 3, Tübingen, 1970).

AEOLIS, NORTHERN IONIA, AND THE NORTH AEGEAN

Old Smyrna

Akurgal, E., *Die Kunst Anatoliens* (Berlin, 1961) 285, pl. 251.

———, *Ancient Civilizations and Ruins of Turkey* (Istanbul, 1970) 119–121; (1973) 119–121.

Anderson, J. K., "Old Smyrna: the Corinthian pottery," *BSA* 53–54 (1958–1959) 138ff.

Boardman, J., "Old Smyrna: the Attic pottery," *BSA* 53–54 (1958–1959) 152ff.

Cook, J. M., "Archaeology in Greece, 1951," *JHS* 72 (1952) 104–106.

———, "Old Smyrna, 1948–1951," *BSA* 53–54 (1958–1959) 1ff.

———, *The Greeks in Ionia and the East* (New York, 1963) 71–74, 81, 83–84.

———, "Old Smyrna: Ionic Black Figure and Other Sixth-Century Figured Ware," *BSA* 60 (1965) 114ff.

———, "Old Smyrna: Fourth-Century Black Glaze," *BSA* 60 (1965) 143ff.

Jeffery, L. H., "Old Smyrna: Inscriptions on sherds and small objects," *BSA* 59 (1964) 39ff.

Mellink, M. J., "Archaeology in Asia Minor," *AJA* 71 (1967) 169; 72 (1968) 141; 73 (1969) 221; 74 (1970) 172; 75 (1971) 176; 76 (1972) 183.

Nicholls, R. V., "Old Smyrna: the Iron Age fortifications and associated remains on the city perimeter," *BSA* 53–54 (1958–1959) 35ff.

Neandria

Clarke, J. T., "A Proto-Ionic Capital from the Site of Neandreia," *AJA* 2 (1886) 1–20, 136–148.

Gerkan, A. von, "Zum Tempel von Neandreia," *Neue Beiträge zur klassischen Altertumswissenschaft* (Festschrift B. Schweitzer, Stuttgart, 1954) 71–76.

Koldewey, R., *Neandria* (51. Programm zum Winckelmannsfeste der archäologischen Gesellschaft zu Berlin, 1891).

Mallwitz, A., "Zum äolischen Kapitell von Neandria," in "Der alte Athena-Tempel von Milet," *IstMitt* 18 (1968) 135ff.

Martin, R., "Problème des origines des ordres à volutes," *Etudes d'archéologie classique* I (1955–1956) 117–131.

Schefold, K., "Das äolische Kapitell," *JOAI* 31 (1939) 42ff.

Weickert, C., *Das lesbische Kymation* (Leipzig, 1913) 33ff.

Larisa on the Hermos

Boehlau, J., and K. Schefold, *Larisa am Hermos* I: *Die Bauten* (Berlin, 1940).

———, *Larisa am Hermos* III: *Die Kleinfunde* (Berlin, 1942).

Kjellberg, L., "Das äolische Kapitell von Larisa," *Corolla Archaeologica Principi Hereditario Regni Sueciae Gustavo Adolpho dedicata* (Lund, 1932).

———, *Larisa am Hermos* II: *Die architektonischen Terrakotten* (Stockholm, 1940).

Schefold, K., "Das äolische Kapitell," *JOAI* 31 (1939) 42–52.

Klopedi

Åkerström, Å., *Die architektonischen Terrakotten Kleinasiens* (Lund, 1966) 27ff.

Evangelides, D., "(12η Ἀρχαιολογικὴ Περιφέρεια I) Ἀνασκαφαὶ ἐν Λέσβῳ," *Deltion, Parartema* (1924–1925) 41–44.

———, "Ἀνασκαφαὶ ἐν Λέσβῳ," *Praktika* (1927) 57–59.

———, "Ἀνασκαφὴ Κλοπεδῆς Λέσβου," *Praktika* (1928) 126–137.

Hatzi, D., "Εἰδήσεις ἐκ Λέσβου, Κλοπεδή," *AAA* 5 (1972) 43ff.

Koldewey, R., *Die antiken Baureste der Insel Lesbos* (Berlin, 1890) pls. 16–17.

Perrot, G., and C. Chipiez, *Histoire de l'art dans l'antiquité* (Paris, 1898) vol. VII, 622, fig. 276.

Mytilene

Burn, A. R., *The Lyric Age of Greece* (New York, 1960) 266ff.

Condis, J. D., "Capitello eolico di Eresso," *ASAA*, new series, 8–10 (1946–1948) 29–30.

Mendel, G., *Catalogue des sculptures grecques, romaines et byzantines* (Constantinople, 1912) II, 36f., no. 276.

Page, D., *Sappho and Alcaeus* (Oxford, 1955).

Schefold, K., "Das äolische Kapitell," *JOAI* 31 (1939) 46, fig. 18.

Eressos

Condis, J. D., "Capitello eolico di Eressos," *ASAA*, new series, 8–10 (1946–1948) 25ff.
Walter, O., "Archäologische Funde in Griechenland von Frühjahr 1939 bis Frühjahr 1940: Inseln des Aigaion," *AA* (1940) col. 288.

Thasos

For the literary sources, see A. R. Burn, *The Lyric Age of Greece* (New York, 1960) 157ff.
For the archaeological remains, see *Etudes thasiennes* (Paris, 1944–), with annual reports in the *BCH*.

Delos

For the archaeological remains, see *Exploration archéologique de Délos* (École française d'Athènes, Paris, 1909–), with annual reports in the *BCH*.
Additional bibliography is listed in R. Vallois, *L'Architecture hellénique et hellénistique à Délos* (Paris, 1944), and in P. Bruneau and J. Ducat, *Guide de Délos* (Paris, 1965) 9ff.

Paros

Annual reports of the excavations may be found in the *BCH* and in Tὸ Ἔργον τῆς Ἀρχαιολογικῆς Ἑταιρείας. For specific references to the Aeolic monuments see the catalogue in this work.

Other studies include:

Fastje, H., "Der Rundbau von Paros," *AA* (1972) 421ff.

Gruben, G., "Naxos und Paros. Dritter Vorläufiger Bericht über die Forschungskampagnen 1970 und 1971," *AA* (1972) 319ff.
Kondoleon, N. M., "Νέαι ἐπιγραφαὶ περὶ τοῦ Ἀρχιλόχου ἐκ Πάρου," *ArchEph* (1952) 32ff.
——, "Πάρια ἰωνικὰ κιονόκρανα," *AAA* 1 (1968) 178–181.
Rubensohn, O., *Das Delion von Paros* (Wiesbaden, 1962).
——, "Parische Künstler," *JdI* 50 (1935) 49ff.
——, "Paros I," *AthMitt* 25 (1900) 341ff.
——, "Paros II," *AthMitt* 26 (1901) 157ff.
——, "Paros III," *AthMitt* 27 (1902) 189ff.
Welter, G., "Der altionische Tempel in Paros," *AthMitt* 49 (1924) 22ff.

ATTICA

For general bibliography for Archaic Athens, see V. Ehrenberg, *From Solon to Socrates* (London, 1967).

For the Aeolic capitals from Athens see:

Borrmann, R., "Stelen für Weihgeschenke auf der Akropolis zu Athen," *JdI* 3 (1888) 275–276, fig. 16.
——, "Altionische Kapitelle aus Athen," *Antike Denkmaeler* 1 (1891) 8 and pl. 18.
Dinsmoor, *Architecture of Ancient Greece*, fig. 53, upper right.
Durm, J., *Die Baukunst der Griechen* (Leipzig, 1910) fig. 284, nos. 4 and 6.
Kübler, K., "Ausgrabungen im Kerameikos I," *AA* (1938) col. 605, fig. 16.
Meurer, M., *Vergleichende Formenlehre des Ornaments und der Pflanze* (Dresden, 1909) 492, pl. 2 no. 4, 502, pl. 8 no. 7.
Raubitschek, *Technik und Form*, 162ff.
Trowbridge, S. B. P., "Archaic Ionic Capitals found on the Acropolis," *AJA* 4 (1888) 22ff.

Index

Abydos, 52, 62
Achaemenid palaces, 77ff
Achilles, 98, 149, 153
Adriatic Sea, 90
Aegina, *see* sphinx columns
Aeolic league, 58f
Agamemnon, 149-50
Agathon Painter, 150
Ahab, 35, 48
Aigai, 60, 62-63, 70
Aigisthos, 149
Akrisios, 148
Akropolis collection of National
    Archaeological Museum,
    Athens, *see* vases, Attica
Alâzeytin, 51ff; Aeolic capitals,
    51, 53ff, 103, 120, 137, pls.
    29-35; bibliography, 160;
    Building 26, 51; Building 30,
    51, 53f, 56f, 121, 137, pls.
    29-31; Building 31, 51, 53,
    55ff, 103, 105, 121, 137, pls.
    32-35; fortifications, 51;
    theatral area, 51
Alexandria Troas, 62-63
Alkaios, 87
Altamura Painter, 149
altars, 93, 123, 147, 150; Larisa,
    74; Neandria, 64, 69;
    Perachora, 57
Alyattes, 59

Amasis II, 128
Amathos, 33, 48, 52
Amazons, 148
Amenhotep II, 18
Amorgos, 90
Amsterdam, Allard Pierson Mu-
    seum, *see* vases, Attica
Amurru, 78
Amynanda, 51
Anatolian Aeolic columns, 116-
    17; *see also* Gordion; Hittite
    volutes
Andros, 90
antefixes with Aeolic-like motifs,
    106
Antissa, 62
Aphrodite, 150
Apollo, 105, 147ff; *see also*
    Bassai, temple; Naukratis
    (temple); Thermon (temple)
Apollo Napaios, temple of, *see*
    Klopedi, temple
Aponia, 151
Archestratos, 88
Archilochos, 88
Argos, 90
Ariadne, 148
Arslan-Tash, 19, 119, 143
Artemis, 149; *see also* Ephesos
    (temple)
Ascalon, 28

Asklepieion, *see* Paros
Assos, 62f, 98, 152; *see also*
    vases, Assos
Assurbanipal, 143
Assyrians, Aeolic columns, 42-
    43, 57, 60f, 70, 78, 95, 116f;
    Ionic columns, 123; palaces, 78
Asteria, 150
Athena, 59, 105, 147-48, 150;
    temple of, at Larisa, *see*
    Larisa, temple; at Miletos, 65;
    at Old Smyrna, *see* Old
    Smyrna, temple
Athenian vases, *see* vases, Attica
Athens, 57, 88, 90, 98ff; Aeolic
    capitals, 100ff, 120, 130, 140f,
    145, pls. 52-59, 67; Aeolic
    building, 55f, 103ff, 120, pl.
    59; bibliography, 162;
    plaques with Aeolic capitals,
    105, pls. 63-64; *see also* New
    York, Metropolitan Museum;
    vases, Attica
Athens 2025, group of, 151
Athens, Agora Museum: Athens,
    capital A 4273, 100f, 105, 140,
    pl. 52; *see also* vases, Attica
Athens, Akropolis Museum:
    Athens, capital 3794, 100, 102,
    120, 130, 141, pls. 53-55;
    Athens, capital 9980, 55f,

Athens, Akropolis Museum (*cont*).
103ff, 120, 141, 145, pls. 56-59;
Athens, capital 10261, 100,
102f, 120, 130, 141
Athens, Kerameikos Museum:
Athens, capital without no.,
100, 105, 140
Athens, National Archaeological
Museum: Sykaminon, capital
4797, 106ff, 141, pl. 67; *see
also* vases, Attica
Ayia Paraskeve, *see* Klopedi

Babylon, 39, 49; facade with
Aeolic capitals, 21, 35, 61, 71,
97, 117, pl. 16
Badari, 52
balusters, 42f; *see also* Ramat
Raḥel, balusters; "Woman at
the Window"
Bareiss col., *see* vases, Attica
Basel, Antikenmuseum, *see*
vases, Attica
Bassai, temple, 132
Bayrakli, 58
Beazley col., *see* vases, Attica,
Oxford
Beni Hasan, 52
Berlin 2415, group of, 150
Berlin 2536, Painter of, 150
Berlin, Staatliche Museen, *see*
vases, Attica
Beth ha-Kerem, 40
Beth-Shan, 28
bit hilani, 31, 33, 45, 77f
Black Sea, 90, 111
block capitals, 130-31
Bodrum, 51
Bodrum Museum: Alâzeytin,
capital 2251, 51, 53f, 57, 137,
pl. 29; Alâzeytin, capital 2252,
51, 53f, 56, 137, pls. 30-31;
Alâzeytin, capital 3582, 53,
55ff, 103, 105f, 120, 137, pls.
32-34; Alâzeytin, capital 3583,
53, 55ff, 103, 105f, 120, 137,
pl. 35
Bologna, Museo Civico, *see*
vases, Attica
Boston, Museum of Fine Arts,
see vases, Assos; vases, Attica

Brunswick, Maine, Bowdoin
College Museum of Art, *see*
vases, Attica
Brygos Painter, 149, pl. 71
Bryn Mawr, Ella Riegel Memo-
rial Museum, *see* vases, Attica
building models, *see* Istanbul,
Archaeological Museums,
Larísa model; Jerusalem,
Israel Museum, Megiddo
shrine; Tell Taʾannek shrine;
Tell el Farʿah shrine; "Trans-
jordan" shrine; Philadelphia,
University Museum, Amathos
model
bull led to sacrifice, 147
Byblos, 46, 52, 57

Cádiz, 21, 46, 70
Cádiz, Museo Provincial: stele,
21, 40, 70, pl. 28
Caeretan hydriai, 93
Cairo, Archaeological Museum:
Medinet Habu, relief 59891, 19
Carchemish, 88, 119
Carian rock-cut tombs, 105
Carians, 50ff; *see also* Alâzeytin
Carlsruhe, Badisches Landes-
museum, *see* vases, Attica
Carthage, 46, 110
Caunus, rock-cut tombs, 105
cavalrymen, 149
chariots and charioteers, on
vases, 146f, 150f
Chersiphron, 124
Chicago, Field Museum: bronze
stand, 18f, 37, pl. 1; bronze
jar, 18
Chicago, Oriental Institute:
Khorsabad, ivory, *see* "Wom-
an at the Window"; Khorsa-
bad, relief A 11255, 123;
Medinet Habu, relief 14089,
19, 48, pl. 3; Megiddo, capital
3657, 21, 32ff, 35, 41, 44f, 48,
135, pl. 10; Megiddo, miniature capital, 18, 34f, 38, 44,
135, pl. 14; Megiddo, ivory
B 2009, 19, 119; Tell Tainat,

relief, 21, 40, 70, 77f, 95, 117,
119, pl. 24
Chios, 62, 97f, 153
cocks, 150
coin hoards in Egypt, 111
Comacchio Painter, 150
composite capitals, Egyptian,
19ff, 23, 34, 44f, 115, pl. 2; *see
also* Medinet Habu
Copenhagen Painter, 148
corbeled buildings, *see* Alâzeytin,
Building 30; Building 31
Corinthian capital, origin of,
132f
Crocifisso del Tufo, *see* vases,
Attica, Orvieto
Croesus, 78, 125
Cybele, 79; (?), 147
Cycladic Aeolic style, 91, 121;
see also under individual
islands
Cyprus, *see* under individual
cities
Cyrene, 106f
Cyzicus, 88

Danae, 148
Dardanos, 62
Darius I, 118
Dar-u-Dukhtar, rock-cut tomb,
123
date palm, 18f, 21
David, 27, 37
Dead Sea, 28
Delian League, 88
Delos, 90ff, 106ff, 122, 128, 131f,
140; bibliography, 162
Delos, Archaeological Museum:
Delos, capital, 91ff, 140
Delphi, 90, 106ff
Didyma, 90, 93, 107, 122, 125f,
131
Dionysos, 148, 150
discus thrower, 148
Dokimasia Painter, 149
doubled volutes, *see* Eressos;
Ionic capitals with doubled
volutes
Douris, 149
Douris, vaguely akin to, 149

"Dragon Houses," 57

Early Bronze Age spirals, 17
Elaia, 62
Elaious, 62, 111
Emporion Painter, 147
Ephesos, 69, 90, 96, 107, 111, 119, 122-29, 131
Erechtheion, 103
Eressos, 62, 88f, 139f; bibliography, 162
Erythrai, 62
Esarhaddon, 125
Etruscan Aeolic capitals, 59f, 63, 95, 110, 117; origin of, 63
Euboea, 57
Eucharides Painter, 148
Eudaimonia, 151
Eukleia, 151
Euphrates River, 77
Euranion, 51
Eurynoe, 150
eyes in capitals, methods of manufacture, 96

Ferrara, Museo Nazionale di Spina, see vases, Attica
Florence, Museo Archeologico Etrusco, see vases, Attica
flute players, 148
foot, length of in Aeolis, 79
Foundry Painter, 149
fountains, 98, 146, 151, 153
friezes on Aeolic buildings, 81, 83; see also Larisa, Old Palace; temple; Neandria, temple
furniture, relation to Aeolic capitals, 92, 94f, 103, 119, 146; see also Chicago, Oriental Institute, Tell Tainat, relief

Gaza, 28, 52
Gezer, 28ff, 39
giants, 148
gigantomachy, 148
Golgoi, Cyprus, 19, 21, 37f, 46, 117, pl. 20
Gordion, 52, 97, 110, 117, pl. 69
Gotha, Schlossmuseum, see vases, Attica

grain trade in Athens, 111
gravestones, see stelai
Greenwich, Conn., Bareiss col., see vases, Attica

Half-Palmettes, Painter of, 146-47
Halikarnassos, 90; see also Alâzeytin
Harrow Painter, 149
Hazor, 27ff, 39, pl. 7; Aeolic capitals, 21-22, 29, 33, 36, 44f, 48, 59, 61, 134, pls. 4-6; bibliography, 158; Building 3090, 29, pl. 7; building with pillars, 29; casemate wall, 27, 29; gateway, 27
head of goddess, in a sanctuary, 147
Heidelberg Painter, 91, 145f
Helen, 150
Hera, see Olympia (temple); Samos, temple
Herakles, 89, 93, 146, 148, 151
Hermes, 88, 105, 147f
Hermonax, 149
Hermos River, 73; see also Larisa on the Hermos
Herod, 39
Hieron, 150
Hippodame, 150
Hiram of Tyre, 39
Hittite volutes, 18, 21
hoplite, 149
hoplitodromoi, 149
horsemen, 149f
Huleh Plain, 27
Hygieia, 150

Ialysos, 143
Iaso, 150
Ilion, 63
"International Style" of the Bronze Age, 21
Ionic capitals with doubled volutes, 88
Ioulios Plocamos, stele, 132
Istanbul, Archaeological Museums: Chios, krater, 98, 153; Klazomenai, sarcophagus 1426, 98, 152; Larisa, capital

1924 (Mendel no. 277), 56, 73ff, 95, 110, 138, pls. 42, 44; Larisa, capital 1925 (Mendel no. 278), 59, 69, 76f, 83, 94f, 138, pl. 46; Larisa, capital 1926 (Mendel no. 279), 59, 69, 76f, 94f, 138, pl. 47; Larisa, capital 1926, 59, 79f, 139, pl. 48; Larisa, capital (unfinished), 79, 138; Larisa, clay capitals, miniature, 139; Larisa, clay krater, 152; Larisa, clay basin, 152; Larisa, leaf drum, 60, 70, 74ff, 79, 81, 91; Larisa, model 72.4, 60, 70, 79ff, 88, 97, 139, pls. 39-40; Mytilene, capital 985 (Mendel no. 276), 59, 85, 87, 97, 100, 139, pl. 50; Neandria, Aeolic capitals, 58f, 64ff, 70f, 73, 75, 77, 83, 87, 95ff, 100, 138, pl. 41; Neandria, leaf drums, 60, 64ff, 70f, 73, 75, 77, 83, 91, 96f, 138, pl. 41; Roman stele 237, 132
ivory plaques, 19, 37, 40, 42, 46, 119, 142-43, pl. 19; see also "Woman at the Window"
Izmir, Archaeological Museum: Old Smyrna, capitals, 59ff, 64, 95, 97, 110, 138, 143; Old Smyrna, leaf drums, 59ff, 71, 95, 97, 138, 143, pl. 36

Jebusites, 37
Jehu, 35
Jericho, 28
Jerusalem, 28, 34, 37ff, 52; Aeolic capitals, 21, 38, 41, 44f, 48, 136, pl. 21; bibliography, 160; columns before the temple, 39-40; temple of Solomon, 38ff
Jerusalem, Israel Museum: Hazor, capitals, 21-22, 29, 33, 36, 44f, 48, 59, 61, 134, pls. 4-6; Jerusalem, capital, 21, 38, 41, 44f, 48, 136, pl. 21; Megiddo, capitals M 5339 and M 5340, 18, 21, 30ff, 44, 48, 115f, 134, pl. 8; Megiddo, capital

Jerusalem, Israel Museum (*cont.*)
36.2187, 21, 32ff, 35, 41, 44f,
48, 135, pl. 9; Megiddo, capital 36.2189, 32ff, 35, 41, 44f,
48, 135; Megiddo, shrine M
2985, 33, 44, 47, 135; Megiddo,
shrine M 2986, 33, 44, 47,
135; Ramat Raḥel, balusters,
21, 40, 42f, 44, 46, 60f, 70,
117f, 130, 142f, pl. 26; Ramat
Raḥel, capitals, 21, 33, 38, 40ff,
44f, 48, 136, pl. 22; Ramat
Raḥel, frieze 31.345, 42, 70,
136f, pl. 27; Samaria, capitals,
21, 35, 38, 41, 44f, 48, 135f;
Tell el Far'ah, shrine, 37;
Tell Ta'annek, shrine, 33, 47;
"Transjordan," shrine, 19, 33,
36, 44, 46, 117, 136, pl. 18
Jezebel, 48
Jordan River, 28
jumpers, 148

Kadmos Painter, 150
Kato Phana, Chios, 88
Kerameikos, Athens, 100, 105;
see also Athens, Kerameikos
Museum
Kerberos, 147f
Khorsabad, 40, 78, 119, 123, 143;
see also "Woman at the
Window"
"kings," 150
kithara players, 147ff, 150f
Kition, 52
Klazomenai, 62, 98, 152
Klomidados, *see* Klopedi
Klopedi, 62, 82ff; Aeolic capitals,
59, 69, 82f, 85ff, 96f, 139, pl.
49; altar, 82; bibliography,
161; bronze fibula, 82; tem-
ples, 71, 80, 82ff, 96ff, 128f,
131, 139; terracottas, 83, 85, 97
Knidos, 90
Kolumdado, *see* Klopedi
komasts, on vases, 147
Körmen, 50
Kouklia, *see* Old Paphos
Kul Oba, furniture, 120
Kuyunjik, 42f, 57, 60f, 70, 95,
142f

Kyme, 62

Lampsakos, 62
Lapithos, 52
Larisa on the Hermos, 62, 73ff;
Aeolic capitals, 56, 59, 69,
73-76, 79, 83, 94f, 110, 138f,
pls. 42, 44-48; altar, 74, 79ff;
bibliography, 161; clay building model, 60, 70, 79ff, 88,
97, 139, pls. 39-40; clay capitals, 139; Ionic buildings, 81,
132; leaf drum, 60, 70, 74ff,
79, 81, 91, 138, pl. 45; megaron, 74, 76; Old Palace, 73,
74, 76ff, 82f, 94f, 121, 128,
131, 138, pl. 45; stoa, 74, 79;
temple, 69, 71, 73f, 79ff, 95ff,
128f; terracottas, 76f, 79, 81,
97; *see also* vases, Larisa
leaf capitals, in Neo-Hittite
cities, 70; in Greece, *see* under
individual cities
Leagros group, 146
Lebanon Mountains, 29
Lelegians, 50ff
Lemnos, 90
Leningrad, Hermitage, *see* vases,
Attica
Lesbos, *see* Eressos; Klopedi;
Mytilene
Lewis Painter, 108, 150
lily, 19ff, 39f; *see also* compos-
ite capitals, Egyptian
lion-colossi, 78
London, British Museum:
Nineveh, relief 124939, 57,
60f, 70, 95
Nineveh, relief of building
with balusters, 42f, 142f;
Sippar, tablet, 19, 71, 95, 97,
115, pl. 2; *see also* vases,
Attica
London D 14, Painter of, 151
London E 80, Painter of, 150
lotus, 18ff, 60; *see also* composite
capitals, Egyptian
Lycian rock-cut tombs, 105
Lydians, 58f
Lykos, 149

lyre capitals, *see* New York,
Metropolitan Museum
lyre players, 147ff, 150f

maenads, 147, 150f
Maplewood, N.J., Noble col.,
see vases, Attica
Mari, 77
mason's marks, 29
Maussolos, 51
Medeibîyeh, 21, 28, 41, 43ff, 48,
131, 137, pl. 25
Medinet Habu, 19, 20, 48
Megiddo, 28ff, 35, 39, 43; Aeolic
capitals, 18f, 21, 30ff, 35, 38,
41, 44f, 48, 115f, 134f, pls.
8-10, 14; Assyrian buildings,
30; bibliography, 159; Bronze
Age temple, 22; Building 338,
33, pls. 11-12; Building 1723,
30ff; Building 6000, 31; Gate-
way 1567, 30ff; gateway to
city, 27, 30; ivories, 19, 119,
pl. 19; "stables," 30-31, 35;
terracotta shrines, 33, 44, 47,
pl. 13
Meidias Painter, manner of the,
150f
Melkart, 89f
Melos, 90
Memphis, 52
Metagenes, 124
Methymna, 62
Miletos, 65, 90, 122
Minoan volutes, *see* Mycenaean
and Minoan volutes
Minos, 50, 148
Minotaur, 146, 148f
Moab, *see* Medeibîyeh
Moabite volute capitals, *see*
Medeibîyeh
Mt. Pagos, 58
Münster, Westfälische Wil-
helms-Universität, *see* vases,
Attica
Munich, Antikensammlungen,
see vases, Attica
Mycenaean and Minoan volutes,
18, 21, 40, 117
Mycenaeans on Lesbos, 82
Mykonos Painter, near the, 149

Mytilene, 62, 87f; Aeolic capital, 59, 85, 87, 97, 100, 139, pl. 50; bibliography, 161f; temple, 87
Mytilene, Archaeological Museum: Eressos, capital, 88, 139f, pl. 51; Klopedi, capitals, 59, 69, 82f, 85ff, 96f, 139, pl. 49
Myus, 122

Nabu temple, Khorsabad, see Chicago, Oriental Institute, Khorsabad, ivory
Nabu-apal-iddin, see Sippar, tablet
Naoussa, 92
Nape, see Klopedi
Naples 3169, group of, 149
Naukratis, 52, 129; Ionic (or Aeolic?) capitals, 81, 91, 126f; temple of Apollo, 122, 126-30
Naxos, 90, 106f, 122, 128, 131
Neandria, 58, 62ff; Aeolic capitals, 58f, 64ff, 70f, 73, 75, 77, 83, 87, 95ff, 100, 138, pl. 41; altars, 64, 69, 80f; bibliography, 161; leaf drums, 60, 64ff, 73, 75, 77, 83, 91, 96, 138, pl. 41; roof tiles, 71; temple, 63ff, 80f, 95f, 128ff, 138; terracottas, 71, 73, 95
Nefer-Secheru, see composite capitals, Egyptian
Neo-Hittite volutes, 18; see also under individual cities
New York, Metropolitan Museum: Athens, sphinx on lyre capital 11.185 c d, 104, pls. 61-62; Athens, stele 17.230.6, 104, pl. 60; Golgoi, stele 74.51.2493, 19, 21, 37, 46, 117, pl. 20; see also vases, Attica
New York, private col., see vases, Attica
Nike, 151
Nikosthenes Painter, 148
Nikoxenos Painter, 146, 148
Nimrud, 143
Nineveh, see Kuyunjik
Niobid Painter, 150
Nisos, 149

Noble col., see vases, Attica
North Syrian palaces, see bit hilani
Nymphs, 148

Oidipous, 151
"oikos" of the Naxians at Delos, 122, 128
Old Paphos, 143f
Old Smyrna, 58ff; Aeolic capitals, 59ff, 64, 95, 97, 110, 139, 143; bibliography, 160f; leaf drums, 59ff, 71, 97, 138, pl. 36; pylon, 59; temple of Athena, 59f, 95, 121f, 128, 130, 138
Olympia, 71, 90
Omri, 34-35
Orchard Painter, 149
Orneus, 149
Oropos, 106ff; see also Athens, National Archaeological Museum, Sykaminon, capital
Orvieto, Museo Faina, see vases, Attica
Oumm el-'Amed, 46
owls, 146f
Oxford, Miss., University of Mississippi, see vases, Attica

Paestum, Museo di Paestum, see vases, Attica
Paidia, 151
Pallas, 149
palm columns, 19, 21, 115, pl. 2; see also Sippar, tablet
palmette, origin of, 19, 21, 45
Paphos, 52; see also Old Paphos
Paris, 150
Paris, Bibliothèque Nationale, see vases, Attica
Paris, Louvre: Golgoi, stele, 37f, 46; Trapeza, stele, 46f; see also vases, Attica
Paroikia, 92
Paroikia, Archaeological Museum: Paros, capitals, 92ff, 140
Paros, 88, 90ff, 107f, 122, 131f, 140; Aeolic capitals, 92ff, 140; Asklepieion, 93; bibliography, 162

Pasargadae, 78f
Peisistratos, 92, 99, 111
Peitho, 150
Penthesilea Painter, 150
Perachora, 57
Pergamon, 62
Perikles, 145
Persepolis, 78
Perseus, 148
Persian volute capitals, 117f
Plain of Esdraelon, 29
Polygnotos II, see Lewis Painter
Polygnotos, school of, 151
Polykrates, 92
Princeton, Art Museum, see vases, Attica
Prinias, 120
Pyrrha, 62

Ramat Raḥel, 28, 40ff; Aeolic capitals, 21, 33, 38, 40ff, 44f, 48, 136, pl. 22; balusters, 21, 40, 42f, 44, 46, 60f, 70, 117f, 130, 142f, pl. 26; bibliography, 160; citadel, 38, 40ff; crenelations, 42f; fortification walls, 40-41; frieze, 42, 70, 136f, pl. 27
Ramses III, 19; see also Medinet Habu
"recessed niches," 118f
revellers on terracotta frieze, 83, 97
Rhodes, 90
Rhoikos, 94, 124
Roman Aeolic columns, 132
Rome, Villa Giulia, see vases, Attica

"sacred tree," 17ff, 21, 48
Salamis, 52
Samaria, 28, 34ff, 38, 43; Aeolic capitals, 21, 35, 38, 41, 44f, 48, 135f; bibliography, 159; ivory plaques, 143
"Samarian ware," 36
Samos, 90, 92; anta capital, 121; bronze plaque, 70, 75, 88, 91, pl. 43; pilasters with volutes, 93; temple, 91, 107, 111, 121-31

Sappho, 87
sarcophagi, *see* Klazomenai
Sardis, 90
Sargon, 35, 78
satyr, 150
Scythians, 111
Sea of Galilee, 27-28
Sennacherib, 42f, 142
Sennedjem, *see* composite capitals, Egyptian
Shamash, *see* Sippar, tablet
Shechem, 28, 34ff; Aeolic capital, 21f, 27, 44f, 48, 115f, 136, pl. 17; bibliography, 159; granaries, 22; temple, 22
Shishak, 36
shrines, terracotta, *see* building models
shushan, 40
Sibde, 51
Sidon, 52
Sigeion, 62, 111
silen, 148
Sippar, tablet, 19, 71, 95, 97, 115, pl. 2
Smyrna, 58; *see also* Old Smyrna
Solomon, 27, 30f, 33, 37f, 44, 48
Solon, 111
sphinx, 124, 146ff, 151; on vases, 108f; meaning of, 104; sphinx columns: Aegina, 76, 106, 123, 130; Attica, 104ff; Cyrene, 106f; Delos, 106ff; Delphi, 106ff; Naxos, 106f; Paros, 107f; *see also* New York, Metropolitan Museum
stables at Megiddo, *see* Megiddo, "stables"
stand, bronze, *see* Chicago, Field Museum
stelai, 46, 50, 55ff, 73, 93, 96, 102ff, 116, 120, 123, 132; with Near Eastern volute capitals, 21, 37f, 46; with doubled volutes, 88; *see also* Cádiz; New York, Metropolitan Museum
Stockholm, National Museum, *see* vases, Attica
stone plaques, 142ff
stuccoed columns, 19, 31

Susa, 118
Swiss private col., *see* vases, Attica
Syangela, 51
Sykaminon, 90, 106ff; *see also* Athens, National Museum, Sykaminon, capital
Syleus Painter, 108f, 148
Syrian Aeolic columns, 21, 40, 70, 77f, 117, 143; *see also* Tell Tainat
Syriskos Painter, 106, 146, 149, pl. 66

Tamassos, 47f, 105, 116, pl. 65
Tanit, sign of, 19
Taranto, Museo Nazionale, *see* vases, Attica
Tarsus, 52
Telephos, 150
Telephos Painter, 150
Tell el Amarna, 52
Tell el Far'ah, 28, 34, 37
Tell Halaf, 42, 78
Tell Ta'annek, 28, 33, 47
Tell Tainat, 21, 33, 39f, 60f, 70, 77, 95, 117, 119, pls. 24 and 70
"Temple A" at Ephesos, 69
temple prostitutes, 142
Tenos, 90
Teos, 62
Tereus, 149
Teuthras (?), 150
Thasos, 60, 70f, 88ff, 92, 97, 131f, 140, pl. 37; bibliography, 162; Phoenician colonists at, 89ff
Thasos, Archaeological Museum: Thasos, capital 1385, 60, 91, 97, 140, pl. 37
theater, similarity to earlier palaces, 77
Thebes, Egypt, 52
Thebes, Greece, 90
Theodoros, 94, 124
Thermi, *see* Mycenaeans on Lesbos
Thermon, temple of Apollo, 71
Theseus, 148f; (?), 150
Theseus Painter, 147
thrones, *see* Chicago, Oriental

Institute, Tell Tainat, relief; furniture
Tiglath-pileser III, 29-30
Tirzah, *see* Tell el Far'ah
trainers, 148
transition, wooden to stone architecture, 17, 21, 23, 45, 115
Transjordan, 19, 33, 36f, 44, 46, 117, 136, 159f, pl. 18
Trapeza, 46f
travelers, 150
Troilos, 98, 149, 153
Tübingen, Universität Tübingen, *see* vases, Attica
Tyre, 28, 39f, 46, 52

Umm el'Amad, Jordan, 143

vases, Assos, 98, 152
———, Attica:
Amsterdam, Allard Pierson Museum: no. 2113, 148
Athens, Agora Museum: no. P 8522, 146, 148, 151
———, Akropolis Collection: no. 546, 149; no. 641, 151; no. 735, 106, 149, pl. 66; no. 2547, 105, 147, pl. 63; no. 2549, 105, 147-48, pl. 64
———, National Archaeological Museum: no. 608, 147; no. 14902, 151; no. 17302, 151
Basel, Antikenmuseum: no. BS 426, 150
Basel market, 1961: panathenaic amphora, 148
Berlin, Staatliche Museen: no. 2161, 148; no. 2536, 150; no. 3308, 150
Bologna, Museo Civico: no. Ar. 9, 147; no. PU 354, 151
Boston, Museum of Fine Arts: no. 93.108, 151; no. 95.19, 148; no. 97.370, 149; no. 98.931, 150; no. 03.821, 150; no. 08.31a, 149; no. 63.1246, 149; no. 1971.343, 148
Brunswick, Maine, Bowdoin

College Museum of Art:
no. 1913.8, 151

Bryn Mawr, Ella Riegel
Memorial Museum, Bryn
Mawr College: no. P-215,
151

Carlsruhe, Badisches Landesmuseum: fragment, 151

Ferrara, Museo Nazionale di
Spina: no. 186, 147; no.
16269, 147; from Tomb no.
503, 148

Florence, Museo Archeologico
Etrusco: no. 3910, 149

Gotha, Schlossmuseum: no.
42, 147; no. 43, 147

Greenwich, Conn., Walter
Bareiss Collection: fragmentary kylix, 151

Leningrad, Museum of the
Hermitage: no. 642, 148

London, British Museum: no.
B 49, 147; no. B 506, 147;
no. D 47, 151; no. E 80,
150; no. 64.10-7.182, 147;
no. 64.10-7.184, 147

Maplewood, New Jersey,
Joseph V. Noble Collection:
hydria, 149

Münster, Westfälische Wilhelms-Universität: no. 45,
108, 150, pl. 68

Munich, Antikensammlungen:
no. 1715, 146; no. 8728, 148;
no. S.L. 471, 149

New York, Metropolitan
Museum: no. 06.1117, 150;
no. 08.258.25, 150; no.
09.221.40, 150-51; no.

40.11.2, 151; no. 73.175.3,
151

———, private collection:
Panathenaic amphora, 148;
kylix, 149

Orvieto, Museo Claudio
Faina: from Tomb 2 at the
Necropolis of Crocifisso del
Tufo, 150

Oxford, England, Ashmolean
Museum, Beazley Collec-
tion: fragmentary pelike,
146

Oxford, Mississippi, University of Mississippi: panathenaic amphora, 148

Paestum, Museo di Paestum:
amphora, 148

Paris, Bibliothèque Nationale,
Cabinet des Médailles: no.
269, 147; no. 440, 148

———, Louvre: no. C 201,
149; no. C 222, 149; no. C
11398, 149; nos. C 11404-06,
149; no. CA 1705, 147; no.
CA 1837, 147; no. F 302,
146; no. G 15, 147; no. G
66, 148; no. G 154, 149; no.
G 165, 150; no. G 228, 108f,
148; no. G 246, 150; no.
G 448, 150; no. N 3374,
147; no. S 1351, 149

Perugia, Museo Civico: no. 73,
149

Princeton, Art Museum,
Princeton University: no.
50.10, 147

Rome, Villa Giulia: no. 3579,
149; no. 50391, 149; no.
50407, 149; fragment, 150

Stockholm, National Museum:
no. G 2335, 150

Swiss private collection:
pelike, 148; stamnos, 148-49

Taranto, Museo Nazionale:
no. I.G. 4342, 91, 145f

Tübingen, Universität Tübing-
en: no. D 62, 147

Vienna, Kunsthistorisches
Museum: no. 825, 150; no.
3710, 120, 146, pl. 71; no.
3728, 149

Würtzburg, Martin von Wagner-Museum der Universität
Würtzburg: no. 509, 148

———, Boeotia, 121, 145

———, Caeretan hydriai, 93

———, Chios, 97f, 153

———, Larisa, 98, 152

Vatican G 49, Painter of, 147

Vienna, Kunsthistorisches Museum, see vases, Attica; vases,
Caeretan hydriai

Vounous-Bellapais, 142

"Woman at the Window," 40,
42, 46, 74f, 117, 134, 142f,
pl. 23

wool working, 150

Würtzburg, Martin von Wagner-Museum, see vases, Atitca

Xerxes, 99

youths, 146, 148ff

Zâwijet el-Mêtin, see composite
capitals, Egyptian

Zeus, 148

Zincirli, 119

Pl. 1. Cast bronze stand from Egypt, with openwork decoration. Second half of the eighteenth dynasty. By courtesy of the Field Museum of Natural History, Chicago, no. 30177.

Pl. 2. Foundation tablet from Sippar. King Nabu-apal-idden approaches the god Shamash, who is seated beneath a canopy supported by a palm column with volute capital and volute base. Ninth century B.C. By courtesy of the British Museum, London.

Pl. 3. Medinet Habu. Relief depicting a cluster column with a composite capital, from the western gateway of the mortuary temple of Ramses III. By courtesy of the Oriental Institute, University of Chicago, no. 14089.

Pl. 4. Hazor. Capital from a pillar. About the ninth century B.C. By courtesy of Yigael Yadin and the James A. de Rothschild Expedition at Hazor. After Yadin *et al.,* *Hazor* III–IV (plates) pl. 363.

Pl. 5. Hazor. Bifacial capital from a pillar. About the ninth century B.C. By courtesy of Yigael Yadin and the James A. de Rothschild Expedition at Hazor. After Yadin *et al., Hazor* III–IV (plates) pl. 362.

Pl. 6. Hazor. Pair of volute capitals reconstructed as the crowning members for pillars. Ninth century B.C. By courtesy of the Israel Department of Antiquities, exhibited in the Israel Museum, Jerusalem.

Pl. 7. Aerial view of Area B at Hazor. Citadel 3090 (Strata V to VIII) is at the center. By courtesy of Yigael Yadin and the James A. de Rothschild Expedition at Hazor. After Yadin *et al., Hazor* III–IV (plates) pl. 31 no. 1.

Pl. 9. Megiddo. Capital for a pillar. Tenth to eighth century B.C. By courtesy of the Israel Department of Antiquities, Jerusalem, no. 36.2187.

Pl. 8. Megiddo. Capitals M 5339 and M 5340, found reused in a wall assigned to Stratum III, near Gate 1567. By courtesy of the Oriental Institute, University of Chicago.

Pl. 10. Megiddo. Capital for a pillar. Tenth to eighth century B.C. By courtesy of the Oriental Institute, University of Chicago, no. 3657.

Pl. 11. Reconstruction of Building 338 from Megiddo as
seen from the northeast. For a plan see *Megiddo* 1, fig. 49.
Drawing by L. C. Woolman. By courtesy of the Oriental
Institute, University of Chicago.

Pl. 12. Reconstruction of Building 338 from Megiddo with
the volute capitals used as the crowning members of doorjambs. By courtesy of the Oriental Institute, University of
Chicago.

Pl. 13. Megiddo. Pottery shrine with engaged volutes at the corners, above sphinxes. Tenth to ninth century B.C. or slightly later. By courtesy of the Israel Department of Antiquities, Jerusalem, no. ɪ 4447.

Pl. 15. Samaria. Capital for a pillar. About the ninth to early eight century B.C. By courtesy of the Israel Department of Antiquities, Jerusalem, no. 36.2186.

Pl. 14. Megiddo. Fragment of a miniature capital, of limestone. Date uncertain, probably the tenth century B.C. or slightly earlier. By courtesy of the Oriental Institute, University of Chicago.

Pl. 16. Babylon. Detail of the facade of glazed bricks showing a two-tiered volute capital from one of the decorative columns. Early sixth century B.C. After R. Koldewey, *The Excavations at Babylon* (1914) fig. 80.

Pl. 17. Shechem. Fragment of a capital. Exact date unknown, either late in the Bronze Age or within the Iron Age. By courtesy of the Deutscher Verein zur Erforschung Palästinas. After E. Sellin, "Die Ausgrabung von Sichem," *Zeitschrift des Deutschen Palästinas-Vereins* 49 (1926) pl. 39B.

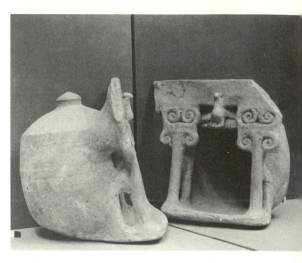

Pl. 18. Pottery shrine said to be from Transjordan, with the entrance flanked by columns with volute capitals (photographed in front of a mirror). Exact date uncertain, but found with pottery of the tenth to ninth century B.C. By courtesy of the Israel Department of Antiquities, Jerusalem, no. 40.286.

Pl. 19. Megiddo. Ivory plaque with incised decoration from Stratum VII A (twelfth century B.C.). By courtesy of the Oriental Institute, University of Chicago, no. B 2009.

Pl. 20. Golgoi, Cyprus. Stele with paired volutes, heraldic sphinxes, and floral elaboration. From about 500 B.C. By courtesy of the Metropolitan Museum of Art, New York, the Cesnola Collection; purchased by subscription 1874-1876 (no. 74.51.2493).

Pl. 21. Jerusalem. Capital for a pillar. Exact date uncertain, probably the eighth to seventh century B.C. By courtesy of the Israel Department of Antiquities, exhibited in the Israel Museum, Jerusalem.

Pl. 22. Ramat Raḥel. Capital from a pillar. Seventh century B.C. By courtesy of the Israel Department of Antiquities, exhibited in the Israel Museum, Jerusalem, no. 55.27.

Pl. 23. Ivory plaque from Room 13 of the Nabu Temple,
Khorsabad, showing the "Woman at the Window." By
courtesy of the Oriental Institute, University of Chicago.

Pl. 24. Tell Tainat. Relief illustrating a volute column, part of the throne for a large seated statue found near the east gate. By courtesy of the Oriental Institute, University of Chicago.

Pl. 25. Medeibiyeh. Capital from the east gate of the citadel. Exact date uncertain, ninth to seventh century B.C. By courtesy of the Department of Antiquities, the Hashemite Kingdom of Jordan.

Pl. 26. Series of limestone balusters from the principal building of the citadel at Ramat Raḥel, used as railings for windows. The right baluster may not belong with this group. Seventh century B.C. By courtesy of the Israel Department of Antiquities, exhibited in the Israel Museum, Jerusalem.

Pl. 27. Broken frieze from Ramat Raḥel depicting columns or balusters with capitals with vertical volutes. Date uncertain, perhaps the seventh century B.C. By courtesy of the Israel Department of Antiquities, no. 31.345.

Pl. 28. Fragment of a stele found near Cádiz, Spain, showing an Aeolic pilaster capital with the volutes rising from a triangle. Date uncertain, probably the Hellenistic period. By courtesy of the Museo Provincial, Cádiz.

Pl. 29. Alâzeytin. Capital from a pilaster, from Building 30. About the second half of the sixth century B.C. Bodrum Museum, no. 2251. By courtesy of Wolfgang Radt.

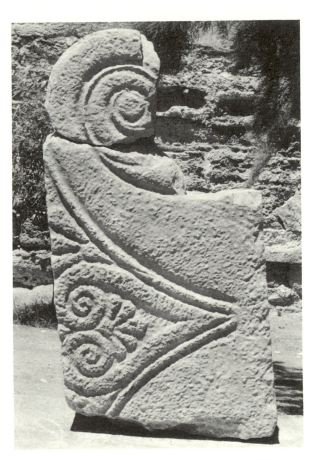

Pl. 30. Alâzeytin. Capital for a pilaster, from Building 30. About the second half of the sixth century B.C. Bodrum Museum, no. 2252. By courtesy of Wolfgang Radt.

Pl. 31. Alâzeytin. Back of the capital with the heart-shaped figure between the whorls, from Building 30. About the second half of the sixth century B.C. Bodrum Museum, no. 2252. By courtesy of Wolfgang Radt.

Pl. 32. Alâzeytin. Capital from Building 31, front of capital. About the second half of the sixth century B.C. Bodrum Museum, no. 3582. By courtesy of Wolfgang Radt.

Pl. 33. Alâzeytin. Capital from Building 31, front of capital showing smooth upper surface of block. About the second half of the sixth century B.C. Bodrum Museum, no. 3582. By courtesy of Wolfgang Radt.

Pl. 34. Alâzeytin. Back of capital from Building 31. About the second half of the sixth century B.C. Bodrum Museum, no. 3582. By courtesy of Wolfgang Radt.

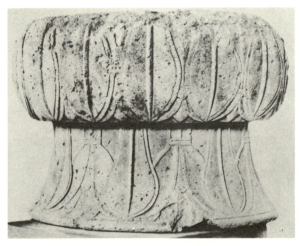

Pl. 35. Alâzeytin. Fragment of second capital from Building 31. About the second half of the sixth century B.C. Bodrum Museum, no. 3583. By courtesy of Wolfgang Radt.

Pl. 36. Old Smyrna. Leaf drum from the Archaic temple. About 600 B.C. After E. Akurgal, "The Early Period and the Golden Age of Ionia," *AJA* 66 (1962) pl. 101 fig. 22.

Pl. 37. Thasos. Leaf drum for a capital. About the sixth century B.C. Thasos Museum, no. 1385. By courtesy of the French School of Archaeology, Athens.

Pl. 38. Phokaia. Column drum and capital or leaf drum from an Archaic building. Sixth century B.C. After E. Akurgal, "The Early Period and the Golden Age of Ionia," *AJA* 66 (1962) pl. 101 fig. 23.

Pls. 39–40. Larisa. Building model with the upper part of
a column, two views. Sixth century B.C. By courtesy of the
Archaeological Museum, Istanbul, no. 72.4.

Pl. 41. Neandria. Capital from the Archaic temple as restored by R. Koldewey, with three superimposed elements. About 575–550 B.C. By courtesy of the Archaeological Museum, Istanbul, no. 985.

Pl. 42. Larisa. Capital with vertical volutes incorrectly re-stored above a leaf drum from another column. Early sixth century B.C. (volute element) and c. 550–525 B.C. (leaf drum). By courtesy of the Archaeological Museum, Istanbul, no. 1924.

Pl. 43. Samos. Bronze plaque illustrating a design like that of the Aeolic capital, with paired volutes rising from a leaf drum. After E. Akurgal, "The Early Period and the Golden Age of Ionia," *AJA* 66 (1962) pl. 102 fig. 27.

Pl. 44. Larisa. Reconstruction of the large stone capital as the crowning member of an isolated column. By courtesy of Walter de Gruyter and Co., Berlin. After Boehlau and Schefold, *Larisa* 1, pl. 29.

Pl. 45. Larisa. Reconstruction of the Old Palace, showing the front facade. About 550 B.C. By courtesy of Walter de Gruyter and Co., Berlin. After Boehlau and Schefold, *Larisa* I, pl. 30.

Pl. 46. Larisa. Aeolic capital with small holes for metal sheathing, assigned to the Old Palace. About 550 B.C. By courtesy of the Archaeological Museum, Istanbul, no. 1925.

Pl. 47. Larisa. Fragment of the left volute of an Aeolic capital, assigned to the Old Palace. About 550 B.C. By courtesy of the Archaeological Museum, Istanbul, no. 1926.

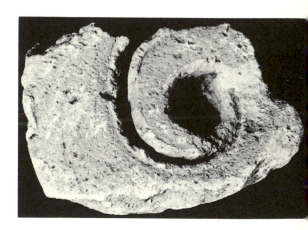

Pl. 48. Larisa. Fragment of a small Aeolic capital, probably from a votive column. Last third of the sixth century B.C. By courtesy of the Archaeological Museum, Istanbul, no. 1926.

Pl. 49. Klopedi. Aeolic capital from the temple. Late sixth century B.C. or slightly later. By courtesy of the Italian School of Archaeology in Athens. After J. D. Condis, "Capitello eolico di Eresso," *ASAA,* new series, 8–10 (1946–1948) fig. 3.

Pl. 50. Mytilene. Capital with double margins and eyes bored completely through the stone. Late sixth century B.C. or slightly later. By courtesy of the Archaeological Museum, Istanbul, no. 985.

Pl. 51. Eressos. Aeolic capital with doubled volutes. Date uncertain, no earlier than the late sixth century B.C. By courtesy of the Italian School of Archaeology in Athens. After J. D. Condis, "Capitello eolico di Eresso," *ASAA*, new series, 8–10 (1946–1948) fig. 1.

Pl. 52. Athens. Fragment of an Aeolic capital found in a well in the Agora. Late sixth century B.C. By courtesy of the Agora Excavations, no. A 4273.

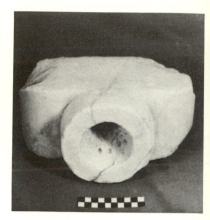

Pls. 53–55. Athens. Capital for a votive column, found on the Akropolis. About 550 to 500 B.C. Akropolis Museum, no. 3794.

Pls. 56–58. Athens. Painted capital from a small building or shrine, found on the Akropolis. About 550 to 525 B.C. Akropolis Museum, no. 9980.

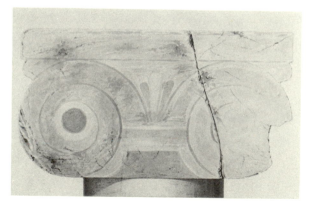

Pl. 59. Athens. Nineteenth-century drawing of the painted Aeolic capital, Akropolis Museum, no. 9980. After R. Borrmann, *Antike Denkmaeler* 1 part 2 (1888) pl. 18 no. 3.

Pl. 60. Athens. Cavetto capital with double-volute design, from a gravestone. About 575–550 B.C. By courtesy of the Metropolitan Museum of Art, New York, Rogers Fund, 1917 (no. 17.230.6).

Pl. 61. Athens. Sphinx on lyre capital, from a gravestone. About 550 to 525 B.C. By courtesy of the Metropolitan Museum of Art, New York, Hewitt Fund, 1911; Rogers Fund, 1921; Munsey Fund, 1936, 1938; and Anonymous Gift, 1951 (no. 11.185 C D).

Pl. 62. Athens. Plaster cast of sphinx on lyre capital, with color restored. By courtesy of the Metropolitan Museum of Art, Hewitt Fund, 1911; Anonymous Gift, 1951 (no. 11.185 C D).

Pl. 63. Black-figured plaque found on the Athenian akropolis illustrating Athena within a shrine, with a table of offerings set before her. Hermes approaches from the right. End of the sixth century B.C. In the National Archaeological Museum, Athens, Akropolis Collection, no. 2547. By courtesy of Walter de Gruyter and Co., Berlin. After B. Graef and E. Langlotz, *Die antiken Vasen von der Akropolis zu Athen* (1925) 1, pl. 105.

Pl. 64. Black-figured plaque found on the Athenian akropolis showing Athena seated within a gabled building while a figure with a lyre, perhaps Apollo, approaches from the right. End of the sixth century B.C. In the National Archaeological Museum, Athens, Akropolis Collection, no. 2549. By courtesy of Walter de Gruyter and Co., Berlin. After B. Graef and E. Langlotz, *Die antiken Vasen von der Akropolis zu Athen* (1925) 1, pl. 105.

Pl. 65. Tamassos, Cyprus. Carved tomb, showing volute capitals crowning pilasters, with dentils above the lintel. About the sixth century B.C. By courtesy of the Director of Antiquities, Cyprus, and the Cyprus Museum.

Pl. 66. Calyx krater illustrating the slaying of the Minotaur by Theseus within a labyrinth supported by Aeolic columns. Attributed to the Syriskos Painter. National Museum, Athens, Akropolis Collection, no. 735. By courtesy of Walter de Gruyter and Co., Berlin. After B. Graef and E. Langlotz, *Die antiken Vasen von der Akropolis zu Athen* II, pl. 61.

Pl. 67. Attica. Capital found built into a church at Syka-minon, near Oropos. National Museum, Athens, no. 4797.

Pl. 68. Skyphos showing a woman running to the right with an Aeolic column at the left and a fire dog at the right. Attributed to the Lewis Painter by D. von Bothmer. In Münster, Westfälische Wilhelms-Universität, Archäo-logisches Museum, no. 45. By courtesy of Klaus Stahler.

Pl. 69. Gordion. Fragments of plaster from the Persian period illustrating an Aeolic column. About 500 B.C. By courtesy of the University of Pennsylvania excavations at Gordion.

Pl. 70. Tell Tainat. Column base in the portico of the *bît hilani*. By courtesy of the Oriental Institute, University of Chicago.

Pl. 71. Detail of a skyphos attributed to the Brygos Painter, in the Kunsthistorisches Museum, Vienna, no. 3710, illustrating the ransom of Hektor. Achilles reclines on a couch the leg of which is decorated with a double-volute motif. After A. Furtwängler and K. Reichold, *Griechische Vasenmalerei* ser. 2 (1909) pl. 84. For photo-graphs and discussion of the vase, see A. Cambitoglou, *The Brygos Painter* (1968) 26ff. and pls. 11–12.